D0518393

THE PARAS

FRANK HILTON THE PARAS

BRITISH BROADCASTING CORPORATION

For Nita

Published by the British Broadcasting Corporation,
35, Marylebone High Street, London W1M 4AA

ISBN 0 563 20099 5

© Frank Hilton 1983
First published 1983
Reprinted 1983

Set in 10/13 pt Monophoto Caledonia
and printed in England by Jolly & Barber Ltd, Rugby

Contents

Picture credits
Page 9, 12 Imperial War Museum, 13, 15 top Frank Hilton, 15 bottom, 16 Sgt Kevin Riley, 19 from *The Glider War* by J.E. Mrazek (Robert Hale), 22 Frank Hilton, 32–5 Homer Sykes, 37 Bill Jones, 39 Frank Hilton, 45, Imperial War Museum, 46 Novosti Press Agency, 47, 48 Süddeutscher Verlag, 49 Keystone Press Agency Ltd, 52 Imperial War Museum, 54 Süddeutscher Verlag, 55 right Imperial War Museum, 63, 65 Bill Jones, 79–93, 94 top left & right BBC, 94 bottom left & right Homer Sykes, 95–111 BBC, 112 Bill Jones, 113–14 BBC, 115 Cpl Andy Whitcroft, 116 BBC, 122 bottom Süddeutscher Verlag, 124 Keystone Press Agency Ltd, 125, 131–9 Imperial War Museum, 145–57 BBC, 164–9 Homer Sykes, 181–9 BBC, 196–9 Imperial War Museum, 200, 201 Keystone Press Agency Ltd, 204–8 Imperial War Museum, 209 Keystone Press Agency Ltd, 210 top UPI, 210 bottom, 211 Keystone Press Agency Ltd, 212 Imperial War Museum, 213, 214 Keystone Press Agency Ltd, 218, 219, 220 top Homer Sykes, 220 bottom, 221 BBC, 222 top Homer Sykes, 222 bottom, 223–5 BBC, 226–8 Homer Sykes, 229 BBC, 231, 232 Frank Hilton, 238 top & bottom 2 Para, 238 middle (Crown copyright), 239 Express Newspapers (photos Tom Smith).

The maps were drawn by Line and Line.

Introduction

Both this book and the television series it is based on were planned and started well before the conflict in the Falklands brought the 2nd and 3rd Battalions of the Parachute Regiment so dramatically to the world's attention. In the summer of 1980 David Harrison, the executive producer, and I met on another project and discovered we had both served in the Airborne Forces during the 1950s. From this came the idea of making a series about the Paras.

Our first intention had been to explore the history of airborne warfare as well as featuring the present-day airborne formations in the armies of Britain and other countries. However, by the autumn of 1981, when the Ministry of Defence authorised us to begin filming, we had more or less decided to concentrate on the training of recruits to the Parachute Regiment and relegate the historical and other aspects to a subsidiary role, and this was subsequently confirmed by Bill Jones, who produced the series. In writing the book, however, I have kept rather more closely to the original idea. By interweaving the story of 480 Platoon with a general history of airborne operations, I have tried to give the reader some understanding of the background to what is still a relatively modern form of warfare, and at the same time relate the life of a present-day Para to that of his predecessors.

Only with the generous co-operation of hundreds of people has it been possible to bring this project to a successful conclusion. Our thanks are due to all those in the Parachute Regiment, No. 1 Parachute Training School, the Ministry of Defence and the many other units of the Army and the Royal Air Force who have provided us with the facilities we needed and shown us such friendly hospitality. We are particularly grateful to the staff at the Depot of the Parachute Regiment for all the assistance they have given us, and to our two project officers, Major Roger Patton and Captain Max Gandell, who worked so untiringly on our behalf. Our special thanks must go to the subjects of our study – the recruits of 480 (or the Hollywood Platoon, as it came to be known) – and to the officers and NCOs responsible for their training. They had to endure our constant presence and scrutiny over a period of more than six months, but they bore this ordeal with patience and good humour, and we wish all of them – whether in or out of the Regiment – success and happiness in their future careers.

There is an omission from the book that needs an explanation. As recruits dropped out of 480 Platoon some of the vacancies were filled by members of previous platoons who had been back-squadded for a variety of reasons. These late-comers figure as prominently in the series as do the rest of the platoon. In the book this is not the case. I felt that the reader would find it difficult enough keeping track of the forty-one original recruits. So – for the sake of simplification and except for occasional references – the back-squads have been left out of the book. For this reluctant omission my apologies.

I should like to express my personal thanks to a host of people for all the help and support they have given me during the writing of the book: Tom Fitch of the Airborne Forces Museum; David Edwards, the BBC photographer; Linda Blakemore and Tony Kingsford of BBC Publications; Bill Jones, the producer, Glyn Worsnip, the reporter, and Caroline Savage, the production assistant, together with the film crews and all the other staff who have worked on the series; Julie Anderson who typed the manuscript; Roger Patton and David Harrison who read it and offered me their criticisms. In the interval between acting as our first project officer and reading the typescript, Major Patton had travelled to the Falklands and back as second-in-command of 3 Para. Nevertheless he still found time to give the book his close attention, as did David Harrison whose constant encouragement while I was writing it helped spur me on to the end. Almost all of their detailed and helpful suggestions have been incorporated into the text.

Last of all, my somewhat ambivalent thanks to the RAF liaison section at the Parachute Regiment's Depot for helping to remind me what a frightening, if exhilarating, business parachuting can be. As the balloon cage I was in swayed to a halt 800 feet above Queen's Parade, Aldershot, I found that all my anxieties about whether I should manage to finish the book on time had totally disappeared. As many parachutists do, I looked beseechingly at my dispatcher in the hope that he had discovered some good reason why it was impossible for us to jump that day, but he merely grinned and invited me to walk forward to the door. It was twenty-five years since I had last jumped. My bones seemed to be made of plasticine. I heard myself shouting 'Go!' and leapt desperately into space . . .

As the Parachute Jump Instructors say: Nothing to it, really. Just like stepping off a pavement.

1 Arnhem Prelude

Sunday 17 September 1944 dawned bright and clear in Lincolnshire. As it did so, John Nicholson was climbing out of the three-ton truck that had taken him and the rest of his stick to the airfield at Barkston Heath. There were aircraft as far as the eye could see, line upon line of them – the transports, the tugs and the gliders that would carry him and a large part of the 1st Parachute Brigade to Holland later that day. This time they knew they were going. In the past three months there had been many false alarms, many briefings, much drawing of equipment, many hours sealed off from the outside world in their concentration areas. But they had never got as far as the airfield before. This time they were going, and the 1st Parachute Brigade would be leading the way.

There were three battalions in the brigade, and John was in the 1st Battalion which he had joined in February 1943. He had fought with it through the closing months of the North African campaign, had jumped into Sicily in the attack on the Primosole Bridge, and was now about to take part in the attack on what would become the most famous bridge in British Airborne Forces' history – the bridge over the Lower Rhine at Arnhem.

Men of the 1st Airborne Division board a Dakota for Arnhem.

At four o'clock that morning John had eaten the special fat-free breakfast provided for them in their camp in the deer park of Grimthorpe Castle. But he was glad of the tea that came round shortly before they emplaned. He was fifth in his stick of eighteen. In front of him were his platoon commander, a signaller and two three-inch mortar men. Behind him was his mate, Paddy McKee, who used to be in the PIAT team with him. The PIAT was an infantry anti-tank weapon, the British equivalent of the American Bazooka, and John was glad his PIAT days were over. It was no joke hitting the slipstream with that awkward lump of stove-pipe – even out of a Dakota which was pretty good to jump from.

Aircraft were beginning to move. But not his yet, not the 1st Battalion. They had been moved to the back of the brigade as a punishment by their brigade commander. A few weeks before Arnhem they had got themselves a new RSM with a mania for show-clean parades at all hours of the day and night. They were veterans. They did not like that sort of nonsense. So just to show him what they thought of it, they had had a little mutiny one day and refused to draw chutes for an exercise. So now the 2nd Battalion would have the honour of leading the brigade in, with the disgraced 1st bringing up the rear.

Ron Holt was in A Company of the 2nd Battalion. Before moving into the concentration area, he had spent the last few months in Eastham Hall at Stoke Rochford. Very pleasant it had been there, too. The local people had been good to them. They had made many friends, and with luck, it would not be long before they would all be back there again, once this operation was successfully over and done with. Burdened with his parachute, his Bren gun and his kitbag of equipment, he climbed aboard the plane and hooked up.

Bill Collard of B Company, 3rd Battalion, felt much the same as the other two. The briefings had filled them with confidence. The opposition would be light. The British 2nd Army would arrive to relieve them by the following afternoon. The Allies would then sweep on into the North German Plain and in a few weeks the war would be over. Still, it was a shame to be leaving Spalding. He and his mates had been happy there, in their camp on the girls' school playing fields, next door to the Odeon.

The first aircraft were beginning to roll forward. Soon the Dakotas were taking off three abreast. Halifaxes and Stirlings were moving into position towing their Horsa gliders behind them. Then the engines of Bill's Dakota fired and roared into life. It was a heart-stopping moment – a mixture of excitement and apprehension, a sudden realisation that this was it. They were about to take off, just behind the Pathfinders. Bill felt the 1st Brigade were lucky to be going in the first wave, before the defences had time to work out what was going on and get ready for them.

Bill Collard had joined the 3rd Battalion at the beginning of December 1942 and had fought right through that winter in Tunisia. Then in July

1943, like Ron Holt and John Nicholson, he had dropped into Sicily too. By that time their brigade had been joined by other parachute brigades and an air-landing brigade, and had become the 1st Airborne Division. But today was the first time they had all gone into action together. They were part of a vast armada of three allied divisions coming from some thirty airfields in western and eastern England, eventually forming two streams of aircraft and gliders heading out over the Essex and Suffolk coasts en route for Holland.

They saw very little of these armadas, although Bill had a better view than the other two. He was at the rear of his Dakota by a window on the port side, and through it he could see something of the fighter escort above them and the other aircraft carrying his brigade over the fields of East Anglia. As the aircraft circled and formed up, he saw people coming out of church in Spalding at about a quarter-to-twelve that morning. Later he saw air-sea rescue boats beneath them on the North Sea, and a glider down on the water. And as they approached the Dutch coast he could see flashes of fire coming from German gun-emplacements. But there was not enough flak to trouble them. Not enough to disturb the steady flight of the C47 Dakotas stretching across the sky around him.

Ron Holt had an uneventful flight as well. He was third in his stick, behind the platoon commander and his batman. Through the open door – its edges taped so that no rough areas could catch on their gear or clothing – he caught occasional glimpses of other aircraft rising and falling beside them. He had begun his army career in the Black Watch, then transferred to the Cheshires, and when late in 1942 an officer from the Parachute Regiment came round asking for volunteers, Ron had been one of those who had put his name forward. The plane rocked a little as it hit an air pocket, and he took a firmer grip on his Bren gun. They were crossing the Dutch coast now. He could hear the occasional burst of flak, but nothing anywhere near them.

For his part, Bill Collard had started his army life in the Gloucesters, and when his battalion was converted to anti-aircraft defence he felt it was time he moved on to something more interesting. So when he heard about the airborne forces he volunteered too. He was young, impatient. He was anxious to have a go.

John Nicholson's battalion was also being used in a defensive role when it was chosen as one of those to be transferred en bloc to the Parachute Regiment. Not everybody had agreed to go, but about seventy per cent had done so, though they had lost a few more later at Hardwick Hall and Ringway. They had been filling sandbags on the East Coast and by that time John was well sick of shovelling sand.

Ron Holt dozed a little over the North Sea. But suddenly it was Action Stations, and they were getting up and checking their static lines, pulling hard on the strops, turning to face the rear of the fuselage. Then the green light was on, and in a second or two he was out in the sunshine over the dropping zone, one of hundreds whose parachutes were blossoming around him . . .

Bill Collard's exit was trickier. Not because of anything the enemy were doing but because the Dakota he was in had got itself a bit too close to the ground. The pilots always went into a shallow dive on the run-in so that the canopies would not catch on the tail wheel as they deployed, but this time it looked as though the last men in the stick were not going to make it. 'We're getting bloody close to the ground,' bawled his dispatcher, as Bill came up to the door and went out. And Bill was forced to agree. To his practised eye they looked hardly more than 200 feet up.

Now it was John Nicholson's turn. As his pilot began the run-in he could not hear anyone firing at them either, and he hoped it stayed that way. He also hoped the generals who had planned all this were right and that there would not be too much opposition and that all the Germans in the area were cooks and stomach-cases, men who ought to be invalided out. That was what they had been told and that was what he hoped, but somehow he found it difficult to believe. He also found himself wondering why he had got himself into this outfit, what exactly had attracted him to the airborne forces in the first place, apart from the extra money and being fed up with shovelling sand, of course. But it was too late for any more thoughts of that nature now. The green light was on. His stick was moving towards the door. It was time to go, go, go, go, go . . .

Troops and containers are dropped at Arnhem.

2 480 Platoon falls in

On Monday 11 January 1982 forty-one successors to those three young men who had jumped at Arnhem in 1944 were due to report at Browning Barracks, the Parachute Regiment's Depot at Aldershot. It was the hardest winter for twenty years, and that weekend southern England had been swept by yet another blizzard. The skies had cleared by Sunday, but on Monday morning the snow lay frozen where it had fallen on the roofs of the barrack-blocks, on the parade-ground, and on the wings of the Douglas C47 Dakota where it stood in its World War 2 markings on a patch of ground in front of the barracks. It was a strangely un-English scene. As was Aldershot High Street too, where the snow was piled high in banks along the side of the road like some Tyrolean ski resort.

The Dakota in its World War 2 markings outside the Parachute Regiment's Depot at Aldershot.

480 Platoon were expected from 0700 hours onwards. So in the freezing pre-dawn gloom, the reception party – complete with minibus – waited as ordered at the station. The NCO in charge was Corporal Danny Lyden, one of the new platoon's instructors, a 24-year-old Glaswegian who had only recently got back to the depot himself off Christmas leave and was still in the process of readjustment.

The recruits came from all corners of the United Kingdom. One of the first to arrive was Ewan Fleming, from Dundee, and it was not long before

Captain Peter Boxall, Personnel Selection Officer (PSO) at the Regimental Depot, was able to put one of his favourite questions: 'What made you leave lovely old Scotland and come all the way down here to join the Parachute Regiment?'

Why recruits wanted to join the Regiment was explored much more systematically on the selection forms the recruits had to fill in. But the PSO liked to hear what they had to say for themselves and found it helped to get things off to a friendly start. Fleming said he had always thought the Parachute Regiment was the best in the British Army and so he had come to give it a good hard try. He was a tall, slim young man, who had worked successively in civvy street as sales assistant, storeman, machine operator and assistant parts manager. He had never been out of a job since leaving school in 1976, but nothing he had done had proved very exciting and he had turned to the Territorial Army for stimulation. '15 Para?' asked Boxall. 'Black Watch,' said Fleming.

Another early arrival was Aly Melvin. A six-footer like Fleming, but a little heavier in build, he was also from Dundee and also a TA member. 15 Para in his case, so he had some idea of what he was letting himself in for. Close behind came Mark Chard, a short, dark-haired lad from London, and Lee Clark, a tall, rather gangling young man from Kent. After a brief, disillusioning spell as a police cadet, he had been unemployed for the last year. His passion was playing the trumpet, his ambition to get into a military band. Why the Parachute Regiment's band? Well, when he went along to enquire at the recruiting office it was the only band that had any vacancies . . .

After them came another Londoner, Ian Woodcock, son of an RAMC major. For him the army was a totally familiar environment; he had spent all his life among soldiers and he wanted to continue that way. Eventually he hoped to follow in his father's footsteps and become an officer. And there was something about the lad that made Corporal Lyden feel sure he would achieve that ambition. As the Corporal said later, whenever he heard Woodcock calling him by name he had the urge to answer 'sir'. That had to be a good start for a potential officer. But these were early days. First he had to get through the twenty-two weeks of training and become a para. Until then he was just a 'crow' – as recruits were called – like the rest of them.

The first minibus load set off from the station, the icy snow crunching under the wheels. As the sun began to rise in a clear sky, they headed towards the Depot, new boys off to a sterner school than the ones they had recently left. Approaching Browning Barracks, they turned off the road and stopped at the barrier to let the sentry check their vehicle. Then they were through and pulling round behind the barrack-block where the minibus halted and let them off.

Now it was their civvy shoes crunching on the snow. Hands thrust into the pockets of raincoats, bomber-jackets, anoraks, they followed the corporal across the yard. Already they were beginning to feel slightly sheepish about their civilian appearance. As they ambled over to the barrack-block, soldiers came and went crisply along the asphalt paths trodden clear in the snow. Only they, the new recruits, walked to where they were going. Everybody else was marching or doubling. And though the RSM might cringe at the sight of them, though the military police might wet their lips and itch to tell them to 'pick 'em up and look a bit effing smart about it', these were early days yet and they would be given time to acclimatise.

Browning Barracks, 11 January 1982. 480's billets are on the ground floor of the block at left centre.

480 Platoon (minus Healey and Byrne) at the end of Selection Week.

Corporal Lyden's section at the end of Selection Week. Left to right, back row: Kentish, Tattum, Preston, Robertson; front row: Moy, Bush, Chard, Ward.

There was much to be done in the first two days – a great deal of administration, as their platoon sergeant explained to them – such things as medicals, kit issue, haircuts, documentation. Sergeant Kevin Riley was waiting for them in their billet, the ground floor of a modern barrack-block, called Ridgway and Blyth, with views out the back over the canal and fields that flanked the northern side of the camp. Like many institutional buildings it had a faintly tatty air, though efficient enough and incorporating the kind of improvements the modern soldier had come to expect. Endless barrack-blocks had gone out with endless hospital wards. Now there were rooms for eight soldiers, subdivided into sections of four to give a greater sense of privacy. But it was still very rudimentary accomodation – a bed, a mattress, a locker, and a chair at a communal formica-topped table. It was pretty spartan in the eyes of the modern young man used to the privacy of his own room and the comforts of his stereo music centre. That was another of the questions Captain Boxall liked to ask. Did they think they could stand living in a barrack-block with forty other people? Would they mind sharing a room with three other guys? And if that caused no problems, would they be capable of looking after themselves, keeping themselves and their lockers clean and tidy, making their beds, polishing the floors and all that sort of stuff?

These might seem very obvious points, but nowadays many young men had very little experience of looking after themselves, and the less these things took them by surprise the better. A new life was beginning for them. The bonds with the past were about to be broken. It was important they knew what to expect in the coming months so that they should not stumble or fall at the first hurdles. That was why the PSO liked to be sure there was nothing in their past to prevent them from going forward into their new careers. No left-over burdens. No debts or crimes. No ailing parents or unhappy girl-friends. Had Fleming, for instance, left a crying lassie at the railway station? No, said Fleming, he hadn't. He'd got that sorted out. Along with everything else that might prove a problem. His decision had been made after due and careful consideration. Nothing had been done on the spur of the moment. He had a very clear idea of what he had let himself in for.

Some of the others were not quite so confident on that score. And the pressures of the next few weeks were going to test their resilience, their ability to throw off their easy-going civilian ways, their resistance to the pull of emotional ties. It would be some time before they saw their homes and loved ones again. Comfort, privacy, girl-friend, leisure, family – all these were about to be blotted out. In their place would be the limited horizons they now saw about them – the room-mates they would have to share their immediate, intimate lives with, and the other recruits who were going to have to train and work with them.

It is one thing to contemplate joining the army, but quite another to do so. Statistically, for all those who go along to an army recruiting office only about half actually go in and make an enquiry. Of those, only about half come back. At which point the man concerned is considered a serious applicant and given a basic intelligence and aptitude test to ensure he is numerate and literate enough to reach the Army's standard. If he passes this satisfactorily he is given a medical examination, usually by a civilian GP, to see if he is fit to proceed further along the line. Only about one in ten of potential recruits reaches this point, and here there is a pause in the proceedings while the man waits for a place at the Recruit Selection Centre at Sutton Coldfield or, if he is in Scotland, the Recruit and Youth Selection Centre in Edinburgh. At these centres the individual is given a further series of intelligence, vocational and physical tests and either advised that the army is not for him or offered a vacancy in an appropriate arm. If satisfied with what he is offered, the recruit then goes home to wait until called to report to his training unit.

In Captain Peter Boxall's view, the urge to join the army must be both powerful and positive. The recruit should not be so much escaping from something disagreeable as searching for something better. Indeed, a study of the reasons given by 480 Platoon for their choice suggested that this was in fact the case. The selection form that recruits filled in listed nineteen different reasons for wanting to join the army, ranging from such vaguely glamorous things as 'adventure/travel' to the hard-nosed, sensible variety like 'job security' or 'learning a trade', and in view of the heavy unemployment figures in early 1982, particularly amongst young people, it would not seem unreasonable to imagine that the practical reasons would be the ones most likely to carry the day. Not a bit of it, however. The glamorous reasons won hands down. The combination of adventure and travel was by far the most popular. And such worthwhile things as 'belonging to a team' and 'getting responsibility' scored very highly too. Admittedly 'learning a trade' figured well up in the list, but such things as 'no suitable job in the area' or 'wearing a uniform' or 'to get away from home' came absolutely nowhere. Of course, it was possible a certain amount of canniness might have influenced the recruits' decisions in this particular section of the form, but it was hard to believe so consistent a choice was merely the result of a desire to impress the PSO. It seemed that most of the young men who joined 480 Platoon knew what they were about, or at any rate thought they did, and the images they had of the army were positive, not negative. Maybe they would not make the grade. Maybe they would change their minds. Maybe the army would not be what they thought it was. But when they walked in through the Depot gate, they had a pretty clear idea what they were looking for and had spent some time waiting for it to become a reality.

In some cases there had been over a year between walking into the recruiting office and reporting to the Para Depot on 11 January 1982. Alex Preston had to wait so long before being summoned to Sutton Coldfield that he had begun to think the army had forgotten about him: 'I mean, I rang them up twice,' he said, 'went round, kept going round, and they kept just saying you'll have to wait.' His room-mate, Dean Ward, was just as keen. He had wanted to join the army ever since the age of thirteen, when he had got a foretaste of military life in the Army Cadets. He had wanted to go in as a junior at sixteen, but his mother would not let him because of the trouble in Northern Ireland. She tried to dissuade him again, when he was eighteen. But as much as he respected his mother's wishes, Dean insisted that his mind was made up. So, bowing before the inevitable, she had given him a big surprise farewell-party the Friday before he joined, and sent him on his way with her blessing. As a rule, the parents were opposed to their sons joining the army. Only rarely did they recommend it as a solution to a boy's career problems, as in Lee Clark's case, and even there it probably had more to do with the educational opportunities available to him as a musician than out of desire to see him patrol the streets of Londonderry. Clark's choices were less romantic than many others. For him 'learning a trade' came first, then 'job security' followed by 'good pay'.

John Hughes, on the other hand, did not join for the money. He had had a job with a photographer but had wanted to try something different. All he seemed to do at home was go from the alehouse to his girl, from his girl to the alehouse, and then back to his ma and his da. It was getting pretty boring. A mate he worked with was a Para for seven years. Hughes used to do a lot of training with him. A lot of weight-lifting. The physical life appealed to him. Outdoor activities. Sport. Adventure. Travel. His eyes had a fairly puzzled look about them. Whatever precisely it was that had brought him there, he no longer seemed sure he would find it. Though of course there was one reason they all had in common, as Graham Harrison explained when questioned on the subject a few weeks later.

It was a freezing cold day and the platoon was standing at attention on the parade ground in open order, being inspected by Regimental Sergeant Major Howard Lewis. They all stared dutifully into the middle distance while Harrison was being interrogated. Not a muscle twitched, not an eyeball flickered. To all intents and purposes they had no idea what Harrison was talking about and cared even less. But in fact every man jack of them was all ears and agreed with every word he said.

'What made you join the Parachute Regiment, Harrison?' said the RSM.

'Because I wanted to fly, sir,' he replied. 'Jump out of the sky.'

'Fly and jump out of the sky, eh?'

'Yes, sir!'

'Then why didn't you become a jet pilot?'

'I just wanted to jump out of aeroplanes, sir.'

'Oh. So you're not intelligent enough to be a jet pilot, but daft enough to be a parachutist? That's what it is, is it?'

'Yes, sir,' said Harrison.

And from all sides, silently, chests out, eyes front, three rows of inner voices echoed, 'Yes, sir, that's what it is!' That was the dream at the end of the rainbow, all right.

But on Monday 11 January 1982 parachuting was still a long way off. More than four months off. Between then and Brize Norton, the Parachute Training School, lay a lot of hard work and physical effort, a lot of drill, discipline, and spit and polish. All the things to be found in any other regiment plus a great deal extra because they were Paras and more was expected from Paras than from other regiments of the line. Especially physically. The medical examination they received on entry paid attention to specific points. As the Medical Officer explained: 'We know that knees, ankles and chests are a problem here, so one checks them specifically.' Any doubt on that score and the recruit was sent to the military hospital for a second opinion from a specialist, who – because he was a soldier himself as well as a doctor – was able to know whether it would be dangerous for a man to start the sort of training Paras were put through.

The Medical Officer came as something of a surprise to the recruits of 480. Captain Bergman was not quite what they expected. Plump, brisk, jolly, efficient – nothing unusual about that. But somehow they had never imagined the Para MO would be a woman, a bit of a tomboy, who serviced her own car and was attracted to the army out of a sense of adventure. Beverly Bergman was the only medical corps woman in the Paras and regarded it as a great honour to wear the insignia of the regiment she was attached to.

'Now then,' she said to Graham Robertson, another Scot, from Perth, who had been born and bred in Rhodesia, 'you've been overseas, I see, and you had a health problem while you were there. You were ill for a while about five years ago, your doctor said. You probably won't remember it. It's obviously not left you with any problems. Now put your hands on your hips, please, and take a deep breath in . . .'

And so the different processes went on for the first two days until all the interviews, medicals, kit issues and documentation had been completed and the recruits were settling down in their sections and getting to know each other and their section leader. Each of the five sections was commanded by a corporal, who was the NCO they would be closest to for the next twenty-two weeks. He would be friend, guide, parent, teacher, warder, judge. He would shout at them, sneer at them, threaten them, loathe them, disapprove of them, like them, protect them and find them superior in every way to the members of all the other sections. Gradually a symbiotic union would grow between them so that temporarily he would need them as much as they needed him.

Well, that was the theory anyway. And it clearly makes a great deal of sense. The section is the basic army unit, the brick from which battalions are built. And the corporal commands the section, in war as well as in training. In some ways it is the best job in the army, close to the men, with lots of responsibility and satisfaction. Already several of the recruits had grasped that fact, had envisaged becoming corporals themselves one day as one of their prime aims. In their eyes, a sergeant's job seemed far less attractive. He was moving out of that charmed area of human contact with his men. He was on the way to becoming an administrator, one of 'them', a man at a distance and – because he was responsible for discipline – a man to hate. Also a man the private soldier could afford to hate. But he couldn't hate his corporal, because his corporal was a sort of mum, dad and big brother all rolled into one.

Corporal Lyden demonstrated to his section how to use a steam-iron. Then how to wear the uniform he was ironing. Ward acted as model. He wore the socks, the boots, the denim trousers, the pullover. Then the beret. The famous beret. The red beret. There was rapt attention as Corporal Lyden showed them how to fit the badge and keep it over the corner of the left eye. Now they were getting somewhere.

Corporal Lyden was earnest, thoughtful, a dutiful mum. In the next room along the corridor, Corporal Baker was addressing his section with an elder brother's twinkle in his eye. 'Nice baggy shorts, just like your grandad used to wear.' He held up a shirt. 'Lovely smooth material – just like sandpaper.' Then he warned them of the dangers of putting their pullovers in the washing-machine. They'd get no sympathy from the quartermaster's stores. Just a new pullover and be told: 'Ten pounds. Sign 'ere. 'oof it.' Next he waxed lyrical about the boots. Lovely boots. Really nice. But they did take some breaking in. The trick was to put them in a sink full of hot water for a bit, then set about them with a tin of polish.

By the end of the first day – rather to the platoon staff's surprise, in view of the weather – everybody had arrived except one. And he was not coming at all. He had had second thoughts since his visit to Sutton Coldfield. But since another soldier – back-squadded through injury – was joining the platoon, the numbers still stood at forty-one. There were twenty-five Englishmen (one of them black), ten Scots, four Welsh, and two Irish. The average age was twenty, the youngest seventeen and ten months, the oldest twenty-five and three months. Half the platoon had, at some time or another, had some close relative (a father, an uncle or a brother) in the forces, and eight of them had served in the Army Cadets or the TA. Here again the bias favoured the Scots. Four out of ten had been in the TA, two of them members of 15 Para.

Although the recession was at its height, very few of them had been noticeably affected by unemployment. Certainly some had – four of them, from Scotland and the North, had been unemployed for a year or more – but this was exceptional, and only in two cases could it really be considered a serious factor in their joining the army. Other unemployment was very temporary – often in the last few months while waiting to be called into the army. In fact half the intake had been involved in some kind of apprentice-ship or training scheme, and a fair number of those had completed their time as tradesmen. So the decision to join the army seemed to have little to do with personal inadequacies or a hostile environment.

The replacement for the missing recruit was Austin Hindmarsh, a dark-haired, dark-browed, tight-lipped young man who had been in the army for more than eighteen months while a leg injury held up his training. He was now setting off once again – a veteran amongst the new boys – in an effort to complete the course. The course was tough and injuries were common. An insulation engineer in civvy street, he had got the sack for swearing. That seemed rather a harsh decision. Was it for swearing in front of a customer? No, said Hindmarsh. For swearing at his boss.

Sergeant Riley arrived to see how Section 1 was getting on. They were lucky having Hindmarsh, he told them. He could help them out with any problems, show them how things were done. Hindmarsh rather resented this suggestion. It was Sergeant Riley's job to teach recruits – not his. He had enough to do looking after himself.

Outside the window night was falling. The temperature – below freezing all day – was falling too. But inside the billets everything was snug. The radiators were thumping out heat, beds were strewn with gear and clothing. Here and there, as tentative work started on the boots, the recruits were also beginning to learn more about their room-mates. It was quite a culture-shock for some of them, to be living on equal terms with Jock and Taff, Scouse and Cockney. John Hughes, the stocky lad from Liverpool, was a bit taken aback by it all. He'd got two Welshmen in his section, he said, and one of them – Taffy Hunt – never stopped talking. If he'd met him in a pub in civvy street, he'd have called him a stupid effing Welsh twit and probably gone and smacked him one. Whereas here he was one of his mates, wasn't he? It made you think, that sort of thing.

On the second day he and the rest of 480 were given a lot more to think about. Captain Peter Boxall and Captain John Baird, their platoon commander, gave the recruits a clearer idea of the difficulties that lay before them. They were reminded that the selection process they had gone through had taken time and effort. To have got this far was an achievement showing a high degree of motivation, but what lay ahead would be even more demanding. The training programme was tough, both physically and mentally. So tough that it was important none of them should embark on it without very careful physical and medical screening. It was for this reason that the course began with a preliminary selection week – a prerogative the Paras shared only with the Guards. The Guards had it because of the special drill emphasis in their training, the Paras because of the special physical emphasis in theirs. If, at the end of this first week, the recruits were found to be fit and there were no other problems, then – as the PSO put it – 'You're in, you're on, and you can get started.' But, as he went on to explain, at the end of eight weeks would come a moment to take stock, a moment for the recruit and the army to decide whether the time had come to part company. Anyone wanting to leave must put in his application before three months were up because, after that date, for those who were eighteen or over: 'You're in, you're ours, and you stay,' as the PSO put it in another series of his pungent phrases.

But while 480 were still digesting this piece of information, and possibly feeling the military web to be closing about them, John Baird presented the other side of the picture. The Paras didn't take any old thing. The eighth week was a sieve they found useful too. And the sieves went on operating right up until the end of the course. Not everybody who wanted to would pass. In fact, if they were to go by the average figures for the last few courses, only about one in three of those who actually started out would finish successfully. And whether they would be amongst that number depended entirely on the way in which they approached the training. It was all about determination and will-power. That was the key. Determination and will-power. That was all that really mattered in the

Captain John Baird addresses 480 Platoon.

end. 'You might not be as fit as the next guy,' he said. 'That doesn't necessarily matter. You might pass because you know you can do it. All you have to do is put the pain out of your mind and say: I can do it, I will do it, and you will.'

One in three. It was a daunting forecast. Roughly fourteen out of the forty-one members of the platoon sitting in the lecture hall that afternoon. Or only two or three from every section. Suddenly your mate became your competitor if that was the case. If him, then possibly not you, and vice versa. Who of those sitting there today would be left in twenty-two weeks' time when those who had completed the course successfully marched on to the square for their passing-out parade? Fleming, the quiet Scot, ex-storeman, ex Black Watch (TA)? Hughes, bored with his trips to and from the alehouse and looking to better himself and become somebody? The musical Clark, the talkative Hunt, the old sweat Hindmarsh? It was impossible to know. The hurdles were so many and various. Maybe it would be the taciturn Melvin or the small and chirpy Chard who, like everyone else, had left a little of his individuality at the barber's. He had heard what Captains Baird and Boxall had to say. Had they managed to put him off at all? Or was he still determined to go through with it?

Oh yes, said Chard. He'd do it. He knew he would. Even if it killed him.

3 Trial Run

It was Wednesday morning and the platoon were out for the first of the many runs to come. 'Basic Fitness Test' it was called on the programme, or BFT in the initial-ridden language of the army. Part of a carefully graded programme of physical activity designed to bring the recruit by degrees to the physical standard required of him in the Parachute Regiment. The distance they had to cover was one and a half miles and, although they did not know it, they were in the process of setting the time they would be judged on during the next twelve weeks. Whatever time they clocked today they would be expected to improve on next week, and the fortnight after, and the fortnight after that.

The snow was still crisp and deep underfoot. A thick mist covered the fields. The platoon had set off in a bunch from the barracks and were now returning in a long straggling line, the pad of their feet and the rasp of their breathing muffled on the morning air, their red vests the only touch of colour in the wintry landscape.

'Come on! Push, push!' Their platoon staff and the PT instructors were running with them, urging them on, goading those who dropped behind. 'Come on! Sprint the last 300 metres! Come on, open those effing legs!'

The hounding went on. Right down the path along the side of the Farnham road, over the canal bridge, through the fence and down into the patch of scrubland behind the barracks, a gap of nearly half a mile between the first and the last of the runners, Gary Price and Michael Healey, both in the same section, both fond of sport and the outdoor life according to the interests they had listed on their selection forms. Price was home in 8 minutes 50, with Fleming hot on his heels, and Tony Butler, a stocky, muscled Judo expert, about fifty yards behind. A Welshman, a Scotsman and an Englishman leading the field home; a Welshman, an Englishman and a Scotsman, in that order, bringing up the rear. The Scot was Andy Cunningham, a big 19-year-old from Ayrshire who, like Woodcock, hoped eventually to become an officer.

Steaming, red-faced, chests heaving, their breath vaporising in the cold morning air, they lined up in front of the billet while their times were checked and recorded by the PTIs (Physical Training Instructors). Now the pressure was on. Civvy street was receding across the mist-enshrouded fields. The two-day period of acclimatisation was giving way to three days of assessment and introduction to the training programme. The army was taking over. The civilian crowd was turning into a military platoon. The long-haired individuals in their jeans and bomber jackets were merging gradually into a uniform group. Up to now they had been shambling about in a bunch, half in, half out of step. From now on some order would begin to prevail. Their heads would come up, their shoulders go back, their arms would swing. And those of them who, in the colourful language of the Company Sergeant Major, had formerly 'walked about with pins through their snotters, in vomit-stained wellies and blood-stained shirts', would have to put all that sort of nastiness behind them and reconcile themselves to dressing correctly.

At the same time, they were going to start doing drill, the aim of which, according to Army Orders, was to 'produce discipline, co-ordination and the habit of alert obedience to the orders of a superior', so that, by learning teamwork, 'the soldier's confidence and pride in himself, his comrades and his superiors will grow and a solid foundation for future training will be established'. And the person whose immediate responsibility it was to inculcate these virtues was the Platoon Sergeant, Kevin Riley, or 'Skull' as he subsequently came to be known. 'Marching is only an extension of walking, nothing more,' he said. And then, as that was sinking in, he added as a faintly menacing afterthought: 'Except it's a very *smart* method!'

The platoon was in the drill shed, an open-sided building giving on to the square, for use when the weather made drilling difficult. The parade ground was still heavily encrusted with snow and ice. The platoon corporals prowled the perimeter of the squad, keeping an eye on individuals, noting any blunder or act of indiscipline amongst members of their own sections. Corporal Al Slater had a spot of advice for them, too. 'Look directly to your front,' he snapped. 'Don't follow anybody around with your eyes because you get noticed immediately.' Nothing wrong with that, surely? Getting noticed was the mark of the interesting individual, wasn't it? The way to get on in the world? Not in the army, apparently. And certainly not while you were just a recruit. According to Corporal Slater, getting noticed was absolutely the last thing you wanted to do.

Up, up. Down, down. Up, up. Down, down. Up, up. Down, down. The cries bounced rhythmically backwards and forwards across the gym that afternoon as the recruits stepped up on to a bench, and back down again, up on to a bench and back down. The Depot PT staff were putting 480 through yet another set of initials, the APFT this time, or the Army Personnel Fitness Test. This was calculated to reveal the areas of physical weakness in each individual so that, by careful application, those weaknesses could be remedied. Attention was paid to the lungs, the heart, the upper and the lower body. Again Tony Butler did well, as did Hughes and Philip Tattum, a tall ex-lumberjack from North Wales. Cunningham, who had been near the back on the BFT, was way down the list on this test as well. Too few press-ups. Too few pull-ups. He was a big man, clumsy at times, as if he'd outgrown his strength. And twice today he'd broken Corporal Slater's golden rule and got himself noticed.

But at least he hadn't run into the trouble facing Stephen Wood and Kevin Byrne. They had been unfortunate enough to fail their medicals and had been sent off to specialists at the military hospital for a second opinion. Wood's problem was his knees, Byrne's his high blood pressure. It had come as no surprise to him. It was diagnosed initially in Liverpool and then again at Sutton Coldfield, and though the doctor there agreed it was a bit high, he had finally decided to pass him. So for Byrne to arrive at the Depot and learn he was not fit to do the training and would have to be discharged had come as a bitter blow to him. He had set his heart on the Paras, waited sixteen months for it. And now it had been snatched away from him, he said, before he had even had a chance to show what he could do. He had packed his job in, too. Wouldn't get that back, he'd be on the dole now, so all hope of saving up to, maybe, marry the girl in the photo propped up on the chair beside his bed had disappeared out the window. Already he had been moved out of No. 4 Section's room, as if to stay there any longer might contaminate the others. Certainly his misery was evident enough, his bitterness towards the army, too. He felt he'd been had. Led up the garden. Given a glimpse of the promised land only to have the gate slammed in his face. It was heart-breaking. He couldn't believe it. He blamed that doctor at Sutton Coldfield. If he hadn't passed him fit for the Paras, maybe he might have got in to some other outfit. Now it was too late, wasn't it? His section commander, Corporal Slater, came in to the tiny room. He was too embarrassed by what had happened to Byrne to be able to look at him. His eyes drifted along the top of the window. It was time Byrne got his kit together. They were waiting for it over in the stores.

At much the same time, Healey, the young man who had come in last on the BFT, was parading in front of Recruit Company's Officer Commanding to explain why it was he wanted to leave the army after so short a stay. It was his right, of course, if he so wished, said Major David Roberts. No question of that. But having gone to so much time and trouble to get there, it seemed rather extraordinary that Healey should now want to jack it all in! There were plenty of poor buggers in civvy street who'd be only too grateful to be in his place. So what was the matter, then? Why had he suddenly decided he wanted to leave? Healey could not find a satisfactory answer to that one. He just didn't like it. No, he wasn't homesick. He didn't think he'd enjoy the training, that's all. And that was that. Right turn and fall out, in a shuffling, civvy sort of way.

Oddly enough Healey came from Corporal Slater's section too. But unlike Byrne, he couldn't wait to hand his kit in. Only too glad to get rid of it and go back to the life he'd been leading before. It was an interesting illustration of how one man's promised land could be another man's desert. Not that thoughts of that kind were any consolation to the company commander. His irritation was perfectly understandable. Every regiment in the British army had an annual quota of recruits allocated to it. Every recruit who fell by the wayside, or was invalided out, or voluntarily opted to leave, was a man lost to that regiment. Healey had simply wasted one of those rare and valuable places.

By the same token Byrne had reason to complain about how he had been treated. It could be argued that by passing him fit at his initial medical examination, only to turn him down at the Depot, the army had, by their own incompetence, effectively wasted about eighteen months of his life. Besides squandering one of the valuable places from their annual quota.

None of the parties concerned could draw much comfort from this particular sequence of events. But it brought to an end the slightly honeymoonish quality this first selection week had possessed. On Tuesday afternoon their platoon commander, John Baird, had addressed them all as gentlemen. By Friday, the gloves were coming off and those who spoke to them were being rather less polite. Company Sergeant Major Sean Lucey, for instance, didn't mince his words. In the course of a colourful and no-nonsense speech he made it very clear what was expected of them in the Army and issued them with a very wide-ranging list of dos and don'ts.

Mainly don'ts. Such things as not making a nuisance of themselves in Aldershot where, as obvious squaddies, they would stick out like 'bulldogs' bollocks'. He also advised against excessive drinking in off-duty hours, especially if it led to unwarranted 'gobbing-off' about being a Para in the presence of other soldiers. Because – if they were foolish enough to indulge in that sort of behaviour – not only would they end up 'looking like a panda in the intensive care unit of the military hospital', but they would also 'appear in front of their Company Commander on Monday morning' who would immediately withdraw £70 or so of their capital off them and restrict their privileges. Then, after a few words on the subject of theft, which he found both abhorrent and nauseous, he went on to warn them of the danger of falling foul of the military police who, besides wearing big daft red hats and being disliked by everybody in the army except, oddly enough, the military police, had exactly the same powers as the civil police and weren't afraid to use them if provoked.

This was a point that Provost Sergeant Brian Kelly of the Regimental Police was also anxious to make, when it was his turn to speak to 480. His points might have been less wide-ranging than CSM Lucey's, but they had the power to send a shiver down the newly-upright spines of every member of the platoon as they stood in the snow before him. He had only four rules, he said. He didn't like people to steal. He didn't like people to get drunk. He didn't like people to go absent. Fourth, and most important, he didn't like catching anybody doing any of those things. But if he did, that was when he and they would come face to face – 'Look to the front, there! Not at me!' he bellowed – and he could assure them, without the slightest shadow of doubt, that that was an encounter he would win.

Behind him as he talked was Kelly's Kingdom. To the casual eye it was set in a barrack-block like any other, at the back of a pleasant inner court-yard suggestive of patio walks and goldfish ponds. Only on closer inspection did one become aware of the bars on the windows, the hatless and beltless prisoners labouring inside, and the guard on the door. Of all his rules, it was rule number three that was most surprising. Going absent. Why should anyone want to go absent in today's army? Like Kelly's Kingdom and its promise of unnamed horrors taking place inside its walls, it was another unexpectedly sinister note that was being struck – and one that sounded from a number of different quarters. Even as early as their second day there, come to think of it, in the PSO's address. He had told them that if they wanted to leave the army after their eight weeks' basic training, they must make sure they got their application in before three months were up. But what happened if they didn't? Well, CSM Lucey had a few words on that subject too.

'Absence and desertion, one and the same, that means you leave here with no intention of returning. Step out of line on that side of life and you'll get done.' No ambiguity there. Nor in RSM Howard Lewis's contribution late that Friday afternoon, even though delivered in the kindest and most understanding of all possible tones. He appreciated what a shock it must be coming from an easy civilian environment into a difficult military one like this. He also appreciated that after a week or two, or even much later, there might creep over the recruit a yen for his mother's cooking, a longing to see his girl-friend, or simply an urge to take the dog for a walk or go and watch Liverpool play Everton on a Saturday afternoon. All these things were very understandable. But if the soldier were foolish enough to succumb to one or other of these temptations and decided after a spell of leave not to return to barracks, then all he would be doing would be making a rod for his own back. Because, when he finally did come back – as they all did eventually, maybe after six months, or a year, or even longer – he would end up in 'that little enchanted cottage at the bottom of the stairs', that Kingdom known as Kelly's, which was not a pleasant place, wasn't meant to be a pleasant place, and where the beltless and hatless prisoner would have ample time to rue the day he'd ever chosen to go absent. That sort of thing simply wasn't necessary in today's army. If a recruit had any problems, he should tell his corporal or his platoon sergeant. No need to be shy in front of them. As CSM Lucey had pointed out, buggery, thuggery, theft and incest, they'd heard it all. It didn't surprise or embarrass them. If a recruit was in trouble, much better he should go to them for help than try and handle it on his own.

All very sensible advice. But like so much advice, seemingly irrelevant to most of 480 at that time. Getting into the Paras was a dream some of them had had for years. So why should they want to go absent? They had far more pressing problems than that to worry about. Their legs were killing them. In some cases every bit of their body was killing them. Every time they went into a lecture and sat down, they knew they were going to be as stiff as planks when they tried to get up again. They weren't used to it yet. They'd had it easy in civvy street, especially over Christmas. Too much to eat and drink, precious little exercise. Not that they were complaining about the effort demanded of them here. Not at all. They liked it. That was what they had come for. And they knew the army had it all worked out. They weren't just going to throw them in at the deep end, to sink or swim as they could. It was all planned. All progressive. Designed to build them up gradually. All right, they were expected to deliver the goods, give a hundred per cent, hundred and ten per cent even, but nothing wrong in that, was there? That was the way they'd get fit, get tough, get fit and tough enough to pass the course. And that wasn't just the individuals' attitude either, not in Corporal Baker's section. Even though they'd only been together a few days, they were getting to know each other, starting to pull together, and that was important, because when times got hard, when they felt like dropping out of the runs, or jacking it in, then all the others could shout at them, call them names, keep them going and drive them on.

Steve Birrell was one of the leading personalities in 3 Section. He had a strong feeling of identity with the group he was in, as well as a sympathetic understanding of his superiors' point of view. He could quite easily see how difficult a task it was for them getting the likes of him into some kind of soldierly shape. Hadn't he taken nearly ten and a half minutes in their first BFT? Plenty of room for improvement there. A similar stoicism emerged from the other sections. Yes, they were a bit fed up with all the cleaning, but that was just part of the job, wasn't it? One of the things you had to get used to. If you were on a battlefield, you couldn't turn round and say: 'I'm fed up with this, I'm knocking off now, I'm going home to have me tea.'

It was late on Friday afternoon. A temporary thaw had set in. For the first time in several weeks the temperature had risen above freezing. The effects of all the inoculations were taking their toll. Polio. Typhoid. Paratyphoid. Tetanus. They had so many bugs in their bloodstream, they needed time to let them settle down. But the working week still wasn't over. The army works till lunchtime on Saturday. Elementary drill and minor team games were on the programme for the following morning, and there were a bewildering number of chores to get on with. Ironing clothes, cleaning boots, polishing floors, tidying lockers, folding all your things in a particular sort of way, and then, if they weren't folded right, refolding them until everything finally achieved a shape and size your section corporal found satisfactory. That sort of thing wasn't so much a physical as a mental strain. But again, if you wanted to be a Para, it was something you had to put up with.

One thing they were all agreed on. Not much chance of doing any of the things CSM Lucey had warned them against. For a start they weren't allowed out till they passed off the Square at the end of the fourth week. So, unless they wanted to take a chance and go over the wall, making a nuisance of themselves in Aldershot was automatically ruled out. And they didn't feel they'd be doing much drinking either. Too busy in the evening for that. Or too tired. And nobody in his right mind would want to do one of those runs with a hangover and Corporal Slater or Sergeant Riley breathing down his neck. But again, that was how it was. They weren't complaining. Certainly not Tattum, who sat bulling his boots, teeth like a row of tent-pegs beneath the dark arch of his moustache. 'I mean if you crack up doing this,' he said, 'you're not going to be much good on the battlefield, are you?'

Again that remark about the battlefield. No one could say they did not realise where their decision might be leading them. At that time, of course, the only battlefield Tattum was likely to see service on was Northern Ireland. But since all the battalions did tours in the Province, he could very well end up there. Worse things could happen to a soldier than having to clean his boots. And Tattum was right to bear that possibility in mind. He was also looking forward to an intensification of the physical work. The bull had to be done but it gave him no pleasure. The running and the assault courses and the outdoor exercise were what he enjoyed. The way he reckoned he'd enjoy the parachuting when he got that far. *If* he did, that is, for at the moment it seemed an awfully long way off, which was another point CSM Lucey was at pains to draw to their attention.

Many of them probably misguidedly thought, he said, that once they had joined the Parachute Regiment all they were going to do was get themselves down here and start throwing themselves out of aircraft. Well, they weren't. It was a long time before they would see that aircraft, it was a long time before they would throw themselves out of that aircraft. Before that they were there to do an awful lot of physically hard and mentally hard training, and only the very toughest amongst them were going to survive. That was a fact of life. He wanted them to remember that. He also wanted them to know that he didn't intend to wish them good luck as those that had gone before him had done, because in his opinion luck played no part in it. What counted, what would see them through, was their ability to absorb information, suffer hardship and drive themselves on.

It was a Churchillian vision. Nothing but blood, sweat and tears. Did Tattum think he'd make it? Have to wait and see, wouldn't they? But no way would he give up of his own free will. He liked it here. If the Parachute Regiment wanted to get rid of him, they would have to kick him out.

4 The Pressure goes on

However, there was no danger of that happening just yet. For those medically fit, the next seven weeks were the critical probationary period in which both the Regiment and the recruits would have the opportunity of finding out what they had let themselves in for. Having survived selection week, the next moment of truth would come after something known as Basic Wales, a week in the field on the army training grounds around Brecon Beacons. That was due in the seventh week and would come as the climax to that section of the programme in which the individual military skills were taught. These skills were common to all arms, but the standard of attainment demanded of the Paras was just that much tougher.

But before Basic Wales there was a smaller group-hurdle to cross at the Depot. An intensive four-week period of PT, drill, fieldcraft and elementary weapon training, which led up to a formal parade where the Platoon demonstrated it was fit to pass off the Square. By then the recruits should have mastered the basic soldierly skills, learnt enough drill to salute officers, march about smartly and mount guard, and acquired some knowledge of the history of the regiment they aspired to belong to. During the first four weeks there was nothing to distinguish 480 Platoon from the recruits of any other unit. They wore denim fatigues, white name-tags across their chests, the peaked DPM (Disruptive Pattern Material) combat cap, and had to call out the time in unison with every drill movement they performed. They also usually had to double from place to place as a platoon. But since that had a great deal to recommend it in the freezing weather they were being subjected to, the recruits did not really consider that a chore. The hats, however, were deeply hated.

What is the first thing that comes to mind when the man in the street thinks of the Paras? The red beret. And for 480 Platoon not being allowed to wear theirs for the first four weeks was a cruel deprivation. Instead they had to wear what they described as craphats – their DPM caps. Usually, craphat was a term used by Paras to describe the ordinary blue beret worn by most of the other regiments and corps in the British Army. But by extension it had come to mean, in 480's eyes, any hat other than their beloved red beret, and so their combat caps took the full brunt of their hatred and contempt. As a result they tended to get thrown about a great deal. Onto beds, against walls, into lockers, or across the room at section

*Birrell in front of his
locker. Note the DPM
cap on the table.*

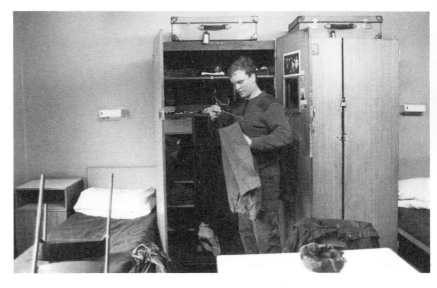

mates who had incurred displeasure. 480 could not wait for the moment
when their endeavours would be crowned in the only proper way for a
Para, by the right to wear their own personal red berets. Until then the
coveted berets sat on shelves in their lockers and were taken out from time
to time to be admired, brushed, tried on and generally fussed over.

It was not long before several of the platoon managed to break the Slater
commandment: Thou shalt not get noticed. Amongst other things, Aly
Melvin's previous TA experience in 15 Para was proving more of a burden
than a blessing. It laid him open to charges of complacency, to knowing it
all, to thinking he could take an easy ride just because he'd done some of
the training before. This was not, of course, how he saw it. In his eyes he
was giving of his best. It wasn't his fault if certain NCOs misjudged him.
Like the time when he was smiling at a passing 'bird' and his section
commander, Corporal Priestley, had thought he was amused about the
drill mistake he'd just made. Melvin denied it, of course, but denying things
in the army had a way of making your guilt seem greater with every denial.
It also made you even more noticed than you were before the incident
occurred. So the truly canny Scot bowed his head and kept his trap shut.

But even silence could not help Cunningham. His lumbering bulk stood
out near the back of the field in all the BFTs. These $1\frac{1}{2}$-mile runs – or 'tabs'
as they were usually called – were the bane of his existence. And plenty of
other people were haunted by them too. Several even confessed to dream-
ing about them the night before, running them over and over again in their
sleep, eyelids and legs twitching as they lay in their beds, running,
running, from midnight to daybreak, over the field by Queen's Parade,
back down the Farnham Road and across the canal and into the barracks.
And when they awoke at Reveille they said they often felt so tired they

hardly had the strength to drag themselves out of bed and into the washrooms and across to the cookhouse for breakfast.

Admittedly Cunningham improved his position in the second BFT, moving from thirty-sixth place to thirty-third. But since, in the interval, two of the recruits had been discharged, and another one was waiting to go, the improvement was rather less dramatic than it seemed at first sight. And it wasn't just the BFTs that were giving Cunningham trouble. He had also failed one part of the fitness test in the selection week and had already come to his Company Commander's notice on that score. So he had been fairly consistently noticed, and as a result got rather more attention from his section leader, Corporal Lyden, than either of them really cared for.

Meanwhile the pressure was gradually being applied in other areas as well. Besides the drill and the bulling of boots and the cleaning out of the lavatories and washrooms – all of which seemed more or less reasonable activities – other weirder demands were being made of them by Sergeant Riley. They were expected to shine their billet floors with black boot polish and to rub away industriously with wire wool at the corridor dustbin till it gleamed like the Officers' Mess silver. Seemingly pointless activities that irritated many of them. Cleanliness they understood. Germs spread diseases. They were all living together at close quarters. Infection could easily spread. But to spend hours polishing a floor with boot polish only to

Woof at work on the washroom floor.

Sergeant Riley wrestles with an administrative problem. Hindmarsh looks on.

have the dazzling surface scuffed and ruined within seconds of anyone entering the room seemed like madness. Riley's madness. A madness, however, in which some of the more philosophically inclined discerned a method. It was all part of the disciplinary process. It was a way of teaching you to do what you were told. Anybody could do something that seemed reasonable. But if, every time you were told to do something you couldn't see the reason for, you started questioning it, then the whole of the army's discipline would rapidly fall apart.

Graham Robertson, the young Scot from Perth, understood this. As he saw it, bull was designed to create good habits in the future. It was all part of the army's very sensible procedures. He had no complaints on that score. He was also one of those whose ambition it was to be a corporal. Their pay was good, they had a good, comradely life together, they weren't subjected to the pressures and expenses that faced the officers and top NCOs. He was only seventeen and ten months, but he had given his future career a lot of careful thought. Before coming into the army, he'd worked in a pet-shop and liked it so much that he decided he wanted one of his own. 'So I thought, if I can get up in the ranks a wee bit,' he said with a quiet gleam in his eyes at the prospect, 'enjoy myself and stay in the army for a few years, I can try and get a bit of capital and buy myself a business.' And with that prospect in view all the bull and the physical effort were no problem to him.

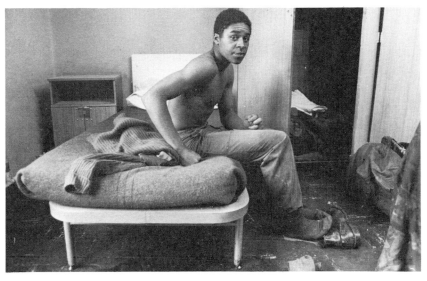

Hooper applies a final touch to a toe cap, while Ward relaxes in the billet.

Unlike Cunningham, however, Robertson wasn't getting noticed at this stage. His quiet manner, his reluctance to push himself forward, his thoughtful, contained approach to the work and to the world in general, all conspired to make him melt into the background. And yet he was scoring well enough in the BFTs and the assessment tests. It would be some time yet before his qualities came to be properly recognised. As was the case with Nick Moy in the same section, another dark horse like Robertson, and also one of the youngest. He had no time for what he saw as useless bull, but he didn't mind the physical work. 'I hate it while I'm doing it,' he said. 'But I get a great feeling of satisfaction when I've finished it.' At one time he'd applied to get into the Marines as an officer, but by the time they got round to processing his application the educational standards had gone beyond what he had to offer, so he'd chosen the Paras instead. More critically-minded than Robertson, he was just as determined and, if any-thing, had joined more for excitement and adventure than out of any deliberate planning about his future.

By week 3 of their training, cross-country runs had been added to the routine 'tabs', and most of the platoon were holding up under the strain. Some, like Cunningham, had improved their BFT times considerably – in his case by almost a minute. And only one – Hunt – had failed to improve. Immediately the PT staff wanted to know why. Was Hunt slacking? Injured? Whichever it was, action had to be taken quickly. Either they had to get a grip on him, or give him extra training when he'd recovered from the injury, to enable him to catch up with the others.

The technical expertise of the PTIs was awe-inspiring. Each part of the recruit's body was carefully monitored so that any failure or difficulty in any particular area could be identified and corrected. The heart and lungs might be strong, but the legs might be letting him down. He might have a good running action, but not have the strength in the upper part of the leg – a possible reason for Hunt's problem. Cunningham's weakness, on the other hand, was in the upper body. A big man, he had difficulty heaving up to the beam – though already there was some improvement since the first APFT.

In week 3 another member of Corporal Slater's section, Peter Richards, decided he had had enough and asked to be discharged. It was a sudden decision, one he retracted a few days later, but by that time he had missed too much of the training to be able to catch up. He was temporarily attached to HQ company, where he would wait to join the next platoon when it was due to form. Corporal Slater's section had now lost half its original complement, four out of eight. Two had been discharged as medically unfit, one was a voluntary discharge, and the latest, Richards, back-squadded, was now marking time. No other section had lost a recruit at all. Was it really just a coincidence all the drop-outs had occurred in Corporal Slater's section? Or was there something about Corporal Slater that had, at least, contributed to the departure of the two that had opted to leave? Most of the platoon agreed that he was a fairly hard taskmaster, who was not liberal with his praise. In fact nobody had ever heard him praise anyone. At the same time, everybody seemed to respect him. They admired his soldierly qualities, the fact that he had come out top in a highly competitive survival course. And, though one of the platoon said that if he ever met Corporal Slater in a pub he'd be tempted to put an effing glass over his head, the recruit in question was rather given to extravagant statements and no doubt that was one of them. In any case, if a glare from Corporal Slater was enough to frighten a man out of the Parachute Regiment, how well would he have been able to stand up in front of an enemy? NCOs, like assault courses and jumping out of aeroplanes, were all part of a Para private's hazards.

The first exercise 480 went on was called Steel Eagle. It was their first practical experience of living rough and they were all looking forward to it. It was a chance to play Cowboys and Indians, go camping, sleep out under the stars, creep about in the woods and blaze off at each other with blank cartridges. And they were lucky with the weather. It was still very cold, but the sun shone and the sky at night stayed clear.

They learned how to turn their poncho into a 'basha' – a waterproof shelter – by stringing it up from its corners to nearby trees or bushes. To do that efficiently they had to use rubber bungees that would stretch and hold it tight. The army didn't provide those bungees. It was up to the recruits to buy them. It was also up to them to buy a compass (the one recommended cost £8), and without it they would have found it very difficult carrying out the NAVEXs that played quite a big part in their four days on Hankley Common a few miles to the south of Aldershot where the exercise was

Opposite: *Cunningham camouflages his basha, and Captain Baird briefs 480 for a NAVEX.*

taking place. A NAVEX was a navigation exercise, a vital part of a Para's training, since he, more than most, was likely to find himself in unknown territory, possibly separated from his unit and dependent on his map-reading skills to get himself across country to his objective or back to his own lines.

A NAVEX was fun. So was discovering the mysteries of the Hexamine stove, a metal burner in which blocks of fuel could be burnt in order to brew up a mug of tea or cook the contents of their 24-hour ration pack. The platoon corporals demonstrated the finer arts of field cooking as they had already done with the basha building. The menus were varied, four different kinds, all with breakfast, a snack and a main meal, which might consist of vegetable soup, chicken curry, rice, apple flakes and biscuits fruit filled.

'Yuk, that's horrible,' said someone.

'Probably be going home again tomorrow with dysentery,' said another.

'Yours looks a bit like Pedigree Chum,' said the first. 'What does it taste like?'

'Pedigree Chum.'

But these were standard jokes. Dysentery was very unlikely. Quite the opposite, in fact. The diet was designed to overcompensate and bind the soldier tight. Corporal Priestley drew his section's attention to the 'brew-pack' – a plastic bag containing such things as packets of dried milk, tea-bags, sugar, coffee, beef-stock. He suggested they add a lump of Hexi to it so if they got separated from their equipment they'd always got the wherewithal to make a hot drink.

Night fell and with it the temperature. Faces streaked with camouflage cream peered into the gloom. They learned how to find their way in the dark by running their hand along a piece of string tied from tree to tree, from basha-area to basha-area. Sentries were posted, guard details arranged. Two hours on, spent shivering amongst the trees, and four hours off shivering in their sleeping bags. Exercises in observation at night. Exercises in moving by night, out on patrol, stalking each other, their rifles loaded with blanks, and then . . . Bang! What was that? 'Who was that?' cried Corporal Baker. 'Cunningham! What are you doing? What *are* you doing, Cunningham? What do you think you're doing! . . . '

What Cunningham was doing is known to the army as a Negligent Discharge. And he was not the only one to be guilty of it that weekend. Hughes' finger slipped on the trigger too, and when asked who'd done it, he owned up out of solidarity to keep Cunningham company. But suddenly they found the games were over. They weren't crawling about in the bracken playing Cowboys and Indians any more. What Cunningham and Hughes had done was no joke. In the army's eyes a negligent discharge was a very serious offence. As they found out back at the Depot the following week.

Corporal Slater adds savour to a meal on Hankley Common.

'Cunningham!'

'Yessir!' They were outside the Company Commander's Office, and the CSM was about to read the charges to them.

'You are charged with neglect to the prejudice of good order and military discipline contrary to the Army Act 1955 in that, at Hankley Common, on or about 5 February 1982, you so negligently handled a self-loading rifle as to cause it to be discharged in the presence of other persons. Do you understand the charge?'

'Yessir!'

'Do you agree with the date of the charge, that being 5 February 1982?'

'Yessir!'

'Did you so handle a self-loading rifle as to cause it to be discharged without the order to do so being given?'

'Yessir!'

'Stand at ease!'

The same questions were put to Hughes, who – in addition – was ordered (a) to lower his chin and stop looking at the ceiling, and (b) not to anticipate the questions, all of which he replied to in the same positive manner as Cunningham had done. They were marched into Major Roberts' office and formally charged, whereupon it was explained to them that they had the right to go before their commanding officer or apply for a court martial, but were advised they would be wiser to accept the OC's punishment. Did they agree to that? 'Yessir!'

The full seriousness of their act was impressed upon them. Weapons had to be treated with respect. Had they been live rounds rather than blanks, some innocent person might very well now be lying in hospital, or possibly dead. Major Roberts dreaded to think how Hughes and Cunningham would actually be feeling if that had in fact occurred. But since it was a first offence and they had not been long in the army he was going to be lenient. Five days restriction of privileges. Left turn and march out. Leftrightleftrightleftright . . .

Cunningham and Hughes were the first to be punished formally for an offence, but a few days later Taffy Hunt came close to being number three. While standing at ease in front of the billet he started, as he described it, 'pulling jibs and going cockeyed' at Hindmarsh, whom he could see through the window of his room on the ground floor of their barrack-block. Unfortunately for Taffy, a sergeant on the floor above happened to glance out of his window at that moment and, observing Hunt's unsoldierly behaviour, drew Corporal Slater's attention to it.

Leftrightleftrightleftrightleft went Hunt, sphincter twitching, under Corporal Slater's guidance over to the guardroom where Sergeant Kelly waited, like some regal spider, monarch of all he surveyed. There then followed, according to Hunt, a conversation between Corporal Slater and Sergeant Kelly that, alternately, made his blood run cold and his heart leap up with hope. Corporal Slater wanted Sergeant Kelly to put Hunt in the cells. In which case, said Sergeant Kelly, Corporal Slater would have to charge him. But Corporal Slater didn't want to charge him, he just wanted to frighten him. Whereupon – after a bit more toing and froing – Sergeant Kelly told them to eff off, but not before warning Hunt that if there was any more effing about from him, Sergeant Kelly would effing have him, oh yes, he'd have him all right, and Hunt would be in there for an effing week. 'Shaking like an effing leaf, I was,' said Taffy, 'over at the guardroom. Everyone said I'd be the first to go in . . .'

They were still only crows, greenhorns, wet behind the ears, and as such not yet subject to the full weight of military discipline. But they had been warned, given a fright, made aware of the consequences of their acts. Next time there'd be no mitigating circumstances, they'd be in the cells, be fined or, worse still, be up for court martial. Hughes took his action very seriously indeed. He agreed with Major Roberts that a negligent discharge was absolutely unforgivable. If it had been live rounds in his SLR he might have killed someone. He was beginning to have doubts about whether he wanted to stay in the Paras. Maybe he ought to transfer to something like the Artillery instead. His room-mates weren't too sure about this. It seemed to them that a negligent discharge in the artillery could do even more damage. In that case, then, what about the catering corps? No danger of hurting anybody there. And he'd done a bit of cooking in a hamburger joint. Be a way of getting a trade, too. After all, when you come to think of it, being a Para wasn't exactly preparing you for the rest of your life in civvy street, was it now? Imagine going along to an employer for a job, and when he asked you what you could do, telling him you could fire an SLR and jump out of an aeroplane! What good would that be to him? Hughes' large pink face was screwed up anxiously. It was difficult to know what to do.

Most of the others felt Hughes was exaggerating a bit. In any case, they were still a long way off being able to say any such thing to an employer. The only thing they had ever fired from an SLR so far was blanks, and the nearest they'd got to an aeroplane was standing looking up at that Dakota outside HQ block. The Maroon Machine, as it was known to initiates, still eluded them. They couldn't even wear the beret till they passed off the Square at the end of the week. Far better, felt Birrell, if everyone concentrated on that at present, learnt their drill movements, called out the numbers and swotted up on their regimental knowledge. Passing off the Square might only be a formality, but they wanted to get it right, if only for their Corporals' and Sergeant Riley's sake. It was important to make a good show of it.

Friday 12 February dawned bitterly cold and stayed that way. In the morning 480 had a spell in the gym, a rehearsal for the afternoon's parade, and a visit to the Education Officer for a Military Calculations test. But all this time their heads were buzzing with the items of regimental history they were going to be examined on, the operations the regiment had taken part in, the colours awarded for these operations, the decorations won by its officers and other ranks for gallantry in the field. Arnhem was easy. Everyone had heard of that. Though it wasn't called Arnhem, of course, it was called Operation 'Market Garden', which wasn't quite as easy to remember. Though easier than Operations 'Biting' and 'Colossus'.

'Which one was "Biting"? Was that Tunisia or Broonevil?'

'Bruneval, idiot.'

'All right, cleverdick. Bruneval then. Where's that?'

'France!'

'Whereabouts in France?'

'South-west?'

'North-west, knob!'

'Same thing.'

They all hoped they weren't asked about the Tunisian battle honours – Oudna, Tamera, Djebel Azzag and Djebel Alliliga. Though one thing was easy to remember about the North African campaign, that was where the 1st Parachute Brigade got the Regiment its nickname. The 'Red Devils' the Germans had called them after the bitter fighting of winter 1942–3. Out of the Brigade's original strength of 2000, there were 1700 casualties.

As the parade came nearer, the names became more jumbled in their heads, and what had seemed a mere formality loomed larger and more threatening. Last-minute adjustments were made to their appearance. Their jumpers were straightened, their berets examined for bits of fluff.

'Come on! Outside. Get outside. Come on. Move out!'

They were falling in for the last time with their name-tags on, they hoped. Already they were wearing their berets instead of the hated DPM caps. It was an advance privilege, a piece of credit extended to them so they might look smarter on parade and do their drill with greater pride and swank.

Drawn up in front of the billet, they were given a last-minute check by Sergeant Riley, who fussed over them like an anxious mother sending her children off in their first school uniforms. 'You're getting me thoroughly cheesed off, Chard. You're a scruffy little individual. If you don't change your attitude, I'll change it for you the hard way.'

Bits on his jumper. White bits sticking on his jumper! And Cunningham could wipe that smile off his face too. Look at his beret! Look at it!

'And when did you last press this shirt, Tattum?'

'Ten minutes ago, Sergeant!'

Sergeant Riley's eyes narrowed. Tattum was living dangerously. 'Then try switching the iron on! The iron, Tattum.' Sergeant Riley's face bored in on him like a meat cleaver. 'Or you and me are going to fall out!'

Finally everything was ready. The moment had come for 480 to march out on to the Square and show their paces. Sergeant Riley reminded them of the three good incentives for performing well today. They would stay with the red beret, get rid of the name-tags, and stop calling out the time of their drill movements.

The temporarily sick and injured had fallen in apart from the main body of the platoon. They would attend the parade in the drill shed and were ordered to 'limp over to it in step'. Then Sergeant Riley called the platoon to attention. 'Righhhhhhhhht turn! By the lefffffft. . . . Quiiiiiiick march!'

They stepped out smartly and headed for the Square. As they emerged from the shelter of the barrack-blocks an icy wind bit into them. It was very unpleasant. But what was an icy wind compared with the hail of lead that had swept through the bocages in Normandy and across the bridge at

Arnhem in 1944? In the course of a few short years the Regiment had won two VCs and twenty-eight battle honours – ten of them on the Queen's Colour. Their backs straightened and their chests puffed out at the thought of it. It was a fine record – a record to be proud of, and if they were tough enough and determined enough and, yes, lucky enough to pass out and be accepted into the Regiment, they too would be heir to its gallant and glorious tradition.

But first they had to get their answers right. Where exactly was the Merville Battery and what the bloody hell had happened there?

5 Germany takes the Initiative

The Regimental history 480 Platoon was trying to commit to memory was little more than forty years old, and most of it had been written during the last three years of the Second World War. In 1939 Britain had no airborne forces, and it needed the brilliant assault by German glider and parachute troops on Holland and Belgium in May 1940 to convince the British – and Churchill in particular – of the usefulness of such a specialised force.

The German blitzkrieg that burst upon the West on 10 May 1940 depended upon three main elements: fast-moving armoured divisions; a close-support air force; and airborne units designed to seize key fortresses, airfields and bridges ahead of the advancing troops. None of these had been invented by the Germans. The Americans, the French and the British were the pioneers of flight. The British invented the tank. And the Italians and Russians both had a strong claim to be the inventors of military parachuting, as distinct from its other use as an emergency means of escape from burning balloons or crashing aircraft. What the Germans had done in all three cases was to grasp the significance of these inventions, see their possibilities in modern war, and perfect the means by which they could be exploited.

The British and the French had plenty of tanks in 1940. Good ones, too. But they used them in penny packets instead of the massed concentrations that brought the German army such success. The British and French were not particularly short of aircraft either. But again they failed to understand how they should be used, tactically, as the modern army's artillery, hitting the defences immediately ahead of the armoured divisions as they raced forward. Airborne forces were another matter. The British had none. The French were in the process of forming. But since, at that time, both the French and the British had defensive military postures, such forces would have been of no use to them anyway.

Historically, an American soldier in the First World War can lay claim to having put forward the first practical plan for the use of airborne troops. In 1918 Colonel Billy Mitchell of the US army proposed that part of the 1st US Infantry Division should be dropped by parachute behind the German lines at Metz while a general advance took place in the same sector. Unfortunately – though fortunately perhaps for the troops earmarked to carry out this novel and hazardous operation – the war ended before his plan could be put into effect, and the next nation to show an interest in military parachuting was Italy. By 1927 the Italians had developed an excellent back-pack static-line parachute, the 'Salvatore', and made their first mass military drop from Caproni Ca 73 high-winged biplane bombers. By the late 1930s they had two army airborne divisions and a naval airborne regiment, none of which was ever used in the role intended for it, though all fought with distinction as ground troops in World War 2.

However, the nation best remembered for its pioneering role in the development of airborne forces is the Soviet Union. Already, in the summer manoeuvres of 1930, the Red Army had dropped a small body of troops by parachute and successfully captured an enemy HQ. But by the mid-thirties such great strides had been made under the enthusiastic direction of Marshal Tukhachevsky that whole battalions were being parachuted into position. The aircraft used for this purpose was the Tupolev ANT–6, a huge four-engined, fixed-undercarriage monoplane with a rather difficult exit through a hatch on top of the fuselage. From there the troops climbed down on to the wing before dropping off and pulling the ripcords of their free-fall chutes as soon as they were clear of the aircraft.

Russian parachute troops free-fall from the wing of a Tupolev ANT–6 in the mid 1930s

Opposite: *A Russian air display in 1935 and* (below) *a battalion drop at Kiev in the same year.*

The Ukraine manoeuvres of both 1935 and 1936 were attended by military observers from most of the major powers and there is no doubt of the impact they had on the Germans. Their military attaché in Moscow immediately sent a top-secret signal to Berlin announcing that what he had seen marked a revolutionary transformation in the techniques of war. The British were less impressed, even though their observer, the future Field Marshal Earl Wavell, had also witnessed in the September 1936 manoeuvres successful heavy drops – both low-level and by parachute – of light tanks, field-guns and armoured cars. Though intrigued by the ingenuity of the Soviet achievement, Wavell did not think that such novelties would have a great deal of influence on the future course of war. And to some extent this British attitude was perfectly reasonable, since airborne forces were essentially aggressive and the British – at least at that time – had no aggressive intentions.

For the Germans, however, what they saw in Russia helped both to fire their imagination and give support to those already thinking along similar lines. General Goering, as he then was, was one of these, and in October 1935 he ordered the formation of the first German parachute battalion as the nucleus of a future parachute corps, though it was not until January 1936 that the corps officially came into being. After that, progress was rapid. A parachute training school was set up. A design team was put to work to produce a suitable parachute. The three-motor Ju 52 transport plane was assigned to them as a troop-carrier. The production of a suitable glider was set in hand, with the stipulation that it should cost no more than ten parachutes and carry ten men.

The diving exit from the Ju 52 is clearly shown in this picture of a 1938 training drop.

On 1 July 1938 Major General Kurt Student was appointed to overall command of the German airborne force, which was then designated (as a deceptive measure) the 7th Air Landing Division. Under his guidance, a firm idea of how those troops should be employed was rapidly formulated. Student favoured the use of airborne troops as an integral part of an assault by major land forces. He did not accept the idea of using them in small parties as sabotage troops. In his view airborne forces could become a battle-winning factor of prime importance by making third-dimensional warfare possible in land operations and by outflanking the enemy vertically. He believed, too, that the element of surprise contributed a great deal to their effect.

Hitler's view was just as enthusiastic, though more romantic. In one of his visions of the war of the future he saw 'the sky black with bombers, and – leaping from them into the smoke – parachute storm troops each grasping a sub-machine gun'. The vision was apocalyptic, as was the German attack on Poland. But one element was missing from that attack: no parachute troops were dropped anywhere. On 27 October 1939 Hitler told Student why. The German airborne forces were too valuable to employ in Poland. They were virtually a new and secret weapon. He intended saving them for a more important occasion – the attack on France, and the piercing of the Western Front, in the following year.

Hitler had very clear ideas about how this should be done. Whereas plans for the use of his new armoured divisions in the coming offensive all originated from General Guderian, the most striking features of the German airborne plan were conceived by Hitler.

Hitler watches one of the earliest German parachute drops, October 1936.

Their role would be a critical one. The main body of Student's forces were to be used in Holland and would be directed against the bridges at Rotterdam, Dordrecht and Moerdijk which carried the main route into Holland from the south over the estuary of the Rhine. The remaining troops were to be used to assist the invasion of Belgium by seizing the bridges across the Albert Canal near Maastricht. To achieve this it would be necessary to capture the modern Belgian fortress of Eben Emael whose guns dominated the area, and it was here that Hitler showed his brilliance. He proposed that glider troops should land on top of the fort and destroy the steel and concrete gun emplacements with another of Germany's secret weapons – the hollow-charge explosive.

Before that could take place, however, Germany invaded Norway and Denmark, and for that campaign Hitler demanded – in spite of Student's protests and contrary to his own previous arguments – the services of a parachute battalion. In the early hours of 9 April 1940, Ju 52 transports carrying the 7th Air Division's 1st Battalion took off and flew north as the spearhead of the German attack. Student's parachutists had mixed fortunes. Some seized their objectives rapidly with few casualties, others were not so lucky. But overall their contribution to the German assault was a vital one, not least in the demoralising effect their presence had on the Allied troops and commanders. So the premature use of Student's airborne arm in Scandinavia did not jeopardise its success in Holland and Belgium. In any case, Hitler had deliberately avoided using his gliders. And they were the key to the Eben Emael and Albert Canal operations, which were planned to begin before the Scandinavian campaign ended.

General Student with his troops.

Gliders had two great advantages over parachute troops. They could carry a unit of men – ten including the pilot, in the case of the DFS 230 – and land them in a group and ready to fight, whereas even the most efficient low-level parachute drop would spread the same number of men over an area at least 200 yards long. Moreover, on landing it would then take them some time to get out of their parachute harness, locate and unpack their weapon containers and get assembled. If they were under fire at this moment they could suffer crippling losses. The glider's other great advantage was its silence. It could, if necessary, be released some distance short of its target and arrive undetected. And when – as was the case at Eben Emael – the target was near the border, there was scarcely need for the aircraft towing the gliders to overfly enemy airspace at all.

Although Hitler had suggested the use of gliders for the attack on the fortress, such tactics were fully in accordance with Student's own beliefs. He favoured the 'short method', as he called it, landing paratroops right on top of the objective whether it were fortress, gun battery, bridge or airfield. He considered the element of shock and surprise achieved by this sudden arrival worth the risk of the heavy casualties the attackers might suffer in the process. And with luck the surprise might be so great that the defenders would be overwhelmed before having the chance to retaliate at all. It was a technique the Germans were always to employ and it brought more victories than disasters, though in Holland the battle hung in the balance for several hours.

Gliders on top of Eben Emael after the attack. The cupola in the foreground has had a hole blown in it by a hollow charge.

The assault formation assigned the task of seizing Fort Eben Emael and the bridges over the Albert Canal consisted of eleven officers and 427 men under the command of Captain Koch. The formation was divided into four groups – one to deal with each of the three bridges to be captured, the fourth to land on top of the fort itself. There were forty-two gliders in all, and they began to take off, towed by their Ju 52 transport tugs, from two airfields near Cologne just before dawn on the morning of 10 May 1940.

Lieutenant Witzig was in command of 'Granite' assault group, whose job it was to put Fort Eben Emael out of action. The fort, manned by 1200 Belgian soldiers, was sited on a plateau overlooking the Albert Canal, and

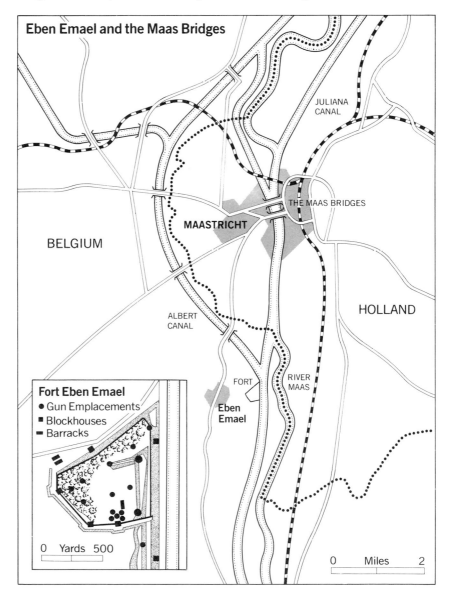

Eben Emael and the Maas Bridges

JULIANA CANAL

THE MAAS BRIDGES

MAASTRICHT

BELGIUM

HOLLAND

ALBERT CANAL

FORT

RIVER MAAS

Fort Eben Emael
- ● Gun Emplacements
- ■ Blockhouses
- ▬ Barracks

Eben Emael

0   Yards 500

0   Miles   2

*A Ju 52 drops
parachutists over
Holland as a Dutch
fighter passes overhead.*

covered an area about half a mile wide and three-quarters long. Its flanks were protected by a forty-metre drop on the canal side and wide anti-tank ditches on all the others. It bristled with blockhouses mounting 120mm and 75mm guns, and any troops who managed to get across the ditches and into the perimeter would be caught in a deadly cross-fire from dozens of machine-guns. To deal with this monster Witzig had some eighty-five pioneers and sappers who had spent most of the previous six months training for the operation.

En route to the target – as a result of near-collisions – two of the gliders parted company with their tugs. Both gliders were from 'Granite' group, and Witzig was aboard one of them. The rest of the force flew on, and when, just after 5 am, they cast off their tow-ropes and swept down towards their targets, they were still unaware that any of their number had turned back. The first the Belgians knew of their arrival was when, with a ripping of fabric on the barbed-wire entanglements, dark shapes came in from the East and skidded to a halt between the blockhouses. In their urgency to attack, the glider troops hurtled out of the doors and in some cases crashed through the sides of their gliders. With them they carried five tons of explosives, some in satchels that were dropped through slits in the bunker roofs and walls, some in the twenty-eight hollow charges designed to punch holes through the gun-cupolas' steel walls and blast molten metal into the bowels of the casemates.

Desperately the Belgian gunners struggled to depress their barrels low enough to engage their enemies as more gliders touched down. Astonishingly, two and a half hours later, when the battle was still raging, the attackers were joined by another glider. Lieutenant Witzig had caught up and had come to take over his command from Sergeant Major Wenzel. But it was not until twenty-four hours later that the weary survivors of 'Granite' group were finally relieved by the advance troops of Reichenau's 6th Army, who proceeded to put an end to all further resistance.

So, for the loss of six men killed and twenty wounded, Witzig's force had captured a fortress the German High Command had estimated would have cost them 6000 casualties in a conventional attack. Of the three bridges Koch's formation had set out to seize two had been captured intact, and within a few hours the Panzer divisions were pouring over them and into Belgium. Fewer than 500 soldiers in forty-two gliders had opened the way for the defeat of the Belgian army.

In Holland, where Student had dropped with the remainder of his division, the battle was more desperate. The attack on the bridge at Dordrecht cost the German parachute troops heavy casualties, and attempts to seize The Hague's airfields were abandoned after many of the Ju 52 transports crashed in flames in the face of Dutch anti-aircraft fire. Nevertheless, constant pressure by the German airborne troops on the ground enabled them to hold on until relieved by the German 18th Army on 12 May at Moerdijk, and the following day at Dordrecht and Rotterdam, where some of the fiercest fighting was going on and where, in the moment of victory, General Student was struck down by a bullet in the head, a wound it took him almost a year to recover from.

But his forces had done their work. What the glider and parachute troops had set in motion in Holland and Belgium, the German armoured columns finally brought about in Luxembourg and France – the collapse and total defeat of the combined Allied armies. It was only by a miracle that over 230,000 men of the British Expeditionary Force escaped back to England from Dunkirk. But they did so with very little of their heavy equipment, even in some cases without their rifles, and they returned to a country in the grip of parachutist fever and preparing itself for a last-ditch struggle against Hitler's airborne hordes.

And 'hordes' was the operative word. Panic, rumour and heated imaginations had considerably inflated the modest numbers of troops that Student had at his disposal. Admittedly, the Germans had also dropped dummy parachutists in order to spread confusion and mislead their enemies into thinking larger forces were being deployed against them, but such was the

Opposite: *German parachute troops drop over Holland in May 1940, and* (below) *take their weapons from the containers during the attack on the Moerdijk bridges.*

Below: *P.E. Popham's booklet on the German parachute forces.*

Below right: *A wartime recruiting poster for the Home Guard.*

extent of the exaggeration it almost seems as if Allied troops and commanders were unconsciously seeking justification for their rapid defeat. For it is quite extraordinary what impact these 4500 airborne troops had on the course of the war.

Wild rumours went round of Germans dropping into Holland disguised as everything from nuns to butcher-boys. Some of the books and pamphlets published at the time helped spread and confirm these stories. P. E. Popham's sixpenny booklet on the German Parachute Corps was clearly meant as a useful handbook for the anti-parachutist forces. Amongst a great deal of accurate information about the aircraft used, the equipment carried, the uniform worn, was also a great deal of delightful nonsense. Popham described how parachutists often disguised themselves as parsons, nuns, postmen and butcher-boys. The parsons had machine-guns under their cloaks and grenades in their trouser pockets, while the postmen had collapsible bicycles and machine-guns in their post bags. Best of all perhaps was the butcher-boy's disguise. The machine-gun and grenades were carried in a meat-basket covered with a white cloth. Professor Low, in another book of the period, pointed out the disadvantage of such disguises for any but the occasional parachutist: 'No one is likely to be deceived if he sees a nun, or even a postman, descending by parachute'.

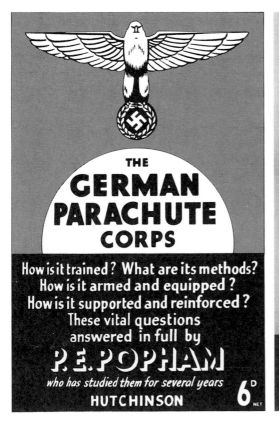

THE GERMAN PARACHUTE CORPS

How is it trained? What are its methods? How is it armed and equipped? How is it supported and reinforced? These vital questions answered in full by

P.E. POPHAM

who has studied them for several years

HUTCHINSON 6D NET

"Let 'em all come"

MEN 41-55

HOME DEFENCE BATTALIONS

Deceived or not, the British took the threat very seriously. The immediate response was to call the nation to arms. 'Dad's army' – the Home Guard as it was later to become, the Local Defence Volunteers or LDV in the early summer of 1940 – was specifically formed to meet this expected aerial attack. The pikes which were to have been issued as a temporary solution to the shortage of firearms were clearly seen as perfect weapons for dealing with parachutists. And throughout the summer of 1940 – while Fighter Command fought the Battle of Britain over London and southern England – not a day went by without the fear that the skies would soon be dark with German transport planes showering down their parachutists.

It was therefore some comfort to learn from Popham that the majority of them would be wearing spring heels, between eight inches and one foot in height, causing them to bounce back up into the air immediately after landing and come down flat on their faces in the prone position, where they would lie helplessly for up to a minute, making it comparatively safe to deal with them during that period. Once dead, it was well to search them for they were almost certain to be carrying lists of the names and addresses of German sympathisers in the district. With these in his possession, the Home Guard soldier could very quickly deal with all the traitors and 'Quislings' in his neighbourhood. Professor Low, though sceptical of most of Popham's stories, has one or two treasures of his own. In particular he tells how the German authorities were anxious to persuade their parachute troops that the operations they were engaged in were not desperate suicide ventures but well-thought-out manoeuvres. And he quotes as an example of the confidence-building equipment used for this purpose the many cases in which German parachutists were 'officially issued with 3 ounces of toilet paper and 3 army contraceptives' – in the belief no doubt that a man with that lot in his pockets would hope to survive at least a week. Funny though some of these pamplets may be, the reality was no joke. Britain came very close to being invaded, and even 4500 parachute and glider troops backed up by one or two air-landing divisions might very well have been enough to tip the scale against the defenders.

Winston Churchill certainly thought so, and in consequence the part played by the German airborne forces in the attack on Holland and Belgium had one last and most important effect. On 10 May 1940, the day the German Army Groups began their attack, Churchill was acclaimed as Britain's new Prime Minister, and even before the French Armistice was concluded with Nazi Germany on 22 June, he had already directed a memorandum at the Joint Chiefs of Staff in which he called upon them to propose measures for 'a vigorous, enterprising and ceaseless offensive against the whole German occupied coastline'. That same memorandum also included demands for the formation of a corps of 5000 parachute troops, a demand that he repeated two weeks later when he argued that such forces could meanwhile play their part as shock troops in the defence of Britain. So even at a moment when Britain seemed on the point of being overwhelmed, the forces she would one day need for a return to Europe were already being envisaged.

But, as in so many other things, the British came late into the field and had to start from scratch. In July 1940 Major J. F. Rock of the Royal Engineers was entrusted with the task of taking charge of 'the military organisation of British airborne forces'. What form they should take and how they were to be trained was left to Rock and a number of RAF officers to resolve. But in order to set them on the right track they were handed a German parachutist's helmet and tunic, and a damaged parachute that had been forwarded to England from Holland. They were also given one of the recently-formed commando units as the first British soldiers to be transformed into parachute troops.

6 Basic Wales

On the square at Browning Barracks on 12 February 1982 what little of this history 480 Platoon had managed to imbibe was rapidly deserting them. The new adjutant, Captain Roger Williams, was posing difficult questions, and in their nervousness some of the platoon found their minds going completely blank – as did Tony Butler, their judo expert, when the adjutant stopped in front of him. First Captain Williams told him he was a lopsided monster who needed a haircut and was standing all wrong. Then he asked him if he knew what kind of decoration his company commander had. Butler was one of the fittest, fastest and strongest men in 480 but, no, he was afraid he didn't know that. Captain Williams told him it was an MBE. Did Butler know what that was? No, Butler was afraid he didn't.

The next man the adjutant came to was Gary Price, a human being's nightmare according to Sergeant Riley, at whose birth they had kept the worst part and thrown the best away.

'Can you tell me where the 3rd Battalion is, at this moment, Price?'

'No, sir, sorry, sir.'

'They're in Tidworth. Do you know where Tidworth is?'

'No, sir, sorry, sir.'

'It's near Salisbury Plain. Have you got your ID card on you?'

'No sir, sorry, sir.'

'Why not?'

'Don't know, sir.'

And, not noticing the anguish on Sergeant Riley's face, Captain Williams passed on.

The next man he came to was Tattum, staring inscrutably into space, shoulders drooping slightly but teeth stowed carefully away for the occasion. Captain Williams soon put a stop to that. He asked Tattum which barracks the 2nd Battalion were in.

'Don't know, sir,' said Tattum, flashing his fangs.

'In Bruneval Barracks. D'you know what happened at Bruneval?'

'Er. Parachute Regiment got their honour there, sir.'

'What for?'

'Don't know, sir.'

Gloom settled on Sergeant Riley. Their only hope now was the drill. Perhaps that would save the day.

It nearly did. The squad drill at any rate. Captain Williams complimented them on that. But their individual drill had let them down. And so had the questioning. They lacked confidence in both those areas, and as a result they were not yet fit to take their place as members of the guard, as individual members stuck there on the gate, who would have to deal with such things as terrorists and stroppy generals. For that reason, they had not passed off the square.

'Sergeant Riley!'

'Sir!'

'Carry on, please!'

Left! Left! Left, right, left! They marched off the square in a daze. Nobody had ever imagined they might actually fail. That had never been on the cards. Falling at the first hurdle was unbelievable.

As soon as they were dismissed, they slammed back into the billet, cursing their ill-luck, kicking chairs, crashing open the doors of their metal lockers and stowing away the beloved berets they would not be wearing for some time yet. Back to the hated craphats. Back to the name-tags and calling out the time of the drill movements. That was one of the reasons they'd failed, that was. Borland was to blame. That stupid effing Jock, John Borland. He didn't call out the time loud enough. And that new adjutant didn't help much either, just trying to throw his weight about, he was, so that everyone would know he'd arrived. What with him and the BBC cameras, no wonder they were nervous. A right effing state they'd all got into.

While they were on parade, Corporal Slater had been working on his boots. And when he heard they'd failed his face broke slowly into a hellish grin – the first time some of them had seen him smile, they said. Sergeant Riley wasn't smiling. Smiling was the last thing he felt like doing. Besides being responsible for his recruits' turnout and the cleanliness of their barrack block, he was also in charge of drill instruction within the platoon. So any blame 480 incurred on that account could be laid at his door. It was almost certain the RSM would think so, anyway, and want to have a private word with Sergeant Riley about it. Just because you were a sergeant didn't mean you weren't subject to criticism and contumely like the rest.

Steve Birrell voiced the platoon's feelings at their failure. 'All our heads went down about two inches,' he said. He also spoke out on behalf of Captain Baird and the NCOs. It might be rotten for the recruits to fail, but think how much worse it was for the staff. They were the ones who'd get torn apart. As individuals they were much more vulnerable. The recruits could always get themselves lost in the pack. Except Borland, of course. It wasn't just calling out the time he'd let them down on. He didn't know his regimental history either.

John Borland did not take too kindly to being made platoon scapegoat. He wasn't the only one who had fluffed the questions or whispered the numbers. A Scot from Prestwick, a slaughterman for three years in civvy street, he didn't need a bunch of effing Sassenachs to tell him where he had gone wrong. The mood was depressed and ugly. To put in so much work, to drill and study and bull and clean and then to be told they weren't good enough and had to go through with it all again – some of them felt like jacking there and then.

They had been due to go out that weekend, have it free, go home if they wanted to and were able to get there and back in time. But that was all done for now. Until they passed off the square they were automatically confined to barracks. It was the first real setback they had suffered and it suddenly revealed all the irritations and discontents that lay beneath the surface. The mood grew bolshier and bolshier. Sod it. Wouldn't catch them hanging about this effing dump all weekend. It was St Valentine's day on Sunday. Some of them had been planning trips to a disco. Sod Sergeant Kelly. They were effing well going anyway, and to hell with the consequences.

Birrell resisted this sort of attitude. Far worse than this would happen to them before they'd finished. Just got to pick themselves up off the floor and start over again, though he had to admit that putting those craphats back on again was a bit hard to take. He'd thought the only time they'd ever have to wear them again would be to go fishing. Still, if that was how it was they'd just have to get on with it, wouldn't they?

A number of them were down to do their first guard that Saturday night. In theory – having failed to pass off the square – they were now ineligible to do guard duty. But since 480 were the only troops left in barracks that weekend, there was no choice in the matter. If they did not do guard, nobody would. So their fitness or otherwise for the task was beside the point. It was another military paradox to add to their growing collection.

Being on guard was a novelty that both intrigued and exhausted them. Two hours on and four hours off sounded fine until you tried to sleep in the four hours off. Quite apart from not being able to take your boots off, there was always something happening in the guardroom. A visit from the orderly officer, chores to be done, or a mate who didn't want to go to sleep and preferred to read or talk to you. Hughes was hollow-eyed by Sunday morning and wondering what other regiment might be worth transferring to. He wasn't the only one. As the pressure went on, it was a thought that crossed several minds. They had done only four weeks so far. There were eighteen more to go. How could they ever possibly make it to the end?

Others – no names, no restricted privileges – had not stayed in barracks the night before. They had gone to the disco, or up to London, showing the kind of drive and initiative the 'Red Devils' were supposed to be famous for. It had been a good night out at the disco. Dancing with a bird in a cream jump-suit. Hughes blinked with fatigue as he listened to their stories. His girl was in Liverpool, but she'd sent him a Valentine card to cheer him up. It was witty and sexy and he read bits out to his mates while, in the room next door, Pete O'Hare got on with his ironing. He'd spent three years in a plastic-bag factory before he'd joined the Paras, and a minor setback like failing the pass-off didn't bother him. He thought life was great. They were doing something different all the time. He planned to stick it out to the end. Not like a couple in his section he could name and another couple in the section next door. Had enough, they had. Already sick of it. Couldn't stand the bull and the runs. Everybody talked obsessively about the runs. They had come to symbolise all the physical effort and pain they had to conquer if they wanted to stay the course. The runs. The tabs. Chest heaving, legs crumpling, muscles knotting in the calf, in the thigh, searing pains in the knees and ankles.

They were due to repeat the pass-off parade the following Tuesday. On the Monday they had a 4-mile endurance march, half-walking, half-running, rucksacks on their backs, goaded and chivvied by the PTIs, medical staff in attendance. On the Tuesday morning Borland came first on the assault course but tore a stomach muscle in the process. That lunchtime they had another last-minute revision of the questions they were likely to be asked and made the same nervous jokes they had made the previous Friday. Who was the Colonel-in-Chief of the Regiment? Haitch Ar Haitch the Prince of Wales. Who was Colonel Commandant? General Sir Anthony Farrar-Hockley, MBE, ABC, GCE, NBG. Nor were the stars any more promising than they had been when Clark had first consulted them. Aries was still going to have a bad time with his boots. It wasn't a good day for Capricorn to be taking exams. And Virgo would probably end up in Kelly's Kingdom along with Hughes and Borland.

The jokes and the questions went on right up to the moment they got the order to fall in outside for inspection before marching on to the Square. There was the same fussing over their appearance. Berets were defluffed, jumpers pulled down, chins lifted off chests. Then they were called to attention and set off, by the left quick march, towards the Square where the adjutant was waiting for them.

This time, to their surprise, the adjutant didn't ask them any questions. And Pete O'Hare reckoned their drill was worse than it had been on Friday. But in spite of this Captain Williams passed them. Why did they think that was? Confidence, said Andy Way, an 18-year-old ex-police cadet, like Clark. Shouting their numbers out. Friday, they hadn't shouted loud enough. But they were loud enough today all right. It was a hell of a relief to get it over with, even though they weren't given much time to congratulate themselves. Straight after the parade they had to fall in again for weapon training, though this time with their berets on. The next stage would be to get rid of the green backing behind the badge. That wouldn't go till they passed Pre-Parachute Selection in week 12. Still, they had made a step forward. They were on their way to becoming soldiers. The men were beginning to separate out from the boys.

That weekend one of the Irish boys had quietly packed his bags and gone back across the sea to Ireland. The first man in 480 to go absent. Soon his place would be taken by an injured recruit who had fallen behind in his training and had been back-squadded. Meanwhile there was an empty bed in Borland's room. It was Corporal Pollard's turn to lose a man. At last Corporal Slater had someone to keep him company.

For the next two weeks the emphasis was on weapon training. They drilled with the SLRs, they fired them on the range, they were introduced to the GPMG, the General Purpose Machine Gun. And at the end of week 6 they all went down to Brecon in South Wales for more fieldcraft and outdoor military training. There the emphasis was still on the inculcation of individual skills. At the same time they were to do recce and fighting patrols and a number of section attacks to get them used to working as a team.

Basic Wales, as it is called, is essentially an extension of what they had already done on their first exercise, Steel Eagle, though with more realism and under tougher conditions. As it happened 480 were luckier with the weather than some platoons. It rained, of course, as it was bound to do at the beginning of March in the Brecon Hills. It was cold too. But not as cold as might have been expected for a winter where temperatures over large parts of Britain were lower than had been recorded for more than a hundred years. Fieldcraft, map-reading, sentry duties – all these aspects of their training were taught and practised at a more advanced level. They ran assault courses. They did ambushes and night attacks, two endurance marches. They learned how to survive in a military environment, how to live off the land if need be. This was where Corporal Slater came into his own. On Exercise Steel Eagle they had killed and skinned rabbits under his guidance, learned how to cut them up and cook them. This time they killed a sheep and Borland – looking like an Indian brave with his cropped head and camouflage-streaked face – put his civilian skills to use and skinned and butchered it.

Most of them enjoyed their week in Wales, found it interesting and invigorating. Those who did not found more good reasons to think about a transfer or even, in some cases, a discharge. The critical week was approaching. Week 8. The one the PSO had warned them about. The point at which the army might want to dispense with them, or alternatively they might want to dispense with it. It was make or break time now. A major assessment was about to take place. And as with most things the army does, it was carried out according to a strictly prescribed brief and with great conscientiousness.

Corporal Lyden and his section follow one of the training staff at Basic Wales.

The actual proceedings were not democratic in the strict sense of the word, but they were not particularly authoritarian either. Though the final decision inevitably lay with John Baird, the platoon commander, he paid a great deal of attention to what his NCOs had to say, and when in doubt was always prepared to accept the opinion of the recruit's section commander as likely to be the most reliable. Tattum's case was a good one in point. He was in Corporal Lyden's section and, when his name came up for discussion, John Baird said he'd always struck him as being 'a little bit fly'. Now there are a number of characteristics the army does not much care for, and being fly stands high on that list. Stupidity, incompetence, lack of physical fitness, all these things can be forgiven, even if they can't all be corrected. But being fly is a different matter. It means the man in question is trying to put one over on his superiors. He is trying to give an impression that he is working when he is not, or is capable of doing a great deal more than he lets on. He is scoring off the army. He is a cleverdick. He needs watching.

So when John Baird passed that remark it could have had serious consequences for Tattum if it were to stick. Fortunately for Tattum, his section commander Corporal Lyden disagreed with the Captain's judgement and – like the good substitute parent he was – he stood his ground and suggested that the reason Captain Baird had got that impression was probably because Tattum tended not to push himself, in an effort to avoid showing the rest of the section up. It was an ingenious argument, but a little excessive in John Baird's eyes, so he stood his ground too and repeated the charge, adding for good measure a variation to the effect that Tattum seemed to be coasting a bit. And, what was more, he didn't impress him as being well-motivated, keen or get-up-and-go. He always hung back. He wasn't willing to commit himself to every aspect of the training. Under this rain of criticism Corporal Lyden had to tread carefully. He grudgingly conceded there might be some truth in what the Captain said but at the same time insisted that Tattum definitely picked things up faster than the rest.

'Well, OK then,' said Captain Baird, yielding suddenly. 'You're the man who knows.'

But just as it seemed the matter was settled, Sergeant Riley threw his weight behind the Captain. Yes, he thought Tattum was coasting a bit too. And he also thought Corporal Lyden should have a word with him about it.

Attacked from this fresh quarter, Lyden had to work fast. 'But if you think he's being fly, sir,' he said, 'then you're the one who ought to chat to him. Because I haven't noticed it.'

'It's just an impression I got,' said Baird, beginning to back off a little. 'That's what I'm saying. But you're the guy who's worked with him. You know him far better than I do.'

'Well, I'll talk to him then,' said Lyden, offering a compromise, 'and tell him what sort of an opinion he's putting across to other people, although I haven't noticed it.'

'OK,' said Baird. 'But the grading is C.'

This was what Lyden wanted. He had fought a dour fight on behalf of Tattum. It would be interesting to see who was right in the long run. 'C' was a fair grading at Basic Wales. No one got more than C+. There would be the opportunity to do better after P Company at Advanced Wales. No point giving anybody swelled heads. After all, just getting to Basic Wales was an achievement. So far only twenty-nine of the original forty-one members of 480 Platoon had actually managed to stay the course to Brecon.

Of the twelve who had not made it, three had been discharged, three more wanted to be, one was AWOL and five had been back-squadded due to injury or other reasons. The last few weeks before Basic Wales had taken a heavy toll. And the assessment threatened to weed out even more. There were now only four sections left out of five. Corporal Slater's ill-starred section had been further reduced by injury until, just before the platoon set off for Wales, only two remained. One of them, Taffy Hunt of Kelly's Kingdom fame, had been dispatched to Corporal Baker's section to make up their numbers, while the other, Gary Price, had joined Section 5 and was filling the gap left by the runaway Irishman.

As a result, Corporal Slater had been freed to devote his energies and talents to the whole of the platoon instead of just one section. At first a number of 480 found the prospect a little alarming. The Corporal's reputation as a rather surly disciplinarian had preceded him. As it happened they need not have worried. Life in the field brought out the best in Al Slater, as one of his section had noticed in week 3 when they were on

Exercise Steel Eagle. He clearly preferred the simpler realities of outdoor life to the more formal routines of town and barrack soldiering. In Aldershot, whenever he got a moment to spare, he was off running over the nearby fields and training grounds. At Brecon he was out in the open all day and every day. By the end of the week 480 were beginning to find him positively genial.

Cunningham did not share Corporal Slater's enthusiasm for physical exercise. There were times, on the assault course, for example, when he came very close to jacking it all in. But his section commander, Corporal Lyden, kept nagging away at him. 'Get up, Cunningham. Up, Cunningham. Get hold of yourself. Up, up, I said. Don't just effing lie there, Cunningham. Get up. On your feet. Keep going, you idle effing man!' At the discussion Lyden suggested Cunningham should fail and be back-squadded so he could catch up on his physical fitness, which at the moment was letting him down on everything. Captain Baird resisted this. He argued that Basic Wales wasn't about physical fitness. It was about fieldcraft and map-reading and things like that which Cunningham had done well on. There'd be plenty of time to back-squad him on fitness when he got to P Company and Pre-Para Selection. He'd tried hard at Basic Wales. He'd shown lots of guts and determination. To back-squad him now, on fitness, would be back-squadding him for the wrong reason. He was the kind of guy who deserved to be passed on Basic Wales.

This time it was Corporal Lyden who gave way and Captain Baird who compromised. He gave Cunningham a 'C' but agreed to talk to him about

Corporal Lyden gives Cunningham some verbal encouragement.

his fitness. And so they continued. Hindmarsh? A bit of a cowboy was one accusation. Running about showing a gross lack of interest. But Corporal Priestley, his section commander, felt there were signs of a light at the end of the tunnel. Waiting about so many months while recovering from his leg injury had been demoralising for him, so he felt they should give him a scrape-pass and a talking-to and take him a little bit further.

There were several scrape passes, 'E's in the army's book. Butler, the physical fitness enthusiast, got one for being a bit weak on 'the academic side', a bit slow picking up some of the fieldcraft. Melvin, on the other hand, who had made the mistake of getting noticed for the wrong things in the early weeks of the course, was now getting noticed for the great improvement he had shown. No longer was he guilty of another offence the Army wasn't too keen on, 'knowing it all'. His attitude was a great deal better now. He'd realised he'd got to pull his finger out. But they mustn't ease up on him yet. They didn't want him falling back into his old ways.

Melvin ended up with a 'C'. So did Hunt, praised for his liveliness and efficiency, criticised for his 'gobbiness'. Never stopped talking, and some of the other members in his section got a bit fed up with it. But as a soldier he was OK. Like Robertson, the dark horse who had finally been spotted. Almost everybody had something good to say about him. Alert, responsible, fit, intelligent, always there. Not only had he come right out of his shell, but he was carrying others with him. A possible 'B', someone suggested, but as they weren't giving that high a mark to anyone, they had to settle for a 'C+', which nine of them got in the end, including Ward, the darkest of the dark horses, who wore camouflage cream anyway just to keep the others company.

How was he doing? Very well. Good for morale. Took lots of stick but gave it back too. Character, drive and determination were others of his qualities to be praised. Though he was a bit violent if someone did something to annoy him. He'd jump in and grab the first bloke there. Plenty of aggression, in fact? Oh yes. Plenty of aggression. Nothing wrong with that, said John Baird. That was good.

But six out of the twenty-nine got an 'F' for Fail. Whether they would be back-squadded as a result was a decision that would have to be made the following week after Captain Baird had discussed their cases with the Company Commander.

All that remained was to choose the winner of the Spender Trophy, a rather double-edged award for the recruit who won it, since it both praised and criticised him at one and the same time. It was for the most improved recruit at Basic Wales . . . Borland marched smartly forward out of the ranks to take his prize.

'What the effing 'ell did he get that for?' somebody muttered.

'Sheep shagging . . .' came the faint reply.

7 Period of Assessment

That weekend 480 Platoon were given four days leave from Thursday evening until midnight on Monday. For the Scottish boys this was not quite as generous as it seemed. In accordance with some penny-pinching army order they had been given the cheapest warrants between two points, which – from Aldershot – meant routing them across country to Birmingham, instead of through London. In consequence, because of missed trains and bad connections, some of them spent as much as half their leave travelling backwards and forwards to Scotland.

Still, it was a break. It was a welcome trip home. They saw their girls, their parents and their friends – some of whom, they discovered, were less friendly now they were in the Paras. Becoming a soldier was rather like becoming a policeman. It tended to isolate you from your civvy peers, put you on the other side of the fence and make you one of 'them'. Well, sod it. If that was how their friends felt, then they would just have to get on with it. At least, that was what the ones who planned to stay in the army thought. Those who had been having doubts on that score merely found their friends' attitude further justification for what they already had in mind. Get out. Admit it wasn't their scene. Admit they didn't have what it took, or want what it took, or didn't feel like going wherever it might lead them. It wasn't a crime not wanting to be a soldier. Anybody could make a mistake. It wasn't their fault they couldn't stay the pace, or stand the life, and hadn't had the sense to realise it in the first few days like that clever-dick of a Welshman.

Someone said it cost £9000 to train a Para. How much of it had been spent on them so far. £3000? Less probably. After all, they hadn't been up in an aeroplane yet. And that must be what cost the money, not marching about at Aldershot, or running about in the rain in Wales. In any case, that was the army's problem, not theirs. They couldn't all be the sort of cheerful Supermen the army seemed to be looking for. Such things as coasting, covering yourself, forgetting your kit, skiving and having a sly kip when you got the chance were just human nature. You couldn't be aggressive, well-motivated, switched-on, full of guts and determination all the time, the way the Captain and Sergeant Riley and all the Corporals wanted you to be. It wasn't reasonable. So they couldn't really be blamed – could they? – if they were thinking of asking for a discharge, as the

Personnel Selection Officer had promised them they could so long as they got their application in on time. In fact, three of them had already got their applications in, and another two or three had been contemplating it and talking about it with their mates for some weeks now. For if they were going to leave, now was the moment to do it. At the eighth week of training, after Basic Wales had revealed the weaknesses some of them were prone to, and when others had had time to decide whether or not the Paras, or even the Army for that matter, was the life for them.

But first those who had failed Basic Wales came up before their platoon commander, who pointed out their deficiencies to them and told them what their fate was going to be. Or rather told them what he thought their fate was going to be. For, just as his Sergeant and Corporals were subject to his will, so he in his turn was subject to the will of his superiors. Each one up the scale listened politely to his subordinate and then either endorsed or overturned his decision. That might well happen to all or some of John Baird's decisions. For the moment, however, he was free to express his opinion to those who had not come up to scratch in the week they had just spent in the Welsh Mountains.

Alphabetically Brian Bush was first. A bricklayer in civvy street, with an older brother already in the Paras, on entering the room he immediately put up a black by forgetting to salute. It was a bad start that did not endear him to his platoon commander. Equally irritating were the light-reactive lenses in his glasses. They were all too novel and sophisticated for the army, a seemingly defiant touch, however innocent the intention. All part and parcel of the image Bush had created, and which came across in the eyes of his superiors as a lack of the correct and positive attitude that John Baird had talked about at the beginning of their course. All the skills in the world could not cancel out this omission. And Bush did not possess all the skills in the world either, said Baird, even though he had been a Blowpipe Operator in the TA at Widnes for eighteen months. People without any previous military experience had already surpassed him. Clearly serving in the TA was no passport to success in the regular army. As Melvin had found before him, and others were to find later. If anything, being in the TA seemed to be a positive disadvantage. It both raised the army's expectations and somehow annoyed them at your presumption. Either you were accused of knowing it all – like Melvin – or knowing nothing – like Bush. Either way you came off badly and had the contempt of your comrades thrown in. You were just a STAB – a Stupid TA Bastard, and, said Baird to the despondent recruit before him: 'You also made yourself conspicuous by being last at nearly everything . . . you were always last and trailing bits of kit behind you. For that reason you failed Basic Wales and will be back-squadded. What have you got to say to that?'

What could Bush say? Except that he felt like jacking. He'd tried hard according to his lights. He'd done his best, or thought he had at any rate.

What more was he supposed to do? He felt he couldn't go through all that lot again. Not another eight weeks. Not right back to the beginning with 482, the next platoon to form. It was asking too much of anyone. Even someone with an older brother in the Paras and the initial and powerful urge to join him in the Regiment. No wonder that urge was beginning to wane. Still, for the time being he'd take his commander's advice and do less talking. Too much mouth had got him into trouble in the past. This time he'd keep his feelings to himself. So what had he got to say? Nothing.

'Right. Fall out . . . Bush!'

'Sir?'

'Come back. You forgot the salute again!'

John Baird worked his way steadily through the others up for interview. Some had his sympathy, especially the injured. Paul Chant, he knew, was keen and well-motivated. The injury to his ankles was rotten luck. But others had suffered injuries too. Young Chard, Woodcock, Joe Killey, who also came from an army family like Woodcock. They had already fallen by the wayside – gone sick with injuries to their ankles and knees. Chant would have to go back and join them. Purely for injury, not for any other reason. Unlike some people's, Chant's attitude was good. He was the sort of man the Regiment was looking for. He mustn't lose enthusiasm because he had to go back to 482. Chant promised not to. Both to his Captain and himself. He meant it, too. He hadn't joined the army on impulse. He'd given it a lot of thought. It seemed to him it offered a great deal more than civvy street for someone with ambition and the urge to earn himself a decent living. Civvy street had been a disappointment to Paul Chant. He'd done his best to get a trade. In 1978 he'd started training as a mechanic in a garage in his home town, Northampton. Or supposedly training. The first garage he was in, all he did in the two months he was there was put petrol into cars, when he was expecting to go to College for City and Guilds. 'So,' said Chant, 'I had it out with him and he said, just as I was leaving: "I was going to send you there on Wednesday for a test," and I said: "Pull the other one, mate".' But he wasn't any luckier at the next place either. It was all right for six or seven months but then he was put on bodywork when what he wanted was to be a mechanic. And when he complained, all his boss said was, the future was in bodywork, which maybe it was, but Chant hadn't gone to him for that, so he told him where to go as well and left to join the army. He'd been enjoying his training when he'd done his ankle in. It was all attitude really. And once you got to P Company it was all downhill. But for the time being he'd have to put up with it, and go back, with the other unlucky ones, to 482.

Fraser Hooper was another TA soldier John Baird wasn't pleased about. He hadn't shown the guts, determination and motivation Basic Wales was all about. This might be because he'd done it all before in 15 Para. But that was no excuse for being as switched off as he had been last week. He was also unfit, so he was another one Baird would like to see back-squadded. It didn't interest him that Hooper had been an Air Cadet, a TA Para, was twenty-four years old and had had five jobs. 'Was it five?' 'It was, sir.' Well that cut no ice with Baird. No ice whatsoever. Hooper hadn't come up to standard at Basic Wales, therefore he would have to go back, do it again, end of story.

Hooper came from Westlothian. The dourest of dour Scots, he had served his time as a tinsmith and, like Chant, was not unduly impressed at the thought of the future being in bodywork. He saw his as being in the Paras. And though he wasn't pleased to hear that his platoon commander was recommending him for back-squadding, he was prepared to accept it. He had managed to put up with eighteen months unemployment, so he didn't see why he wouldn't be able to put up with another eight weeks in 482. Life was hard north of the border. Scotland was a land where you got used to putting up with things. The English weren't so patient. So if that was how Baird wanted it, then Hooper didn't have any complaints. At least he didn't plan to voice any.

Nor did Hindmarsh. He listened while his Captain told him he had scraped through by the skin of his teeth. They were giving him the benefit of the doubt. It was up to him now. He was the only one who could do it. His fitness had to improve. Also his motivation. And his attitude. Admittedly he'd been unlucky. His leg injury had set him back and hacked him off. But these things happened. It was up to Hindmarsh. Baird hoped he wouldn't let them down. He hoped Hindmarsh wouldn't let *himself* down, because he was the only one who would be responsible for it. And so on.

Baird read the riot act to all the others who had failed or scraped a pass or manifested attitudes the army did not like. He was stern with John Stirling, the tallest in the platoon, all six foot four of him from Ayrshire. He was twenty-one, had five O Levels, and had been unemployed for two years since leaving school in 1976. He too had been in the TA, the 21st SAS Regiment. Not that it seemed to have done him much good, in John Baird's eyes. He couldn't even stand to attention properly! 'That typifies your whole attitude, Stirling. You're not doing enough, you're just coasting. All right? You've been spotted. The section commanders and I have noticed. Don't play around with your tongue. Keep it inside your mouth. Oh yes, we've noticed you've been coasting. We expect a great improvement over the next few weeks. Otherwise, you'll be out. All right?' All right. And so on.

Altogether there were six of the original 480 Platoon that John Baird wanted back-squadded. But before that could take place, his recommendation had to be agreed by the officer commanding Recruit Company. Major David Roberts, who had sentenced Cunningham and Hughes to five days Restriction of Privileges for the NDs on Exercise Steel Eagle, had in the interval been posted. In the absence of an immediate replacement his job had been taken over temporarily by the Company's second-in-command, Captain Max Gandell. So the next stage of the proceedings consisted of a meeting between the two captains to discuss the recommendations. Waiting in the wings, of course, was Max Gandell's superior, the CO of the Parachute Regiment's Depot, Lieutenant-Colonel Simon Brewis, who was reluctant to see a recruit back-squadded unless it was absolutely necessary.

Back-squadding was a perfectly normal procedure in all recruit training. And a man who had been injured understood perfectly well that he could not possibly go on until his injury had cleared up. Those who were back-squadded for other reasons might be equally aware of the good intentions behind the decision. They might even agree that they needed to be back-squadded. But there were other, more borderline, cases where the man in question might feel resentful at being penalised. Or might simply feel that he had not got the patience to repeat a process he had found hard enough to endure the first time round. Hard luck, it could be said. In that case, the man in question had not got what it took and the Regiment was well rid of him. There was some truth in that.

But in the case of 480 Platoon there was another complicating factor that needed to be taken into account. The platoon following – 482 Platoon – was an amalgam of 481 and 482 and, as a result, was eight weeks behind 480 instead of the more usual four weeks. So anyone being back-squadded from 480 was not simply obliged to repeat the last four weeks of the course but had to go right back to the beginning and start from scratch. That would be a fairly daunting prospect even for the most enthusiastic and well-motivated recruit. For the less enthusiastic recruit such a prospect might be totally demoralising and not only drive him out of the Parachute Regiment but even out of the army altogether. And the army was not in favour of that. By week 8 it had invested valuable time and money in a recruit. It preferred not to write those resources off without making a considerable effort to save its investment.

So the demands of the training schedule had to be tempered with the subtleties of personnel management. Or, in practical terms, if Bush was told he was back-squadded would he then leave the army and be a total waste of the time and money invested in him? There was another factor too, of course – one besetting all institutions. Once an individual joins the group, the group is reluctant to see him go. Either because they value his contribution, or because his departure seems like a criticism of those who remain behind. And finally there is another, totally unpractical explanation – the Christian urge to save souls, as it were – the satisfaction of bringing a sinner back into the flock. Who knows? Perhaps one day Bush would reform his ways and go back to wearing ordinary glass in his spectacles. Perhaps Cunningham would become fit and agile and beat Fleming home in the BFT. Perhaps Clark would stop being so artistic and give up the trumpet in favour of some more aggressive instrument, like, for instance, the General Purpose Machine Gun?

'But when I joined, sir,' said Clark, his sensitive features showing no trace of the emotion presumably boiling beneath their surface, 'I understood I was only to do eight weeks and then I would move into the band.' He was a tall lad, well over six feet, and did not have the sort of build one automatically associated with Paras. But Stirling was even taller and lankier and the last thing he wanted to do was play a trumpet in the band. So appearances weren't everything, even though John Baird gave the impression of thinking so.

'He's just not a soldier,' he said to Max Gandell in the middle of their discussion.

'No?'

'Just not a soldier. I'm afraid that just sums it up.'

'Probably make the grade as a bandsman?'

'Oh yes, I should think so. As a bandsman. I mean, his musical qualifications are excellent.'

'Yes,' said Gandell, who at that moment happened to be brooding over them in his documents.

'He plays the trumpet very well. And in fact he's graded as an instructor on the trumpet.'

'And educated, I see.'

'Oh yes, he's an intelligent guy,' said Baird. 'He's what you might call a sensitive and artistic type. . .'

And perhaps, therefore, totally unfit to be a Para. So was there really any point in back-squadding him as John Baird had recommended and making him go through all that agony again?

By the time Clark was marched into Captain Gandell's office to have official confirmation of his fate, he had given up all hope of an easy transfer to the band. And nothing Captain Gandell had to say suggested any different. In fact, he seemed to be backing up everything Captain Baird had said. The way it looked to Captain Gandell, Clark hadn't really been trying hard enough to make the grade as an airborne soldier. Would Clark say that was fair comment?

Not really, no. In his opinion, he'd done his best.

But still, he hadn't managed to keep up with the squad. Was he going to find it any easier in the band? The musicians had to be soldiers too, don't forget. They didn't just spend their time banging or blowing things. When the regiment went to war it was their job to act as Medics and stretcher-bearers. So Clark couldn't go around imagining he could get away with doing the minimum, could he? That wasn't the right sort of attitude, was it?

'No sir,' he said, heart sinking in anticipation of being told the back-squadding was confirmed.

'Nevertheless . . .' – Clark's jaw dropped – 'under the circumstances . . .' There was a look of wonderment in Clark's eyes. Both Max Gandell and John Baird felt he would be happier in the band, blowing that trumpet of his, OK?

Clark didn't actually dance down the corridor. The presence of the sergeant major saw to that. But there was no doubt about the song in his heart and the stars in his eyes.

And what about the parachuting? Was he still planning to come back and do that? Well, maybe, in a couple of years' time. After he'd got some extra musical qualifications. He hadn't got anything against parachuting. It just wasn't his first priority, that was all.

Out of the four other uninjured recruits John Baird had wished to back-squad Max Gandell would only agree to one, Graham Harrison, the lad who had distinguished himself on the square by telling the RSM that he had joined the Parachute Regiment because he wanted to 'fly and jump out of the sky'. With the passing weeks, alas, that prospect had become less and less likely. Not because he had lost the urge to parachute, but because he was finding it difficult keeping up with the rest of the platoon. Like Bush, said Captain Baird, he was always last – well, not always last, because Bush was that, but next to last, and always slow picking things up and absorbing information. Before they went to Basic Wales, he had understood that Harrison wanted to put in for a transfer to the Royal Tank Regiment. Did he still want that?

He did.

In that case, as Baird had already explained, Harrison would have to get to week 12 with a good grade first. Otherwise the RTR weren't going to look at him. It wasn't just a question of the Parachute Regiment dumping its rejects on other arms. A transfer wasn't a cop-out, but a privilege. It was something a man had to earn the right to, by showing he was made of something worth transferring elsewhere. Only when he had demonstrated that would his application be considered. If, on the other hand, he found he couldn't make the grade, then he would have to take a DAOR, which a number of others were putting in for.

At this stage of the course the DAOR – the Discharge as of Right – was available on request. With the payment of a nominal £75 – roughly a week's wages – the reluctant soldier could make good his escape back into civvy street. And although it was not something the army encouraged, three members of the platoon had already put in for their discharge. One was Paul Kentish – a former trainee office-manager from London. Another was Alex Preston, who had had to wait so long to get into the army he thought they'd forgotten him. The last was the other Irishman, and all three had been transferred to HQ Company while the necessary for-malities were going through. As in that first selection week, any defector was instantly removed from the others to avoid a spread of the infection.

It was at this point, too, by a strange twist of fate, that John Hughes, the man of many alternatives, the man who had contemplated transferring to branches of the army as various as the Royal Artillery and the Catering Corps, had all his options removed from him at one fell swoop. He was discovered to be suffering from asthma – a disability he had failed to mention when filling in the appropriate section of his medical form. He too was moved over to HQ Company to await his discharge – in his case a variety described as IE, the army's shorthand for Illegal Enlistment plus Injury or Illness. Both Byrne and Wood had been discharged under that category in the first weeks of the course. Still others were to go later. Its significance lay in the fact that, since the recruit had arrived in that condition, his disability was no legal or financial responsibility of the army.

And for the time being that seemed to be that. The critical eighth week had come and gone. All those who wanted a voluntary discharge had applied for it. The medically unfit had been invalided out. The lame, the halt and the backward had joined 482 Platoon, now forming. The first of the two Irishmen was still absent, Hughes's questioning voice was silent, and Clark was off somewhere blowing his trumpet. A leaner, tougher platoon had emerged, phoenix-like, from the ordeal. There were now only twenty-six left out of the original forty-one. As somebody said: 'Now that the wimps are gone, we can really get down to some hard work.'

Hard work in weeks 8 to 11 meant all the usual physical exercises plus weapon training, or Skill at Arms as it is called in the training manual. For the infantry soldier in the British Army this involves handling and firing a wide range of weapons, from the Self-Loading Rifle to the 84mm Anti-Tank Gun. The first of these, however, the SLR, is the private soldier's personal weapon, and he is expected to reach a high standard of proficiency in handling and shooting it. All the other weapons he may be called upon to fire are described as alternative personal weapons, and the level of skill he is required to achieve in handling and firing them is proportionately less. The pistol, the submachine-gun, the general purpose machine-gun, the hand grenade, the 2-inch mortar, the 66mm LAW and 84mm MAW (light and medium anti-tank weapons) are all weapons the infantry soldier has access to.

The recruit is therefore given the opportunity to familiarise himself with them – both on the range and in the field, where battle conditions can be simulated. The only limitation as far as live firing is concerned affects the anti-tank weapons. They are expensive – each high-explosive missile for the 84mm MAW costs some £500 – so not everyone gets a chance to fire one himself at this stage. But with the small arms the restriction is much less, and by the time the course is over a recruit will have fired some thousands of rounds of 7.62mm ammunition at a cost of 35p per round. And the poorer the shot, the more he will have fired off. The standard SLR shooting test involved the firing of seventy shots. Some might fail the test twice or three times before satisfying their instructors. Skill with a rifle was not something that came to everyone easily. And the test demanded quick reactions as well as quiet precision. Many of the targets were what is known as opportunity targets that popped up at various distances down the range in unexpected places. The man who could get his shot off quickly and instinctively might do better at this than his slower, more accurate comrade.

Some had already fired guns before joining the army and so had an advantage. Ewan Fleming was a good shot, the best in his TA unit. As a result, when it had become his section's turn – a favour granted only once every three years – to fire one of the 84mm MAW high-explosive missiles, Fleming had been chosen for the job. Unfortunately, he missed, and his section commander was so upset he didn't speak to Fleming for three weeks.

But it would be some time before he would get the opportunity to miss again. First 480 would have to concentrate on their small arms training.

It was the end of March. Spring had arrived. Some of the afternoons on the ranges were almost balmy. While the details that were firing went to the butts, the others stretched out on the grass behind the firing-point, chatting and ribbing each other. As usual Ward took a lot of stick. Most of it from Tattum who got a lot of stick back from Ward. They were both in Corporal Lyden's section, were rarely seen apart, and never publicly said anything nice about each other.

'Stingy bastard.'

'Bloody Rasta.'

'I've a lot of white friends in Loughborough.'

'Not here, though.'

'Quick, aren't you?'

'Slow ones went after Basic Wales.'

All except Gary Price, that is. He waited until the end of week 9 and then went suddenly on the Sunday evening, after a game of football and tea in the canteen with his mates. Over the wall and away, like the Irishman whose bed he had been occupying for the last few weeks ever since Section 5 had been disbanded. According to Taff Hunt – now the last of Corporal Slater's original section – Price had asked if he could get out, and they'd said no, he had to stay there, he'd got to stay . . . So he'd just done a runner. Legged it. And it wasn't because he was no good, either. Physically he was one of the best. He was up front in the BFTs all the time. On all the tabs he was up front. He could do anything, he just didn't like it, that's all, he wanted out, and they wouldn't let him . . .

Gary Price was the soldier who didn't know where the 3rd Battalion was when questioned on the subject by Captain Williams. He had also narrowly escaped back-squadding after Basic Wales, on the grounds that he got flustered easily, lacked self-confidence and started to flap under pressure. But keen enough, John Baird had decided. Keen enough to go on . . .

AWOL. Absent Without Leave. Shades of Kelly's Kingdom and RSM Lewis' dark forebodings, according to whom all Price would be doing was making a rod for his own back. Some day they would get him. Some day he would be brought back. Some day he would end up in 'that little enchanted cottage at the bottom of the stairs'. But meanwhile he was off and away. He had done a runner and now there were only twenty-five left out of the original forty-one.

Colin Atkins was another one who was beginning to have second thoughts. He had been having them since week 7 apparently, since the end of Basic Wales, while he was at home on the four days' pass they had been given. He was a Scot and bothered at the idea that if he were to go he'd be the first of the Scots to let the side down. He was a solidly-built young man, serious, mature, a time-served mechanic. He had done a four-year apprenticeship and he was worried what might have happened to his skill after three years in the Paras. He was afraid no garage would look at him when he came out, he'd be out-of-date, have forgotten his skills. It was a problem. He had thought of going to Canada or South Africa and starting a new life out there. But he had £2000 worth of tools and shipping them out would have cost a packet, so he'd abandoned all that. It seemed to him the best solution would be to get a transfer to the REME and service their vehicles. That way he wouldn't lose his skill. But Captain Baird had avoided him when he'd tried to get an interview. Didn't want to know. It was all very difficult. He wanted to stay in the Paras. But, like Hughes, he was beginning to feel that back in civvy street there weren't many employers looking for people who could jump out of aeroplanes and fire an SLR. His dad felt he ought to think very seriously about it. So did he. At the same time, as he'd said before, he didn't want to be the first Scot to drop out.

Ten of the original forty-one had been Scots. Now ten of the twenty-five remaining were Scots. It was quite a record. One that clashed somewhat with the PSO's figures. According to him a higher proportion of Scots dropped out than English. Something to do with the selection procedure, he believed. They didn't pass through Sutton Coldfield as did the rest. He felt that was a more efficient centre than the ones they came through. So far he had been proved wrong. Sutton Coldfield hadn't done at all well. But with another thirteen weeks to go it would be interesting to see what the final figures would be. Meanwhile Atkins resisted setting a precedent. Perhaps he didn't really want to go at all. Perhaps he had just been unsettled by what had happened to some of the others in his section. The Irishman and Price, the two who had gone absent, were room-mates of his. And this trouble with his feet wasn't helping either. He'd had to go sick and miss that afternoon's BFT.

Fleming came first again, the fifth time running now. The only one ever to have beaten him was Gary Price who had just legged it for good, and anyway that had been one of Fleming's off days. He had knocked a whole minute off his original time. One inspired morning he had actually got it down to 7.49. It was a mistake really. It was unlikely he'd ever do it as fast as that again. Yet the staff expected you to improve on it every time. Butler was more sensible and consistent, for instance. In the last three BFTs he had clocked two 8 minute 29 seconds and an 8 minute 30. Cunningham was pretty consistent, too. Last, as a rule. Or next to last on a brilliant day.

Meanwhile the physical pressure never slackened. Steeplechases, assault courses, endurance training. Road walks, runs, cross-countrys. Four miles, six miles, seven miles, ten. An introduction to the Trainasium and the confidence test. All the elements of the Pre-Para Selection programme they were gradually building up to and would have to face in week 12. And this would be crunch-point. All the other hurdles they had had to cross since their arrival at the Depot had been ankle-height compared with this one.

8 P Company

Pre-Parachute Selection – or P Company as it is more familiarly known – is one of the toughest physical and mental tests in any army. Anyone in the British Army wishing to train as a parachutist must first satisfy P Company's requirements before progressing to the Parachute Training School at Brize Norton. Those who come from outside the Regiment join an All Arms Course and spend three weeks at Browning Barracks, where they have two weeks of preparation followed by a third week of tests. That third week of tests is the twelfth week of the Parachute Regiment's Recruit Company course, and on occasions – if the numbers make it necessary – Para recruits mix in with officers and men from other arms and regiments.

480 Platoon was large enough, with a number of recruits back-squadded from previous platoons, to go it alone. As the great day approached, so the feeling of nervous apprehension at what lay ahead of them increased accordingly. In theory this should not have been so. They had already done most of the tests before, some of them, like the assault course, several times, and had managed to complete them in the times expected of them. All they had to do now was produce a result according to schedule and they would emerge at the end of the three days of tests as recruits who had satisfied the stringent but not impossible P Company requirements.

But this was the most critical moment of their training, and it was not unreasonable they should feel some nervousness. It was better than feeling over-confident, like some clowns who, according to Corporal Priestley, as P Company drew near, went down town to the tattooist, in the Shot, like, and got a bulldog with a red beret on its head, with wings and 'Airborne' and 'I'm a killer' and all the rest of it, tattooed on their arms, and then failed, like. No, they weren't that stupid. They didn't intend asking for trouble. They just assumed that if everything went all right, if they didn't sprain an ankle, if they weren't ill or injured, then with a little bit of luck by Wednesday night it would be all over and they would have got enough marks on all the different bits of the test to satisfy the P Company people. And if they did, then – after three weeks of Advanced Tactical Training in Wales – they'd be off to Brize Norton to get their jumps in – that was what really counted, get their wings up on their sleeve, and their best red beret on, they'd be made then, real Paras, ready to go to the battalion.

The weekend before Pre-Parachute Selection – while they were busy

Corporal Priestley's section prepare for Pre-Parachute Selection. Left to right, Hindmarsh, Melvin, Fleming, Way, Stoner and Atkins.

psyching themselves up for the test that lay ahead – something happened which at the time seemed to have very little connection with any of them. A certain Argentine General Galtieri ordered the invasion of the Falkland Islands. A touch of comic opera in the South Atlantic was what it seemed like then. The really important things in life were going to happen between Monday and Wednesday of the following week.

There was, however, another little touch of drama that struck closer home. One of 3 Para's company commanders arranged for loudspeaker announcements to be made at various London mainline stations instructing all members of the battalion to report back to barracks immediately. A slight overreaction, perhaps, but since 3 Para was Britain's 'Spearhead' battalion, on standby to go anywhere in the world at short notice, the officer concerned had assumed, not unreasonably, that it might not be long before they were needed. So that did make a certain amount of impact in Browning Barracks. Almost as much as the fact that Ossie Ardiles, Tottenham's Argentine player, was booed off the pitch that Saturday afternoon during Spurs' defeat of Leicester City in the FA Cup Semi-Final.

Atkins, Way, Woof and Hindmarsh, however, were not very interested in any of these things. They had injuries that prevented them from doing P Company. There would be further months of training before they could present themselves again. It was very galling, particularly for Hindmarsh, whose morale was taking yet another battering. Once more he had to sit on the sidelines while his platoon mates went into action. Andy Way was more philosophic about the setback. Come injury, hell or high water, Andy planned to stick it out regardless until the day he qualified. Nigel Woof was less determined. He had been having doubts for some time about his suitability for the Paras. He now felt even more inclined to put in for a transfer to some less physically demanding outfit. And though Colin Atkins was despondent about his injury, at least he was no longer in danger of being the first Scot to drop out of the course. A fellow Glaswegian, Steven Burns – an apprentice plant-fitter in civvy street – had decided the army was not for him and had applied for a DAOR. There were now only twenty of the original platoon left to take P Company.

The P Company team consisted of five people: Captain Gandell, Sergeant Major Lionel McNally, Staff Sergeant Dick Parker and Sergeants Benoit Registe and Mick Champion. Max Gandell was therefore filling two separate posts at one and the same time – Officer Commanding Pre-Parachute Selection as well as Second-in-Command, Recruit Company. And at 0800 on Monday 5 April 1982, he introduced himself as such to 480 Platoon as they waited nervously for proceedings to begin.

The programme he then outlined to them was one they had all known by heart for some time. It had been instituted originally in the 1940s and had long since crystallised into a form that no one seemed to question any more. On Monday there was something called Milling, followed that afternoon by a 10-mile Battle March. That night the platoon dug trenches and slept out on the training area. On the Tuesday morning they filled in the trenches and took part in the Stretcher Race, after which they marched to the Trainasium, an outdoor structure of scaffolding, nets, catwalks and ladders where they carried out confidence tests. This was followed by three circuits of the Assault Course. Wednesday began with a Steeplechase and concluded with the Log Race, at which point the programme was complete and the staff met to discuss the results and decide who had or had not passed. All very straightforward, and superficially not a very crowded programme. As Sergeant Major McNally pointed out in his introduction, the actual events themselves came to a total of a mere four hours over the seventy-two. But there were other factors that helped drain their energy during this period. They did not get very much sleep on Monday night, and digging trenches was a strenuous activity. Nevertheless, as they sat listening to the introductory talks, there seemed little cause for alarm.

The Pre-Parachute Selection process had nothing to do with the actual business of parachuting. It was not designed to test whether people had a head for heights, or the courage to jump out of aeroplanes, or the right kind of ankles for landing by parachute. It was designed to test more fundamental qualities, like courage, endurance, and determination under conditions of stress, in order to assess whether the individual had the ability to serve with the airborne forces. Max Gandell also said it was a test of military aptitude, but in fact that was only true in the most general sense of the words. No weapon skills were required, no drill, no fieldcraft, no map-reading. 'The men we are looking for', said Gandell, 'will always be outnumbered by the enemy, and their light scales of ammunition and supply will make their hardship even worse. They must be physically fit and strong to march quickly from the dropping zone into battle. They must have a strong reserve of stamina to survive ten days of fighting, as at Arnhem. They have to be physically courageous to stand and fight when the odds are against them. They have to be self-disciplined to curb all their natural fears.'

The first event designed to test some aspects of these qualities was Milling, a rough-and-tumble version of boxing, according to Sergeant Major McNally, where opponents of approximately equal weight and height, wearing 16-ounce gloves, demonstrated their ability to fight with controlled aggression and the will to win, non-stop for a minute. On his left, Tattum. On his right, Thomas. A hundred and eighty pounds apiece and somewhere around six feet tall or as near as dammit. Lay on, MacDuff. No whining, whingeing, whimpering, crying, turning your back on your opponent or refusing to fight. Nor would there be any illegal use of the head, the knee, the foot, etcetera. Milling, he said, was a good way to start the parachute selection and he urged them to reach into the spirit of things and come up with a really good performance. A non-stop performance, for what was sometimes called the longest minute in the world.

The Tattum–Thomas bout, under the guidance of Staff Parker.

The battering began. Arms flailing, heads down until told otherwise, they went for each other like bulls. Tattum v Thomas, Fleming v Birrell, Borland v O'Hare . . . At the end of each bout, Captain Gandell and his staff sitting at a table on a platform above the proceedings raised either a red, a blue or crossed batons to indicate the result, more as a formal close to the occasion than as something to be recorded.

Some of the recruits were much better at it than others. Some found it difficult to keep their head up and their face exposed to an opponent's fists, even if they were cushioned by the padding in the gloves. Non-stop flailing fists can get in somewhere around a hundred blows in the course of a minute. And if you are lucky enough to take only twenty-five per cent of them on your face, then you are still not doing terribly well. Some were overwhelmed by the violence of their opponent's attack. Fists pounded them to their knees, sent them sprawling on the floor of the gym. Through watery eyes they saw their opponents' blotched faces, bared teeth, whirling gloves. Vaguely too they could hear the cries of the crowd, the urgings of the staff, to get in there, get your head up, kill him, kill him, kill him! Biceps bulging, mouth open in a terrible snarl, Butler flailed away blindly. Stephen Thomas, who had worked in the hotel trade as a trainee manager before joining the army, tried to weave his way out of trouble with a bit of fancy footwork, only to have the staff bellow at him that this was not 'Come Dancing', they were actually allowed to hit each other. Robertson's rather slight figure kept falling down. O'Hare went in for a bit of wrestling. Scrumpy Barrett, from Ashcott, Somerset, in cider country, slugged his way through the endless minute and won the encounter. Any man driven back by the force of his opposite number's onslaught came up against a living wall of recruits whose job it was to fend him off and push him back into the ring to take the rest of his punishment. Only had to last a minute. Knocked down, get up. Knocked down, get up. Get up, get up, get up!

Finally the wheel had turned full circle. The only one left to fight was Bush. He was odd man out, so Spider Craddock, who had fought first and won his bout, was matched against Bush, same size, same weight. How Craddock had the strength to repeat the minute was a mystery, but nobody asked him whether he had or not. He was in the army now and he did as he was told. So he fought as ordered, and won again – a stocky, compact figure, 10 stone, 5 feet $8\frac{1}{2}$, tough, wiry, with a quick infectious grin. A plasterer after leaving school in Lancashire in the summer of 1980, he had joined the Paras in search of a better life, travel and adventure. They called him Spider because of the long-johns they had found him wearing during the bitter weather at the beginning of the course. And the nickname had stuck, though the long-johns were not needed any more.

Those whose performance had been judged unsatisfactory the first time were rematched, fitted out with gloves again and exhorted to give each other a further battering. It was interesting to see how much they had improved. Their punching was better aimed, their stance more aggressive. Dazed and bloody, they staggered back to their corners and offered their gloved fists for unlacing. Some said later that the milling had exhausted them, given them headaches, undermined the strength they were going to need for the rest of the test. But at the time they seemed to recover quickly enough. And in any case, as the Sergeant Major pointed out, the total work that morning was finished by half-past ten. No more physical activity would be taking place until Exercise Tiger Shark, which started at two o'clock with the 10-mile Battle March . . .

The dress for the Battle March was denim trousers, combat jacket, the hated DPM cap, SLR and Bergen rucksack packed to a weight of 30 lbs. The cap was a new departure ordered by the CO, Lt-Col. Brewis, to add realism to the event. Often recruits wore no hats at all for the Battle March. But what began as a seemingly trivial factor took on more significance as the afternoon wore on. A surprisingly warm afternoon, touching 70 degrees Fahrenheit in Farnborough that day, the temperature of many an English summer's day. And totally unexpected by the staff and the recruits, whose bodies had got accustomed to temperatures a great deal lower and most of whose training had been done in very cold weather.

The run took place on one of the many training areas around Aldershot, a sandy landscape of heath and sparse woodland just to the south of Farnborough airfield. The centrepiece was Long Valley, an area used for testing tanks and other tracked vehicles, so that in wet weather the ground was a morass of glutinous mud and evil-smelling pools of yellow water. Disappointingly – as the P Company Staff saw it at any rate – there was little water and less mud on this occasion. A succession of dry days had made the going good by normal standards, bad by P Company's. What they wanted was something to put a bit of difficulty into the course, some interesting places where a careless recruit might lose a boot, or flounder up to his waist in yellow filth. There were none of these. Only a few shallow puddles which were easily avoided or, as the afternoon wore on, deliberately run through as refreshment for hot feet and aching ankles. At the edges of Long Valley were a series of hills – to the south Hungry Hill and Flagstaff, to the north Miles Hill, all good vantage points from which to observe the pack toiling through the valleys below or struggling up the trail to the summit.

Shortly after taking part in the Milling, Andy Cunningham received the news that his father had died. So he was sent home on compassionate leave and took no further part in the proceedings. That brought the numbers down to twenty-four, five of whom were back-squads. So only nineteen of the original 480 Platoon lined up that afternoon for the Battle March. Par for this event was 1 hour 45 minutes. Before they started, Sergeant Riley reminded them they had all done it in that time, they had proved they were capable of it, so all they had to do now was summon up guts and determination, drive into it, get going and not worry about the weather. After all:

'What is pain, Ward?'

'In the mind, Sergeant!'

'No, it isn't,' snapped Riley through his teeth. 'It's but a mere sensation. Just grin at it. Smile at it.'

Ward could have sworn pain had been in the mind last time it had come up for consideration. But you didn't argue with sergeants. You just shut your trap, got on with it, and concentrated on making sure you came home as near 1 hour 45 as possible. If you did that, and were at both check-points on time, you got the full ten points. If you only made one check-point, you scored nine, and then, on a declining scale, eight, seven, six points through 1 hour 50, 55 to 2 hours, after which you had technically failed, though you could still score a few points, for effort, which might come in useful at the end if you had done particularly well on everything else.

Staff Parker (white vest) and Sgt Major McNally lead the way in the Battle March. Tattum, Whitton and Bush are immediately behind, and Sergeant Champion is on the left at the rear.

A Battle March is half-running, half-walking. Or half-doubling, half-marching in army parlance. And you were not supposed to do one when everybody else was doing the other, as Bush soon discovered. He was right

up at the front, next to two of the biggest men in the platoon, and matching their stride without actually running was very difficult for him. As Sergeant Major McNally's sharp eye soon spotted. 'No need for you to run, young fellow,' he rapped out briskly. 'No need for you to run at all.' Until it was time to run, of course. And then the last thing you were supposed to do was walk. Bush found he could not match the big men's stride at that either. Gradually he began to slip behind the pack. He did it in the face of a great deal of advice to the contrary. A great deal of urging to keep up, come on now, open your legs, close up, don't drop behind, push, push, come on, keep going . . .

The staff nagged at the marchers like sheepdogs at a flock of sheep. At the head of the column were Sergeant Major McNally and Staff Parker. At the rear, as back-marker – the 2-hour man behind whom no one was supposed to fall – was Sergeant Registe. Between them roamed Captain Gandell and Sergeant Champion with Captain Baird and the NCOs of 480 Platoon. Although they were not carrying weapons like the men, they all wore Bergens with the standard 30-lb load. They were certainly bulky enough, though rumour had it that some of them were more bulk than substance. Others in attendance were the medical men, Corporal Gary Organ and Lance-Corporal John Peka, who followed in their Land Rovers or, where the terrain made that impossible, cut across country in advance of the squad to be waiting at some critical point – on top of the hills, for instance, places where the greatest demands would be made and where they were most likely to be needed.

In the past, in training, the squad had stayed as a squad from beginning to end, with only a slight stretch towards the end. Today, however, the squad began to disintegrate very rapidly, and it was not long before individuals had broken away even from the smaller groups and were running blindly and desperately on their own. Not quite on their own, of course. They could never shake off one of the staff for very long. Hard as Bush tried, he never managed to lose Sergeant Riley for more than a few seconds while he darted away to snap at some other unfortunate.

'Come on, Bush. Goots and drive, goots and drive. I'm bloody well *walking* and I'm going faster than you. Come on, open your legs. What? Can't? No such word as can't in the Parachute Regiment. You're going to be a candidate for the dusty-bin, Bush, at this rate. What's your brother going to think, eh? Go on, that's right. Overtake him, Campbell. Show him what a bum he is. Campbell's overtaking you, Bush. You're letting a Jock in front of you. A Jock! We built a wall to keep them out. Now come on. You've had it. You've had it now. If you don't get on the top of Flagstaff now, you've had it!'

Aly Campbell was a Scot from the Highlands. He had joined the Paras for adventure and travel and the outdoor life, and because he wanted to belong to a team. Although he had managed to overtake Bush, his knees were giving him trouble and he wasn't sure he would be able to stay the course. But he plodded grimly on.

Precisely who was first to flake out was never clearly established. Certainly Bush was amongst the earliest. So were Thomas and Robertson, struck down like Bush with heat exhaustion against all odds and expectations. Very much against the odds in Robertson's case. He was a first-class runner in his day, always well up at the front in the BFTs and Steeplechases. Another early, unexpected casualty was Taff Hunt, who pulled a muscle in his leg and dropped out long before Flagstaff, which was roughly the half-way mark. Up to that point Butler was doing splendidly. He was first up the slope at Flagstaff, teeth bared, mouth open, feet pounding the dusty, rocky outcrops of the track. From the top of the hill there was a good view over the road to Long Valley but Butler never made it that far. Going down the northern slope of Flagstaff he stumbled and turned his ankle, an old injury he had done his best to strap, and came back to camp in the Medics' Land Rover.

Another of the Land Rovers was in action on the top of Flagstaff. While one lad was wandering aimlessly about in the gorse bushes not knowing quite where or who he was, another collapsed unconscious, was revived, and in spite of his protests that there was no longer anything the matter with him was taken off for treatment at the military hospital. That was Barrett, a former machine-operator in a sheepskin factory, and as tough as anybody on the course. Another good runner, like Robertson, he was outraged to find he was being prevented from completing the course simply because he had happened to faint for a few seconds. The medical staff knew better. Heat exhaustion can be very dangerous. Dehydration wrecks the body's temperature mechanism. In an effort to prevent any further loss of water, sweating stops, the temperature rockets, delirium and fever set in.

'What's your name, lad? Tell me your name? What is it? Come on. Tell me your name!' It was one of the lads from 479 and Sergeant Champion of P Company knew very well who he was. He was just trying to make contact with him. Break through the daze, bring the lad back to himself. Very soon he would be shipped off to hospital along with the others. Meanwhile the remnants were crossing Long Valley – a place so prehistoric in appearance, according to Atkins, that you wouldn't be surprised to come across an effing dinosaur or two. By the look of most of them, that would have been the least of their worries. By now the platoon was stretched out over a distance of more than a mile, many of them alone, never in groups of more than two or three, and Sergeant Registe, the back-marker, was having trouble keeping them all in front of him. At one point he was pushing Birrell along by his Bergen. Three and a half miles to go. Don't jack, don't you effing dare jack.

Far off along the track another figure jogged wearily along, lashed by

Corporal Lyden has a word with Bush.

Staff Parker's tongue as he came alongside. 'Come on. The group's up there. See 'em? Right, then. Keep pushing.' Staff Parker drew away, disappeared round a bend. For a moment the weary figure, hunched under its bulging pack, was alone on the track. Not a blue jerkin or a white sweat-shirt in sight. The figure slowed to a walk, straightened its back. Oh, what bliss. What peace. What a marvellous afternoon. If only they didn't have to flog round this effing course. But the peace was only momentary. Floating down the path came the sound of that well-hated Geordie voice singing a merry little song.

'Hi-ho, hi-ho, it's off to work we go, with a shovel and a pick and a great big stick, . . . O'Hare! What do you think you're doing, eh? Goots and drive! Goots and drive! Come on now. Keep pushing, keep pushing! Push, push, push!'

The final and biggest drama took place on Miles Hill. Tracks led up to its summit through the trees on all sides. As recruits plodded slowly to the top they were greeted by staff carrying plastic cans of water, to drink, to swill their mouths out, to bathe their heads and necks under hand-held showers. While Corporal Slater and Captain Baird, two of the water-carriers, were busy plying their trade, Borland – delirious with dehydration – went berserk. Sergeant Major McNally tried to calm him by grabbing him round the body, but Borland wasn't having any. With McNally hanging grimly on, Borland fought back until finally the pair of them came down with a crash in the dust on top of Miles Hill, the Sergeant Major flat on his back with Borland on top of him, legs thrashing wildly. Other NCOs rushed up to help, but it was not easy getting past those flailing boots and catching hold of some part of Borland's body. Meanwhile the Sergeant Major, a cheerful grin on his face, lay where he had fallen underneath Borland, still clasping him firmly around the waist and giving the others advice and exhortations. It took four of them to control Borland and get him into the back of a Land Rover. And even then, as it pulled away, he was still struggling.

Only sixteen finished the Battle March – twelve originals and four back-squads. The senior staff were not pleased. Failing the Pass-Off the Square had been an embarrassment to Sergeant Riley and Captain Baird. Today's disaster could have even more serious consequences.

'What are you doing with that bloody water?' screamed McNally at Tattum, who was innocently, as he thought, dousing his head with the contents of his water-bottle. 'Don't pour it away! It might save your bloody life.'

'Oh great,' muttered Tattum. 'You get all this way to be shouted at.' But he wasn't that fed up about it. He'd finished, hadn't he? Right up the front with Fleming, when he was only a moderately good performer on the BFTs and steeplechases. He could afford to feel pleased with himself.

'Don't guzzle your bloody H$_2$O!' bellowed CSM Lucey this time, at somebody else. It seemed possible that he and the others might be working off their own irritation. Wasn't it rather unusual to lose so many people on a Battle March even if it was unexpectedly hot? The MO, Captain Bergman, said they always expected to lose a certain number. It would be nice to get through a training period without anyone becoming a heat-exhaustion casualty, but it was too much to hope for.

Seven out of twenty-four?

Well, they were going to have to fight in all weathers. From minus 20 up to 30 degrees Centigrade or above if they went to the tropics, so it was important to know which of them could cope. Max Gandell was less philosophic about it. For his money bad preparation was to blame. No more, no less. Just bad preparation. Some of them actually had lemonade in their water-bottles! No wonder they dehydrated. And Butler had

Stoner at the end of the Battle March.

wrapped up his ankle in a tight bandage after smearing algipan all over it. No wonder he'd ended up in agony. Anybody would. Amazing he'd got as far as he did. But it wasn't Butler's job to try and treat his injuries himself. That's what the medical staff were for. It was just another example of bad mental and physical preparation. Max Gandell wasn't happy about it. None of the staff were. They were fed up with all this stupidity. Now they'd hardly got enough people left for the Stretcher Race tomorrow. It was going to have to be one stretcher of eight and one of nine. The bare minimum. It would make it all the more difficult for the recruits who were left. Unless he could get some of the others out of hospital.

But wasn't that against P Company rules? Once they dropped out they were finished, weren't they? They'd failed the Battle March. Well, yes. But the situation was exceptional. It had been very hot and muggy unexpectedly. It wasn't a decision Gandell had come to lightly. He and the Sergeant Major had discussed it at some length before Gandell had gone to see the doctor in the hospital to ask if some of them were fit to come out. Fortunately, three of them had been pronounced fit enough to continue after a night's rest.

So next morning Bush, Barrett and Robertson lined up in their teams with the others, waiting for the thunderflash to be set off and start the race. The weather had broken during the night. A refreshing rain had fallen. Dehydration was extremely unlikely in this event, though exhaustion, leg injuries and shoulders rubbed raw were very much on the cards. The stretcher was made of steel and weighed 180 lbs, representing the joint weight of a stretcher and casualty. The race simulated a withdrawal across country with an injured comrade, and, for some reason nobody was able to explain, Sergeant Registe's team always won.

The thunderflash went off. The two teams raced for their stretchers, and within a hundred yards the matter was more or less settled. Like the Oxford and Cambridge boat-race, the team that was first to get its nose in front was usually the team that made the running all the way. Which proved to be the case on this occasion. Unlike the Battle March, the Stretcher Race was very much a team event. At any given moment there were four recruits shouldering the stretcher while the others carried their SLRs for them – with the two groups changing places at regular intervals. No. 2 squad – Sergeant Registe's – lost a man in the early stages of the race. Stirling stumbled and was struck on the head by the stretcher, the blow stunning him. It meant a little more work for his team, but since they were out in front at the time and their morale was high, they carried on without complaint.

As far as each individual was concerned, whether you were a member of the winning team or not made no difference to your score on the event. You were marked on effort, leadership qualities, cohesive work within the group. A man on the losing team could get full marks. A man amongst the winners could score nought. The staff were watching, appraising, marking all the time. But they were not allowed to help. Even if the stretcher stopped, they were not to lay a finger on it. It was the recruits' test, and they had to pass or fail on their own. Uphill was worst, of course. That was where the steel bit into the flesh while boots struggled frantically to get a footing. But downhill the stretcher had to be held back. And though the staff were not allowed to help, there was no ban on shouts of encouragement: 'Stop whimpering, there! Don't pull down on it! Watch your footing! Open your legs! Bring it up! Work it, work it, work it all the way! In, in, in, in, in, in!'

The losing squad in the Stretcher Race.

They were coming down the home straight. It was the last few hundred yards of the 7½-mile course that followed much the same path as the Battle March but in the opposite direction. No. 2 Squad was a quarter of a mile in front and Corporal Slater and Sergeant Registe were urging them on. 'Come on, let's have a sprint finish here, keep coming, don't stop, straight up to the four-tonner and get it in the back. Straight in the back!'

Crash! The stretcher slammed down on to the floor of the truck and Tattum's team had won.

'Well done, Tattum,' said Captain Gandell as he handed him the pennant. 'Squad 2 again. Course, stand at ease. I would have thought Squad 2 deserve a cheer for that. Not only from its own team, but from Squad 1 as well. So let's hear it.'

A dutiful cheer rang out. Breakfast would now be served. Followed by the confidence tests on the Trainasium, a not very illuminating term to describe the structure, set some thirty feet up in the air amongst a patch of trees by the side of the assault course. The way to do it apparently was just to get on with it without thinking about it too much. Once you started thinking, planks that you had previously run along without any difficulty could begin to seem rather narrow. But first there was breakfast in the rain, under the trees, hot and filling, beans, bacon, sausages, tea. For some of them, seven miles with that stretcher had taken all their appetite away.

Others were ravenous. Like Tattum. As he'd said before, he enjoyed the food. And he was glad to get rid of that stretcher, too. It did terrible things to your shoulder.

Most people gave a good account of themselves on the confidence tests. Up the ropes, along the catwalks, into the nets. Two failed, however, both back-squads, one because he was unable to jump a gap of about five feet between the planks, the other because there was something telling him not to run along the catwalk. Neither of these were difficult things to do compared to crossing the shuffle bars which they had done at the beginning. The problem appeared to be psychological in one case, somewhat more calculated in the other. Probably just working his ticket, Max Gandell thought. Anyway, no point wasting any more time on them now. Back to the barracks for lunch, then on to the assault course and three times round in less than 7 minutes 30. Moy was caught cheating on that one. A slight misdemeanour, as Sergeant Major McNally called it, for which he didn't deduct any points. Moy had missed out some of the obstacles apparently.

'Why was that, Sergeant Major?'

'Because he didn't think he'd be able to cross them, sir.'

That seemed logical enough. And he was only a youngster. Just eighteen. So it seemed only fair to turn a blind eye and see how he got on in the rest of the tests. Only two more left now. The Steeplechase and the Log Race on the following day.

'During the last two days,' said Sergeant Major McNally, 'we have seen varying forms of effort, seen a few people whingeing and crying. And there have been a number of you who have produced a little bit of the old melodramatics, obviously looking for the Academy Award. There are not many of you left and this is your last chance today to impress the pre-parachute selection staff. Some of you are doing well and you must know you're doing well. My advice to you today is not to be complacent and really give it everything you've got. And to those of you who have found yourself at the back on the assault course and when you finished the stretcher race realised you could have done a little more, you've got it all to do today. Now, Staff Parker will brief you in a minute and I'll say one final thing. On the steeplechase, one hundred and ten per cent, is that clear?'

'Yes sir,' came the faint and ragged reply.

'Is that clear?' said the Sergeant Major sharply.

'Yes sir!!! '

Opposite: Tattum starts the Confidence Test and Robertson finishes it. Below: Stoner, Robertson, Ripley, Craddock, Barrett and Ward watch how some of the others make out.

They got down as if for a sprint in the field in the fine drizzle that was falling. The statutory thunderflash was thrown behind them. A flash, a bang, a drift of smoke, and they were up and away on the steeplechase course. There was the usual hounding and nagging over the jumps and ditches. Fleming won this one as he had won every other before. But several came in after the outside limit of nineteen minutes and therefore failed to score.

Lt-Col. Brewis and Captain Baird discuss the platoon's performance.

Left
Above: *The Assault Course. Melvin and Copley.*

Below: *The Steeplechase. Robertson is encouraged by Sergeant Riley, as Fleming leads them home.*

All that was now left was the Log Race – a sort of inverted Stretcher Race, with rope handles this time, mimicking a load of ammunition or a gun barrel perhaps. It was a short course, fifteen minutes only, but under far greater pressure, and many confessed afterwards they had found it the hardest test of all. Squad 1 were first for a change, but the overall winners in the team events were Squad 2, and Tattum came forward to receive the pack of twenty-four cans of beer as the team's prize. This time the presentation was carried out by the Depot CO, Lt-Col. Brewis, who told them he heard it had been a 'below-average performance from an above-average platoon' – a phrase that was repeated many more times that afternoon. So while 480 went back to their billet, the staff of PPS, together with John Baird and Sergeant Riley, met to discuss the results.

It was impossible not to be struck once more by the care and attention given to all aspects of each recruit's performance, both on PPS and during earlier platoon training. But the one shattering event no care and attention could smooth away was the disastrous drop-out rate on the Battle March. Of the original 480 Platoon, seven out of nineteen failed to finish, and however good the subsequent performances of the three who had been released from hospital on the Tuesday morning, there was a strong feeling in the meeting that failing to complete the Battle March automatically ruled out a pass in PPS. They came to this conclusion more reluctantly in some cases than others, but by the end of the meeting it was a conclusion

Opposite: *Preparing for the Log Race.*

Above: *The dash for the lead.*

Right: *Sergeant Registe watches the finer points.*

they all shared. As Max Gandell said, since the Battle March was the main individual endurance test, it was impossible for a man to pass Pre-Parachute Selection without passing that. So he told the rest of the meeting he intended asking the CO's approval for Barrett, Bush and Robertson to be allowed to do another Battle March the following day. If they were to do that, Max would be happy to see them pass, though he realised other P Company staff wouldn't agree with him there.

He was right on that point. Staff Parker immediately objected. Then Captain Baird and Sergeant Riley. If Barrett, Bush and Robertson were to do the Battle March the following day, they would not be doing it under proper test conditions. Sergeant Major McNally backed up the dissenters. In his opinion, the three in question must retake PPS. Captain Gandell accepted their point of view but explained that there was another consideration, one the CO had in mind, about the continuation of 480's training. It was a consideration that became even more compelling when the meeting had finally assessed all the recruits and come to the conclusion that only ten out of the twenty-four should be given a pass. Of those ten only eight came from the original forty-one who had lined up at Browning Barracks on 11 January. It was a wastage rate that seemed quite unacceptable. And probably because of this, Captain Gandell made one final effort to persuade his team of the need to give at least Robertson and Barrett another stab at the Battle March. But he found their resistance to the idea as strong as ever. It would be a dangerous precedent, said John Baird. A lot of soldiering work in the battalion included a lot of marching, said Staff Parker, and they'd failed the Battle March . . .

The Battle March. It was just such marching as this that would get 2 Para to Goose Green and 3 Para to Mount Longdon a few weeks later. Clearly in everybody's minds it lay at the heart of a soldier's capabilities. Especially a Para's. The Para had no transport except his LPCs – his leather personnel carriers – in other words, his boots. A man who flaked out in action would not get another chance tomorrow after a good night's sleep. He would be dead, or a prisoner, or useless. He might be a skilful parachutist and a first-class shot, but without the strength and the endurance that the Battle March was designed to test none of those skills would be meaningful. Max Gandell knew that as well as his team did. But he also knew it was virtually pointless going down to Advanced Wales with a handful of men. They would be unable to carry out anything other than section attacks and manoeuvres. And so small a group would be a waste of staff's time. He was under pressure to produce a reasonable number of acceptable soldiers. Fate in the shape of a hot day had decided that seven would collapse with heat exhaustion, two would be injured and another five would fail due to a generally unsatisfactory performance. It was dismal news to carry to his Commanding Officer, but it was news backed up by the unanimous decision of his team, who believed, he said, that pre-parachute selection was a psychological barrier individuals must pass, that one of the tests was the ten-mile Battle March, and that it would be quite wrong to pass anyone who failed to complete it.

He and the Colonel discussed the matter for some time, then Gandell went into the Central Lecture Hall where 480 Platoon were waiting with their officer and NCOs. He told them they were an above-average platoon with a below-average performance. He told them it was inexcusable to have lemonade in their water-bottles. He told them it was foolhardy to put bandages on their own feet. He then read out the results, telling the failures they would have to come back again, telling the sick they must get themselves fit as soon as possible so that they too would shortly be able to attempt P Company. Then he went back to fetch the CO.

The CO made a long, quiet speech that the platoon listened to attentively. First he presented the award for best student on the course to Fleming. He then announced they would not be going to Wales, but would be held back for retraining to give those who had failed P Company a second opportunity to pass it. Meanwhile he was sending them all on leave in the hope that very shortly the majority of the platoon would be wearing their beret without the green backing. In conclusion, he took off his own beret, told them an ordinary one was free in the quartermaster's stores, a special one downtown cost a fiver, but reminded them that whether they bought it downtown or got it on issue, for him and for everybody else in the Regiment this beret was priceless. Then he wished them all the best for the immediate future and hoped all those who had been unlucky this week would not be put off by their failure but would decide to come back and give it another go.

The platoon liked his speech. They liked the bit about the beret in particular. And they also liked the fact that they were not going to be split up and that those who had failed were going to get another chance to stay with them. Spider Craddock was pleased about that. He valued the platoon's team-spirit. If it hadn't been for Birrell's encouragement during the Battle March, he reckoned he might not have kept going. Birrell had come up alongside him during the ten-miler and started shouting at him to get going. So he'd got going and they went on pulling each other along all the way until they finished.

Ward felt much the same about it too. They'd all been living and working together for nearly three months. It would be a pity to split up now. Tattum agreed. After living with blokes all that time you got to know them pretty close. And it made you feel pretty sick to hear your mates had failed. It was great they were all sticking together for another three weeks and then going straight on to Brize Norton. Dean Ward was pleased about that, too. If they'd gone to Brecon first to do Advanced Wales training, as they were supposed to, he might have failed there and been back-squadded. But he wouldn't fail at Brize because the only way you could do that was by refusing to jump, and he didn't plan to refuse, he definitely wouldn't refuse, he hadn't come all this way, through all this hell, to refuse. So this way, even if he failed Brecon afterwards, he'd still have his wings up.

The wings bit was less important to Tattum. Soldiering wasn't just parachuting. If he'd just wanted to do parachuting, he could have joined a parachuting club. The reason he'd joined the Paras was because they were the best there was. It was a great regiment, the best, and that was what attracted him. When the Paras went into battle – as everybody kept telling you – they were always outnumbered and low on ammunition and had a pretty short life expectancy. But after you'd been at the depot a few weeks you didn't give a damn, you began to think like that as well, you began to think, so what? And you looked on other regiments like they weren't really soldiers at all. They were just a load of craphats. Because what they'd been through on P Company in the last few days, nobody else went through that, did they? And when you looked at other soldiers you thought, Christ, they hadn't done anything compared to what the Paras had to do. They were the toughest soldiers, weren't they? It wasn't just a matter of jumping out of a balloon or an aeroplane. It was what you did on the ground when you got there that counted.

Nevertheless, only eight of the original 480 Platoon had managed to pass their PPS: Birrell, Craddock, Fleming, Melvin, Moy, Stoner, Tattum and Ward. Of the remaining twelve, one had been absent on compassionate leave (Cunningham); four had failed due to a generally unsatisfactory performance (Campbell, Hooper, O'Hare, Stirling); seven had collapsed or been injured during the Battle March (Barrett, Bush, Borland, Robertson, Thomas, Hunt, Butler). Until then Rod Stoner's unobtrusive efficiency – though appreciated by his section commander, Corporal Priestley – had gone more or less unnoticed by the rest of the staff. Now he had suddenly emerged as one of the best recruits in the Platoon. But that was small consolation to Sergeant Riley. As platoon sergeant he felt the disappointment very keenly. To have only eight out of forty-one pass P Company had come as a terrible shock to him, he said. It was like kicking a brick wall with your toe. When 480 started going down on that ten-miler, his morale had gone down like an express train out of control. It really had. Those guys' careers were in his hands, don't forget. All the staff realised that. They also knew you couldn't start shifting your standards around because of that. The PPS was like the driving test. P Company was an outside organisation who had a job to do. And they set the standard the Parachute Regiment wanted for its men. Still, he had to admit it was hard to take. You got to like the guys. You picked some of them and thought they were going to be all right. He'd reckoned there were going to be a minimum of twenty out of the twenty-five who'd pass. He was that confident, he really was.

Opposite: The Battle March begins.

To try and pin down exactly what had gone wrong was extremely

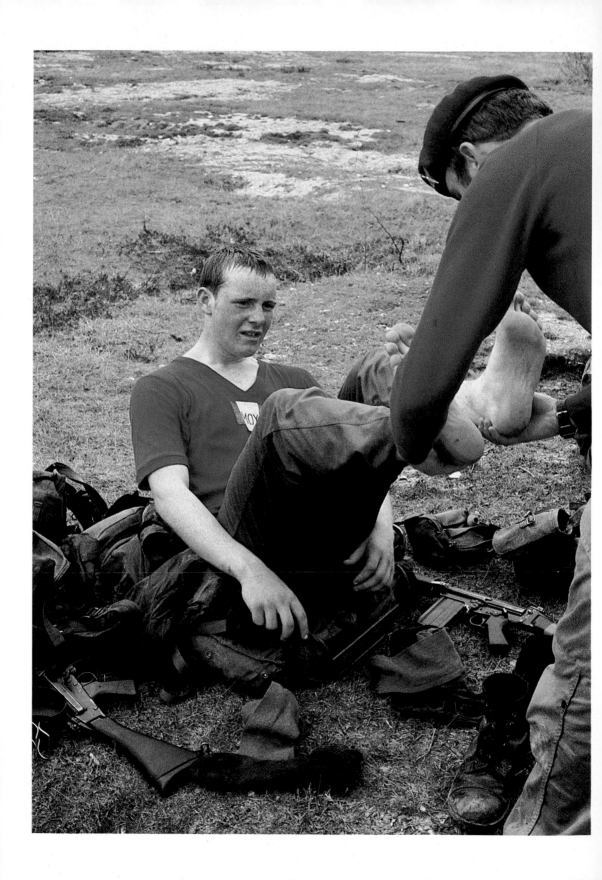

Left: *Checking for any damage at the end of the Battle March.*

Right: *Last-minute adjustment before the confidence test on the Trainasium.*

Below right: *On the parallel bars.*

Below: *480 head for the Trainasium.*

Right: *The longest minute in the world.*

Below: *Craddock takes a left.*

Opposite: *The Stretcher Race.*

Left: *The Assault Course.*

Right: *Craddock beats Stoner home in the Steeplechase.*

Below: *Sergeant Major McNally notes the times.*

Opposite above: *O'Hare waits his turn on the tower while flight drills are practised.*

Opposite below: *Adopting the parachuting position, and at the end of the line on the Exit trainer.*

Right: *Watching the balloon go up at RAF Hullavington, while (below) Ward and Tattum wait their turn to jump.*

Elbows in, toes up, and coming in to land.

Opposite: *Down safely.*

Right: *480 climb the Brecon Beacons in Wales.*

Below: *On parade at Basic Wales.*

Above, left to right:
*Corporal Slater;
camming up at
Advanced Wales;
Corporal Priestley.*

Right: *Birrell provides
covering fire.*

Right: *Corporal Baker briefs his section.*

Below: *Fighting through.*

Back row: *Moy, Sheehan, Barrett, Craddock, Day, Danvers, Hunt, Ward.*
Middle row: *Stirling, Cunningham, Robertson, Stoner, Copley, Melvin, Witton, Tattum, Fleming.*
Front row: *O'Hare, Birrell, Sgt Riley, Capt. Baird, Sgt Slater, Cpl Baker, Butler.*
Four members of the Platoon are missing from this picture: Hooper and three of the back-squads – Galasso, Mincher and Payne – all of whom were in Wales repeating some of their training at the time the photograph was taken.

HRH the Prince of Wales takes the salute at the march past of the 2nd and 3rd Battalions of the Parachute Regiment at their Falklands Memorial Parade on 1 October 1982. Partly obscured on the right is General Sir Anthony Farrar-Hockley.

difficult. They would have to sit down and analyse all the factors. Things like the sudden heat, the bad preparation, the psychological barrier that P Company represented, the lack of aggressive determination – they'd have to look at every possible aspect, so that when they started retraining them they could build up their morale again to the point where they could get through the second time round without any difficulty. Because the bulk of them would get through in the end, he was sure of that. And if they didn't and it was due to the staff's negligence, then obviously those staff would have to go. They all joked about such things – the posting to Ascension Island, or 'Call me Mr Riley, I'm a civilian now' – but if that was what the CO decided, if he thought the staff weren't up to scratch, then nobody would complain about it, they'd just take their posting and disappear. No point having people at the Depot who couldn't teach the recruits. If you taught a guy a bad habit and he took it from the Depot up to the Battalion, then that habit would escalate. That was why it was vital they were taught everything the right way all the time. So they would carry good habits, correct methods, correct drills, all the way through their army career. Normally it boiled down to one thing, that each guy had to do those things to keep himself and his buddy alive. That's what they were training them for. They were training for war. There weren't any ifs or buts about it. They were a peace-time army training for war. They had to train for war because that was what they were paid to do by the taxpayers. That was what the taxpayers wanted. They wanted an army capable of doing a job. And that was what the training staff intended to produce – along with a pride in the Regiment. That was what they were after down at the Depot.

A few days before Sergeant Riley said these things, 3 Para had sailed in the *Canberra* for the South Atlantic. 2 Para would not be sailing for another ten days or so. It would be some time yet before the two battalions would be called upon to demonstrate the qualities that the Para training was designed to inculcate and that PPS set out to test. They were qualities all parachute forces had always set a premium on from the very beginning: guts, drive, physical endurance, and disciplined aggression were the essential elements required of the men. And these – along with a number of other things – were all incorporated in the German Code issued to their airborne soldiers in World War 2. Sergeant Riley had actually pinned a copy of it up on the platoon notice board in the early weeks of training.

It took the form of ten commandments and itemised the need for such qualities as endurance, courage, comradeship, the will to win, aggressiveness, a parsimonious attitude to ammunition, and the ability to go on fighting after officers and NCOs had been killed or put out of action. Some idea of the tone of these commandments can be gained from the last and longest of them: 'With your eyes wide open, nerves keyed to the highest pitch, swift as a greyhound, tough as leather, hard as Krupps steel, you will be the embodiment of the German Warrior.'

Not surprisingly, Sergeant Riley finally decided to take the document down off the notice-board. It was much too po-faced for British consumption. Its heavily teutonic attitudes invited mockery rather than imitation. And though many of the points it made were ones he and the depot staff fully approved of, he felt they could probably make them in a more up-to-date and anglicised form. Nevertheless, it was the code that imbued German parachutists with the will to win they demonstrated in World War 2. And nowhere more noticeably than in the only airborne attack in which a strategic battle was fought and won exclusively by an airborne army – the German assault on Crete in May 1941. It was a battle in which all the qualities outlined in these Commandments were at one time or another demanded of the attacking troops, and it was a struggle that put General Student's airborne forces to their very severest test.

9 Battle for Crete

Between May 1940 and Hitler's attack on Greece in April 1941, General Student had been unable to find any employment for his airborne forces. This was not due to any unpopularity of his troops in Hitler's eyes. On the contrary, Hitler had been delighted with the brilliance of their performance in the Low Countries. But after the fall of France he was indecisive about what his next move should be. He would have liked the British to come to the negotiating table and had been prepared to offer extremely generous terms. When, however, they defied him and fought on, he contemplated invasion. Not enthusiastically, however. Like Napoleon before him, Hitler was uneasy in naval matters. The thought of attacking prepared defensive positions across the sea filled him with anxiety. Nevertheless, he did discuss the possibility of invading Britain, and an important role in the planned operation was assigned to General Student's airborne forces.

At the time Student was still out of action as a result of the severe head wound he had suffered in Rotterdam, so the planning went forward without him. The intention was to use both the 7th Parachute Division and the 22nd Air-Landing Division, whose task it would be to seize a bridgehead some twenty miles wide and twelve miles deep near Folkestone. Air reconnaissance, however, revealed that the British were erecting stakes and obstacles on all suitable glider-landing areas, and presumably installing minefields as well, so at the end of August it was decided an airborne attack was no longer possible.

In January 1941, when Student had recovered sufficiently to take over command of his forces again, the subject came up for discussion once more. But since the British had had even more opportunity to strengthen their defences in the interval, Student was reluctant to commit his forces to such an operation. Instead he proposed a surprise descent on Northern Ireland, as both a diversionary attack and an aid to a sea invasion of southern England. In the event of disaster, he argued, his troops could withdraw into Eire and internment to avoid destruction. Hitler heard him out, but proposed alternative operations in the Mediterranean – attacks on Gibraltar, Malta or the Suez Canal, all obviously useful strategic targets. But before any of these could be put into effect a more attractive option presented itself, at least in Student's eyes.

In October 1940 Germany's Axis ally, Italy, had decided to match Hitler's conquests by invading Greece. Unfortunately for Mussolini, the Greeks after some initial setbacks counterattacked and drove the Italian forces back into Albania. The British then sent aid to the Greeks, and Hitler, who was planning his attack on Russia, suddenly found his right flank in danger. On 13 April 1941 he drove through Yugoslavia and into Greece in a lightning campaign that overwhelmed the Greeks and their British allies, who were driven off the mainland in a second Dunkirk, withdrawing either to Egypt or to Crete as reinforcements for that island base.

Hitler wanted to break off the Balkan campaign at this point and turn his attention back to Russia. When Student heard this he flew to see Goering and proposed his plan for capturing Crete with the use of airborne forces alone. Anxious for the Luftwaffe to distinguish itself in some major feat of arms after its failure over Britain the previous summer, Goering urged Student to go and see Hitler. And on 21 April, after some misgivings, Hitler agreed to Operation Mercury, as it was called.

The units Student had available for the attack were the 7th Air Division, the Airborne Assault Regiment and the 5th Mountain Division – altogether a force of some 20,000 men. Of these some 8000 were parachute and glider troops and the remainder would be brought in, either by air once an airfield had been captured, or by sea, on the first night of the assault. The Luftwaffe's 4th Air Fleet was also providing 500 Ju 52 transports and 72 DFS 230 gliders to carry the troops, and some 500 fighters, fighter-bombers and bombers as escorts and in support.

For their part the British had far more troops on the island than German intelligence was aware of – some 32,000 men in all. Six thousand were the original garrison and the remainder were remnants of formations evacuated from the Greek mainland plus some reinforcements from Egypt. These troops were poorly equipped, however, having little artillery, few tanks, and – by the time the Germans attacked – no aircraft, as it had finally proved impossible to operate them from the island in the face of over-whelming German air superiority. Nevertheless, their New Zealand commander, Major-General Bernard Freyberg VC, had done a great deal to organise the defences in the short time at his disposal since his appointment on 30 April. Though not as confident as Churchill – who saw the German attack on Crete as 'a fine opportunity for killing parachute troops' – he felt his forces had a good chance of success. The island might be difficult to defend, with its narrow coastal plain in the north and its spiny mountain range making any interior movement of forces difficult, but by the same token it was difficult to attack. Apart from the two airfields at Maleme and Heraklion and the airstrip at Rethymno, there were few places suitable for landing aircraft. The rest of the northern plain was indented with gulleys, criss-crossed with stone walls, and planted with olive and citrus trees. Both Luftwaffe reconnaissance and German intelligence failed to give due notice of these hazards.

There was disagreement amongst the German commanders about the plan of attack. General Lohr, the overall commander of the operation, wanted them to concentrate their forces in the Maleme sector, seize the airfield, reinforce the landing by air and sea, then advance eastwards along the plain from a secure base. Student favoured multiple drops, with a widespread occupation of key points on the island from which the troops could radiate until each area had linked up. The final plan was a compromise, the attack being directed at four main points – Maleme, Khania, Rethymno and Heraklion. Freyberg, in an effort to cater for all emergencies, decided to spread his troops out along the northern coast to cover all possible air- and sea-landing sites. As a result his troops were well placed to counter the German attack when it came.

The other possibility open to the Germans – that of landing at some distance from the defended areas, then forming up and making an ordinary ground attack on the British positions – was never apparently given much consideration. It went against the German theories of Blitzkrieg, and also against Student's instincts. But the decision to drop right on top of the defenders was one that many of the German parachute and glider troops had cause to regret. Another error that 480 Platoon would have appreciated was the German quartermaster's decision to kit the parachute troops out with the same uniforms they had worn in Norway – thick woollen battle-dress and heavy waterproof smocks. As a result many of them suffered from heat exhaustion in the early stages of the battle, though some solved the problem by discarding everything except their boots and their smocks.

For six days German aircraft carried out a softening up bombardment of the island. Then, at breakfast time on 20 May 1941 – just after the daily dive-bombing and machine-gunning attack on the British positions had ended – the first of the gliders and transports started to fly in. There were not enough aircraft to take all the parachutists in one lift, so it was decided that the attack on the Maleme–Khania area would take place in the morning, and that on Rethymno and Heraklion in the afternoon. The defenders knew an attack was coming: it was what they had been preparing for during the last month. But when it came they were momentarily caught off balance. Although they knew about the gliders, they had never seen them before, and suddenly there they were above their heads – huge, sinister shapes winging their way towards them with their cargo of death. They knew about the Ju 52s as well, but when they came they also took the defenders by surprise as they roared over in formation and the sky began blossoming with hundreds of parachutes.

One glider battalion and three parachute battalions were dropped around Maleme and its airfield. A further four battalions were dropped in the Khania and Suda Bay area. Most of the landings were fiercely opposed by the defenders. The glider force lost half its strength within a few minutes of landing and the 3rd Parachute Battalion dropped on top of New

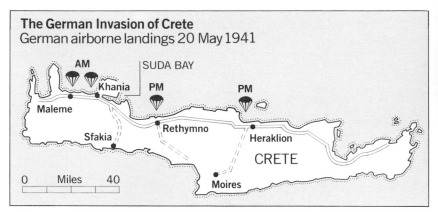

The German Invasion of Crete
German airborne landings 20 May 1941

Zealand infantry and engineers who killed or wounded 400 out of the 600 men of the battalion in the first few minutes of the assault. Colonel Leckie, the CO of the 23rd New Zealand Infantry Battalion, shot five parachutists himself without moving outside his headquarters. Like duck-shooting, one of his soldiers said. For the critical twenty seconds or so that the Germans were helplessly suspended beneath their parachutes, they were easy targets for men who kept cool and took careful aim. 'Suddenly you'd see one go limp then give a kick and kind of straighten up with a jerk, and then go limp again, and you knew he was done for,' said one of the infantrymen. Marcel Comeau, an airman in 33 Squadron of the RAF, found a glider was skidding through the olive trees straight towards his foxhole. It stopped a few feet from him and started disgorging its cargo of soldiers. He shot one at almost point-blank range, then a second, and fired a shot into the mass behind before his rifle jammed and he was forced to run for his life.

Another critical period was during the few seconds it took a man to get out of his parachute harness and hunt for his weapons' container. Here again was an opportunity for the defenders to cut down many of those who had survived the flight. But in spite of the German losses – many of the German commanders were killed or seriously wounded, and in some cases whole companies were wiped out practically to a man – those that did manage to survive went to ground and began the process of regrouping and making their way towards the targets allotted to them. It was here that the value of their training made itself felt. As soon as a commander was put out of action, the next in rank took over, and this went right on down to the private soldier. A great deal of the fighting took place at section level, for the initial scattering of the parachutists, and the casualties they had suffered, left many small groups who had become separated from the main body waging their own private war until able to rejoin a larger unit. These groups, though seemingly inconsiderable at the time, were later to prove a great nuisance to the British in hindering their lines of advance during attempts at counterattacks.

Ju 52s over Crete.

Student's second wave arrived in the middle of the afternoon and fared even worse. At Rethymno one of the two battalions dropped also suffered 400 casualties out of 600 in the course of the afternoon. The other battalion suffered severely too, some units being dropped as many as eight kilometres from the DZ. The remnants of these two battalions regrouped, dug in and waited for the morning. At Heraklion the drop was equally disastrous. Many planes were shot down during the run-in and many of the parachutists were killed in flight. Those that survived were grateful when darkness came and brought them respite.

Back on the Greek mainland Student did not know the full extent of his losses, but he did know that none of his units had as yet achieved any of their objectives. In particular they had not captured an airfield. Without that he could not fly in the men of the 5th Mountain Division with their heavier weapons. The whole operation hung in the balance, and with the sinking and dispersal of the German seaborne attempt to bring in reinforcements during the night the German situation looked even bleaker. The British, however, did not know the extent of the Germans' plight. Radio communications had broken down and General Freyberg was unaware of the true situation. The reports of mass parachute attacks on all sides created the impression Student had intended, convincing Freyberg his situation was worse than it really was.

Left: *A still from a German propaganda film of the attack on Crete.*

Above: *The reality.*

Meanwhile the Germans at Maleme persevered in their task, to seize the airfield as ordered and bring in the transport planes loaded with reinforcements. They were rewarded with a piece of unexpected luck. During the night the New Zealand defenders on Point 107, a hill dominating the airfield, withdrew – under the impression they had been cut off – and when the German infantry returned to the attack at dawn, they found their opponents gone. The chink in the defences that the Germans had been searching for was open. Next morning the Luftwaffe helped block all British counterattacks, and by five o'clock in the afternoon of 21 May the Ju 52s had begun to fly in the men of the Mountain Division. The planes came in regardless of the anti-aircraft fire. Many crashed on landing and were bulldozed out of the way with captured British armoured vehicles. Gradually the Germans began to gain the ascendancy in the Maleme–Khania area, and started to push east along the coastal road.

When finally the British troops in Heraklion and Rethymno were given the order to retreat, they found it hard to believe. As far as they were concerned the parachutists in their area had been defeated or fought to a standstill and were no longer capable of offensive action. But Freyberg felt he had no choice. With the failure of his last counterattack against Maleme it was only a matter of time before the German forces, with their total air superiority, would be in a position to cut off the British Army's retreat to the southern ports. And so the withdrawal began. Another humiliation for the British. Another triumph for German arms. But a bitter and blood-stained victory, drained of the rejoicing associated with those won in Belgium and Holland.

There has always been some doubt about the true figures of German casualties in Crete, possibly because of their severity. However, out of the attacking force of 22,000 it seems clear that some 5000 were killed. And most of those came from among the leaders – corporals, sergeants, young officers, and even amongst the senior officers, who are often as exposed as their men, at least in the initial stages of a parachute operation. Obviously German air superiority contributed significantly to their victory in Crete. At the same time, it was a battle that they also won by the exercise of two of Sergeant Riley's favourite qualities – 'goots and drive'. There had been plenty of guts on the British side too. Many brave men had fought and died without benefit of airborne training. But there had been less drive and less determination once units had been broken up and rendered leaderless, and the British showed less enterprise and initiative at middle command-levels than the German parachute and glider troops did.

Student was apprehensive about Hitler's reaction to the heavy losses suffered in Crete – and not just in troops. About 150 Ju 52s were either destroyed or so seriously damaged in the battle that they had to be written off afterwards. But when the two men met in August 1941 Hitler was as friendly as he had ever been – so much so that Student felt tempted to propose further airborne attacks, possibly against Cyprus or Malta. But before he got the chance to do so Hitler dropped a casual bombshell. The day of the paratroops was over, he told Student. In future they would be used as the Führer's Fire Brigade – élite infantry troops to be rushed to whichever part of the German front was under threat. Only rarely would any of them parachute into action again, and then only on a small scale. Crete was the 'graveyard of the German airborne troops', as Student once said, in more ways than one.

Paradoxically, the reaction in British and American military circles was quite the contrary. German success in Crete, as they saw it, was a stimulus to the development of their own airborne forces. In particular, it provided Churchill with powerful arguments against all those who had dragged their feet or put obstacles in the way of the rapid growth of the British Airborne Forces. On 27 May, as the last shots were being fired in the Battle for Crete, he wrote to General Ismay, for the attention of the Chiefs of Staff, saying that he felt himself to blame for allowing himself to be overborne by the resistance offered by both the Air Ministry and the War Office in the attempts to develop a glider and parachute arm. What Britain needed, he urged, was an Airborne Division on the German model, with any improvements which might suggest themselves from experience.

Four days later the Joint Chiefs of Staff approved a proposal to form two parachute brigades and a glider force sufficient to lift 10,000 men and their equipment. Ten medium-bomber squadrons were to be converted as parachute transports and glider tugs. Two operational gliders were to be put into production: the 25-seater Horsa, and the cargo-carrying Hamilcar with a payload of seven tons. The British were at last seriously engaged in the business of producing an airborne army. Until that time they had done little more than experiment on a relatively small scale, with a force of 500 men from No. 2 Commando as their guinea-pigs. Between the setting-up of the parachute school in June 1940 and the German capture of Crete almost a year later, they had carried out only one small parachute operation.

In November 1940 No. 2 Commando was renamed the 11th Special Air Service Battalion (no connection with the later SAS). In January 1941 – when its commander asked for volunteers for a raid on enemy territory – every man on parade stepped forward. Finally seven officers and thirty-one other ranks were chosen for Operation 'Colossus', and an intensive period of training began. The aim of the operation was to destroy the Tragino aqueduct in southern Italy and so deprive some two million Italians of their regular water supply. The operation was as much a test of the new airborne arm's efficiency as a serious attempt to incapacitate the Italian war effort. It was also an aid to morale. Many of the troops were becoming restless and eager for action.

Though not entirely successful – the aqueduct was only partially destroyed and most of the force was captured – the raid was a portent of things to come, and was recognised as such by the British public. In the dark days of the Blitz the first British parachute troops had gone into action. There had not been many of them, but their numbers would grow. And with the impulse given them again by Churchill in May 1941, their future was guaranteed.

In September of that year, the 11th SAS Battalion was renamed the 1st Parachute Battalion and the 2nd and 3rd Battalions were raised by volunteers from all branches of the Army. At the same time the Brigade was given a permanent home at Hardwick Hall near Chesterfield in Derbyshire. As volunteers arrived they were put through a series of tests designed to sort the sheep from the goats, and out of this there grew a selection process from which today's P Company testing has descended. There were assault courses, road work and endless physical training. Also included were a number of parachute aptitude tests, such as swinging from trapezes and exit jumps, together with air-sickness tests. The threat of being RTU'd, or Returned to Unit, was held constantly over the applicant's head. And a visit to the 'trick cyclist' was also thought useful as a means of judging the qualities that made a man suitable for parachuting.

Not everybody who went through the training at Hardwick approved of these methods. Especially some of the senior officers who found the physical training harsh and, in their opinion, not very relevant to para-chuting. Certainly some of the apparatus caused unnecessary injuries. There was one trapeze designed to accustom men to a back landing from an oscillating parachute. At the top of the swing they were ordered to let go, which meant dropping backwards from a height of fifteen feet. It caused so many casualties that it was very rapidly given up. The intense physical training, however, was not abandoned. Two-mile and ten-mile bashes, milling and boxing, assault courses and gym work were constant ingredients at Hardwick as they are at the Parachute Regiment's Depot today. The only additional elements in Derbyshire were cliff-scaling and abseiling – a local facility not available in Aldershot. The recruits always passed from one activity to the other at the double, and the supervising officers and NCOs studied every man's performance intently for the slightest sign of physical or mental weakness. Endurance and determination were the most highly valued qualities then, as they are now, and no distinction was made between officers or men. All-arms and all-rank courses were the norm at Hardwick.

Some forty years later, those of 480 Platoon who had failed their first attempt at Pre-Parachute Selection were about to join an All Arms Course and present themselves once more for the test. In the interval between their first and second attempts, the Falkland Islands crisis had worsened and turned into undeclared war. The Argentine cruiser, the *General Belgrano*, had been torpedoed and sunk by a British submarine; and HMS *Sheffield*, the British destroyer, had been hit and eventually sunk by an Exocet missile from an Argentine Super-Etendard. Both 2 and 3 Para were en route for the Islands and a landing seemed imminent. Against this background, passing P Company took on even more significance. It was the next step on the road leading to qualification as a Para and possible dispatch to the Falklands as replacement troops in the event of casualties. This possibility caused no alarm amongst those who had already passed P Company. On the contrary, some of them fervently hoped the war would not end too soon. They looked forward to joining their chosen battalion on the Islands and 'helping to give the Argies some well-deserved stick'. After all, that was what it was all about, wasn't it? That was what they were being trained for.

This time everything went off relatively smoothly, at least for those nine of the original 480 Platoon who were taking the test again. On this occasion even Cunningham's constant bad luck deserted him. Described a month before by one of the staff as a 'wanker who wasn't worth his rations', he came good when it was needed. To his delight he was one of the nine who started on the Monday and passed out successfully on the Wednesday. The other eight were Barrett, Butler, Hooper, Hunt, O'Hare, Robertson, Stirling and Thomas.

Two of those who had failed the first time were receiving medical discharges. Alistair Campbell, the Scot, was found to have a problem with his knees that could not be corrected. Brian Bush, the lad from Widnes with the reactive lenses – who had allowed that very same Jock to pass him on the Battle March to the horror and outrage of Sergeant Riley – had been found to be suffering from asthma. Their discharges were therefore carried out under the category of Illegal Enlistment plus Injury or Illness – as were those of Byrne, Hughes and Wood before them. And before anyone had quite realised what had happened they were gone – their army careers unexpectedly ended. John Borland, who had collapsed on Miles Hill, was not yet fit enough to retake PPS so he had been back-squadded to 482 Platoon.

That weekend the seventeen of the original Platoon who had now satisfied P Company of their suitability to proceed for Parachute Training set off for Brize Norton. Behind them they left seven members of the platoon with injuries that would delay them for varying periods of time, and three others who were applying for transfers. Mark Chard had been unlucky enough to add a dislocated shoulder to his previous leg injury and had decided to transfer to the Royal Tank Regiment when he was fit again. Nigel Woof had opted for the Royal Pioneer Corps and Graham Harrison for the Royal Corps of Transport.

Those who set out for Brize Norton had only limited sympathy for the ones they left behind. It was a hard life in the Paras. Only the tough survived. They had passed PPS. They had cleared the biggest hurdle. From now on it should be downhill all the way. Brize Norton had a reputation for being a holiday camp – a place where they could escape the irritations of the Depot for a few weeks and enjoy the pleasures of the parachuting course in relatively luxurious surroundings. So far there had been some kind of hitch at every stage of their training. With luck, they would be leaving all that behind them now.

Even above the noise of the bus, they could hear the sound of an aircraft turning above them, as it came in to land. Soon they would reach the airfield. Just over the hill, through the village and round the corner, and they would be there. Been looking forward to this, they had. Maybe jumping out of aeroplanes wasn't the be-all and end-all of being a Para but it was certainly one of the nicest bits. And they planned to enjoy it.

10 Early Days at Ringway

RAF Brize Norton in Oxfordshire is the home of No. 1 Parachute Training School whose badge bears an emblem of a parachute with crossed torches underneath it and the reassuring motto that Knowledge Dispels Fear. In June 1940, when Major Rock and Squadron Leader Strange were given the joint task of organising the training of the British Airborne Forces, the Training School's first home was at Ringway Airport, Manchester, and its first title was the Central Landing School (later the Central Landing Establishment).

In many ways Ringway was a very unsuitable site for a parachute school. Either the visibility was so bad that flying was impossible, or the winds were so strong as to make parachuting out of the question. But it had one great virtue. It was a long way from the southern and eastern coasts of

Ringway, summer 1945. The public flocks to an open day.

England, and hence from intruding German aircraft. So whenever the weather was good enough, training could go ahead in peace.

Rock and Strange had other problems, too. The six obsolete Whitley bombers the Air Ministry had grudgingly provided them with were also highly unsuitable. Their dropping speed was too fast; they were cold, cramped and badly ventilated; worst of all, the door in the side of the fuselage was far too small to be used as an exit. So the fundamental business of actually getting a parachutist out of the aircraft was beset with all sorts of difficulties. In spite of these drawbacks, however, the first parachute descent was made on 13 July 1940, by what was known as the 'pull-off' method, from the tail-gunner's position on the Whitley. The technique was one the RAF had made use of in the prewar years to train their airmen. Platforms were built on the wings of Vickers Vimy biplanes. The parachutist stood on one of these platforms and pulled the ripcord of his chute. As the wind dragged the parachute open, so he was carried off with it – sometimes, it was said, still clutching the wing-strut.

The early tail-exit from the Whitley.

In the following months hundreds of successful descents were made, and a great deal was learnt about the art of parachuting by a process of trial and error. There were the inevitable failures, the first on 25 July when Driver Evans of the Royal Army Service Corps fell to his death after his parachute failed to open properly. By this time the tail 'pull-off' was being abandoned in favour of an exit through a hole in the floor of the Whitley's fuselage where a gun turret had once been. And before long the modifications that were to be made to the static-line version of the Irvin parachute they were using was to give the British one of the finest military parachutes in the world.

There are basically two kinds of parachute: one operated manually by the wearer, the other operated automatically by means of a static line attaching the parachutist to the aircraft or balloon from which he is jumping. The first reliable parachute was of the automatic kind and was widely used in World War 1 by artillery spotters in cages suspended beneath observation balloons. The problem as far as the occupants of

Two ways of storing a 'Guardian Angel' – on the rigging and on the basket.

these balloons were concerned was their enormous vulnerability to enemy aircraft who attacked their huge hydrogen-filled gas bags with incendiary bullets. Without the parachute, casualties amongst these spotters would have been even more intolerable than they actually were.

British observers used what was called the 'Guardian Angel' type of parachute, which was stowed in a container on the side of the basket or attached to the rigging some feet from the edge of it. A rope ran from the parachute to a primitive harness round the observer's body. When he jumped over the side, the parachute was pulled out from the container, rigging lines first, followed by the canopy until – with the parachute at full stretch – it parted from its container and deployed, taking the observer safely to the ground. This was the basis for all static-line chutes, but after World War 1 they were overshadowed by the manually-operated parachute

A descent by 'Guardian Angel'. Note the single-cord harness attachment.

designed by Leslie Irvin as an aircrew life-saver. And it was not until military thinkers began to consider the use of parachute troops in battle that the static-line chute came back into favour.

The Italian 'Salvatore' parachute was a development of the old 'Guardian Angel'. The difference was that the pack was on the man instead of the basket, and the static line that opened it had to be attached to a strong point inside the aircraft. The 'Salvatore' was reliable and quick to open, its main disadvantage being its single-point harness attachment which left the jumper hanging face forward and unable to control his flight in any way.

The first Russian military parachutes were manually operated by a ripcord, which caused a number of problems. First, the parachutists had to jump from a higher altitude to allow time for the chutes to open. Secondly, the exit from the aircraft had to be carried out with great care. After 1936, however, the Russians changed to static-line chutes, which enabled them to get more men into the air more easily than with their former method.

The Germans watched the Russian experiments with interest and rejected the manually-operated parachute from the outset. Their RZ series was a canopy-first static-line chute, apparently based on the 'Salvatore'. The static line pulled the canopy out of the bag immediately in one bundle. This made for quick opening, as with the 'Salvatore', but was more likely to lead to entanglement failures than the later British X-type, where the rigging lines emerged before the canopy. Another disadvantage of the German RZ models was the retention of the single-point suspension in the middle of the back. In consequence the parachute could not be steered and all landings were forward ones, hence the rubber knee-pads often worn by German parachute troops.

The problems experienced with the British automatic version of the Irvin chute in July 1940 led to its being redesigned in such a way that the rigging lines were drawn from the bag before the canopy. This was achieved by a series of ties at various stages of the packing process which broke in sequence as the parachute developed. At the final stage the parachute was drawn out, undeployed, over its full length, with the last tie, at the apex of the canopy, attached to the inside of the bag. When that tie broke, the jumper and his parachute were free of the aircraft and the canopy then deployed, virtually without any shock to the parachutist's body, just a light tug at the shoulders.

The other virtue of the X-type was its harness. It was also evolved from the original Irvin harness and had four lift-webs, or canvas risers, each running to a set of rigging lines. The seat was therefore more comfortable, the position gave more control, and the lift-webs permitted some elementary steering. It was a parachute that continued with little modification until the early 1960s when the PX type was introduced. This had a larger, more deeply-rounded canopy, giving greater stability and a lower rate of descent, but was in all other respects an X-type.

REMEMBER A MANS
LIFE DEPENDS ON
EVERY PARACHUTE
YOU PACK

Parachute-packing in 1942.

Attempts that summer of 1940 to make similar improvements with the exit procedures, by persuading the Air Ministry to replace the Whitleys with a more suitable aircraft, were less successful. After a week's suspension of parachuting by Rock while awaiting the Air Ministry's decision, Churchill had to intervene, and on 14 August training with Whitleys began once more. Until the C 47 Dakota became available in the autumn of 1942 British parachute troops had to make do with the Whitley. In spite of its deficiencies, in the first two months at Ringway twenty-one officers and 321 other ranks had taken the course. Out of these thirty refused to jump, two had been killed and fifteen were too badly injured to continue.

By now, jumping through the Whitley's hole was standard procedure. When the green light came on, each parachutist dropped through the hole, his arms to his side, his body erect in the attention position. One of the hazards of exiting through the hole – which was three feet in diameter – was that, as the parachutist's feet left the aircraft, the top of his body tended to be thrown forward so that he hit his face on the opposite edge of the hole. This was known as 'ringing the bell', and very few managed to get through the course unscathed.

Above: *Dropping through the Whitley's hole, 1941.*

Right: *The view from below.*

A balloon cage with the simulated Whitley hole.

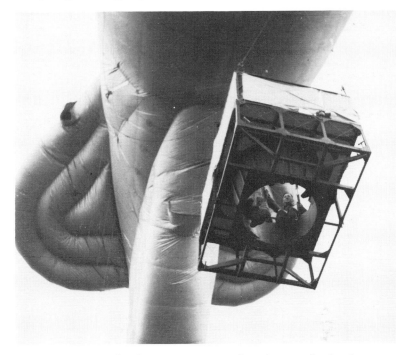

Every aspect of airborne training and equipment had to be researched and produced from scratch. In July 1940 Major Rock had been asked to supply Ordnance with a sample German parachutist's tunic, which was copied in six sizes and produced in sufficient quantity for a thousand men. So zealous was Ordnance in its endeavour to protect every part of the British parachutist from damage that it even asked Rock to inform them if jockstraps as well as anklets would be required. Early British headgear included a black balaclava-style pilot's helmet, a canvas hood, and a flat-topped canvas hat filled with foam-rubber. Every piece of equipment other countries had tried in the search for the perfect parachuting gear was tested.

Such things as containers and gliders were at first modelled on those used by the Germans. But as time went on the kind of improvement brought about with the parachute took place in other areas, too. One useful discovery made early on in British military parachuting was that a man could drop with a load almost equal to his own weight, provided it hung beneath him in flight and hit the ground in time to allow his descent to slow sufficiently before he hit the ground. The Germans never developed this technique. In consequence, as the New Zealanders had discovered in Crete, their troops were at a grave disadvantage during the first few minutes after landing while they hunted for their containers. The kitbag invention introduced an additional hazard, however. Any kitbag that broke free from its line during the descent was a danger to other parachute troops, both in the air and on the ground.

The most original contribution made by the British to the training of parachutists, however, was with the use of the balloon. Though forced on them as an economy measure because of the shortage of aircraft, it had certain advantages over an aircraft as a training device. It allowed pupils to make straightforward exits free of twists, somersaults and other complications. It also made it possible for the staff to give each pupil personal instruction through a loud-hailer as he floated down to the ground. Mist was also less of a problem, and night jumps could often be made when flying was not practicable. As a result its use has persisted to the present day.

In fact, most of the training is virtually as it was forty years ago. Even the organisational structure of No. 1 PTS today is very much as it was at Ringway in 1942. In those days an intake of prospective parachutists was split up into syndicates, each under an RAF officer assisted by a flight sergeant. A syndicate consisted of six sections of ten men (a Whitley stick was ten men). Each section was in the charge of a PJI sergeant (a Parachute Jump Instructor) who was responsible for every aspect of his section's ground and air training. Forty years later, in May 1982 when 480 Platoon arrived at Brize Norton, they joined Basic Course 891, consisting of A & B syndicates, each of which was split into four sections of eight or seven men. Each section was in the charge of a PJI sergeant who was

The wartime parachute tower.

responsible for every aspect of their ground and air training. The only real difference was the size of the aircraft. The C130 Hercules can drop sixty-four men, in two simultaneous sticks of thirty-two which exit through doors on each side of the fuselage. And although there are still certain hazards attached to the exit procedure, 'ringing the bell' is no longer one of them.

A mock-up of the Whitley hole.

11 Joining the Airborne Brotherhood

'It's not a bad mixture,' said Squadron Leader George Sizeland, the officer commanding the basic training squadron at No. 1 PTS. 'You guys have got the courage and the commitment to come here. We've got the skill and the expertise. So let's put it all together and see what comes out.'

It was 8 o'clock on the Monday morning of the first week of the course. The recruits of 480 had made it. Seventeen of them. They were there at Brize Norton as they had dreamed they would be one day. In strange but somehow familiar surroundings. It was the Brize Norton of their imagination, plus a Brize Norton that greatly outreached their imagination. It was as big as a fair-sized town – an airfield plus a camp, family quarters, messes, canteens, clubs, bowling alleys. A dense network of roads and hangars and billet-blocks, and every so often the roar of an aircraft landing or taking off, during which time everyone automatically raised their voices to make themselves heard and then dropped the volume again as the sound of the engines died away.

Brize Norton is the home of RAF Transport Command. A constant traffic of VC10s is interspersed with the occasional C130 Hercules or smaller aircraft. No. 1 PTS was just a small part of the vast, straggling complex that the rest took very little interest in. A part sited in one small administrative block and a hangar, where all the indoor training took place. Also allocated to the school's use was a patch of ground by the main gate where the fairground equipment was set up – the Tower and the Exit Trainer, or 'Knacker-Cracker' as it was called. For the next four weeks – assuming there were no more hitches – the recruits from 480 would spend most of their waking time in the hangar, practising the skills they would need for their one leap out of the balloon car and the seven brief excursions by aircraft to the dropping zone (DZ) at Weston-on-the-Green, some twenty miles to the north-east.

The Para billets were a row of dark-green huts on the edge of the airfield out with the guard-dogs and the parked aircraft. They were long, low concrete huts holding some twenty men each, and more like the wartime image of an army camp that some of 480 had been expecting when they first arrived at the Para Depot. The RAF bussed them to and fro. Marching was not allowed – it cluttered up the roadways, obstructed the passage of vehicles, irritated the unmilitary minds of most of the staff at Brize. The

Pongos – which was the name the RAF gave the military – had to be there, it seemed. No way of getting rid of them. But they could at least keep a low profile. Stay in their huts or their hangar or their buses. That way you could almost imagine they did not exist at all.

The aim of the Parachute Training School was very simple. As defined by Squadron Leader George Sizeland, it was to devise a system of instruction that ensured pupils did not get injured when they hit the ground. Because that was the only time parachutists did get injured. On arrival. Things might go wrong earlier, on the way out or on the way down, but it was not until they actually reached the ground that the damage occurred. No. 1 PTS wanted to ensure that as few of them got hurt as possible. And their record wasn't bad. On the last four Regular courses, for instance, nobody had been injured on ground training, and only six out of the 215 students on those courses had been injured parachuting. That was less than three per cent, he said. And only five had refused to jump. That had to prove the system was working.

There were sixty-two pupils on Course 891. Flying Officer Chris Simpson was the officer in charge and Butch Casey and Taff Evans were his Syndicate Flight Sergeants. The recruits of 480 Platoon were split evenly between the two syndicates, and most of them were concentrated in sections with their mates, though one or two found themselves amongst strangers. Most of the strangers were Marines from 42 and 45 Commandos and Comacchio Company. Others were Signallers, Engineers, Guardsmen and men from various airborne support units. Nearly a third were officers and NCOs. And as soon as the introductory talks and film were over, they all gathered in the PTS hangar to begin their training.

According to the handbook, there are three main areas of instruction for parachuting – Exit, Flight and Landing. Or Fear, Relief and Panic, as the instructors like to call them. There are also other important skills to learn, such as aircraft drills and putting the parachute on before jumping and taking it off after arrival. But they hardly have the drama of the first three. Nor do they need as much practice. One of the PJIs can help the pupil fit his parachute. Aircraft drills tend to drag him along in the wake of his comrades in the stick. And if he finds he is a little hesitant on arrival in the doorway, the dispatcher can always give him a pat on the back to help him on his way. And once he arrives on the ground, getting out of the harness, though complicated at first sight, is essentially neither dangerous nor difficult.

But the Exit, the Flight and the Landing are things the pupil has to do all on his own. From the moment he steps out of the door until he hits the ground, whatever happens can only be caused, controlled or corrected by him. That is why so much time is spent getting these three operations absolutely drilled into the brain and body of the pupil parachutist. By the time ground training becomes air practice all movements should be so ingrained in the cells of the brain and the nerves and sinews of the body as to be totally automatic processes. They have to be. From exit to landing is a matter of about thirty seconds during an operational descent, and if something goes wrong with the process, then the parachutist's response must be instantaneous and automatic. This is why the whole of the first week of the course is taken up with Exit, Flight and Landing training, with only the occasional hour given over to fitting parachutes, and harness-release and ground-dragging instruction.

In the centre of the hangar was a mock-up of a Hercules fuselage. Each pupil leaped from either the port or starboard door to the ground a couple of feet below him, or jumped from the open-sided mass-exit platform designed to speed up the process. On each side of the fuselage was a heavily-matted area where landings could be practised, either by jumping from low bench-structures or ramps, or dropping from swinging steel chandeliers. When a little more skill had been acquired, it was time to jump from the Fan. This was a device designed to simulate a descent, and involved jumping from a platform twenty-five feet above the mats and being lowered in a harness at a controlled rate of about twenty feet per second, which is the average descent speed in a parachute. The two ends of the hangar were given over to parachute-fitting racks and flight-training swings respectively.

For the next week the hangar echoed with the intermingled cries of the staff as they instructed their sections in one or other of the various areas of training. 480 had expected this part of the training to be boring, but in fact they did not find it so. Naturally they were impatient to get on to the more exciting part of the course, but appreciated the importance of the ground training and the need to do it over and over again until each action was automatic and perfectly executed.

How many times did each pupil's feet hit the mat as he came in for a synthetic landing? Three hundred? Four hundred? Five hundred times? Watching some of them land, it was clear why the operation had to be practised so frequently. Landing by parachute is not a natural activity. Learning to roll properly is not something that comes easily to everybody. The British landing technique – unchanged since the very early days at Ringway – is reckoned to be one of the best in the world. It is adaptable to any kind of landing, whereas the French, for instance, have separate kinds designed for each of the four possible approaches – forward, backward, side left or side right. The British landing works for all of these, merely needing a slight adjustment to deal with whichever kind presents itself.

'Are your arms hurting you, Ward?' asked Sergeant Gary Corkish, the PJI in charge of one of the sections. 'Are they? That's because they're hitting the floor every time you land, right? When your arms are fully extended' – and he demonstrated – 'you get them out of the way, OK? This is for your benefit, fellers. You're the guys who're going to get injured if you don't do it right. Side left this time, parachute position, elbows in, everything tight, all together, go!'

And so on. Time after time after time. They got up on the bench, into the parachute position, then off, knees bent, pushed sideways to the floor, the body turning up and away as the weight went onto the thigh and across the hip and the back and the shoulders, the legs flipping up and over, ankles tight together as the feet slapped down on the ground at the end of the perfect parachutist's landing roll.

Well, that was the theory anyway. But some peoples' bodies did not seem to be designed to move so smoothly and harmoniously from the perpendicular to the horizontal. Instead of rolling, some crumpled. Others snapped in half, arms and legs flying. Clearly the taller you were the trickier it was. The perfect build for a para was short and stocky, like Birrell, Barrett, Craddock and Ward. The six-footers – like Fleming, Melvin and Stoner – were at a disadvantage. And Cunningham, inevitably, was one of the most disadvantaged. Though not the tallest of 480 – only 6 feet 2 against Stirling's 6 feet 4 – he was the heaviest, and nowhere was the old adage of the bigger you are the harder you fall more appropriate than in parachuting. The big ones had to do the best landings. If not they suffered disproportionately. Cunningham weighed 13 stone 2, Craddock 10 stone 2. It was all the difference, said one of the PJIs, 'between coming down like a sack of potatoes and floating to the ground like a fairy's fart'.

Strictly speaking, two of 480 were over the height and weight limits for parachute training – 13 stone and 6 feet 3. Cunningham was over the first, Stirling over the second. They were not the only ones on the course, because several marines were even heavier than Cunningham. But Stirling was the tallest, and inevitably it was giving him problems – problems he was conscientiously struggling to overcome, even to the point of overdoing things a bit. One piece of advice Sergeant Corkish gave them, as they went into their roll, was to imagine they were going to bite something on the floor just round their back. 'That's it now, elbows in, arms extended, lean forward from the waist, chin on the chest. Look down at the ground, look at it, arch the back, that's it, arms extended, side right, ready, go! . . .' And Stirling went, as instructed, but not terribly successfully. 'When I say eat something off the floor, I don't mean it literally. You don't have to go down and chew the mat, Stirling, you're doing a landing . . .'

And again, and again, until dimly, through the awkwardness and the unfamiliarity, the wildly-flailing legs, and the projecting elbows, there began to emerge the shapes and the movement the instructors were striving for. Not all at once, not every time, but here and there the perfect landing occurred, and the man who had executed it got to his feet with a feeling of satisfaction and the praises of his instructor ringing in his ears. 'That's better, eh, Stirling, that's magic!' And then, a moment later, it was all gone again, the different bits failed to come together, it was still too willed, too worked at, not yet the smooth, automatic, unthinking process it needed to be before they were ready to grit their teeth and leap into space from the balloon cage at Hullavington.

The Exit looked simple. All you did was stand in the door with one leg in front of the other and jump out when the green light went on. Nothing to it. Except, of course, that the wind outside was travelling past the door at 125 knots, and as soon as you stepped into it you were likely to be thrown about violently in the space of a split second and end up with your static line wrapped round your neck or your rigging lines twisted right up to the edge of the canopy. Neither very desirable occurrences. Sort of things that could cause you a lot of anxiety if they were to happen to you. So it was most important you entered the slipstream in an upright, compact and symmetrical manner which presented the wind with as few opportunities as possible to muck you about.

The Hercules door is 5 feet 10 inches high, so the reason for the height limitation was at once in evidence. With boots and helmets on, a man who started 6 feet tall ended 6 feet 3, so he had to remember to keep his head down as he went out. The size of the Ju 52 door was the reason why German Paras exited from it as they did, in a crouching dive. It was the only way to get out and well clear of the fuselage – another important aim of a good exit technique. So the pupil was required to step out cleanly and crisply, his arms on top of his reserve chute, and bring his feet immediately together. This importance of keeping the arms on top of the reserve and the feet tight together was constantly emphasised by the instructors. As Sergeant Corkish pointed out to Tattum, the gaps in his teeth were obviously going to cause him problems anyway with the slipstream, but if he had an arm or a leg waving about as well, then he was really heading for trouble. No more smiling now! Next time out of the door, he'd have to close his mouth.

Then there was the Flight. The best bit – the jam in the sandwich, the blissful half-minute of Relief between the Fear of jumping and the Panic of arriving. Unfortunately, the pupil could not just hang there and gawp about. There was a great deal to be done in the interval. Things might happen that would have to be dealt with. Things like an unopened parachute, or a mid-air collision with a neighbour. There was a time at No. 1 PTS, said Squadron Leader Sizeland, when they didn't bother to teach you what to do if you had any canopy abnormalities. With only one parachute at your disposal, there was nothing you could have done about them anyway. But since the advent of the reserve chute in the summer of 1955 it was possible to take remedial action. So the first thing to do after a successful exit was to take a shufty at your canopy to make sure it had developed properly.

For this exercise the pupil got into a training parachute harness hanging from the roof. He then clipped the reserve chute on to the two upper D

rings of his harness and made sure the red handle was on top. Then the bench he had been standing on was removed and he was ready to begin his flight drills.

'On the command Go,' said Sergeant Les Hammond, another of the PJIs, 'you give the safety count, one thousand, two thousand, three thousand, check canopy! Look up and have a good look at it, nice round shape, no holes, no tears, the canopy's formed correctly.'

At which point it was time for the next bit of drill, something called all-round-observation.

'Your hands come off your reserve, you look up and, in a salute-grip, select your front lift-webs and start pushing them away from you, then to the left and to the right, and look all round you at the sky. You're trying to prevent an emergency, aren't you? You're trying to use the old mark one eyeball to get a good look round and make sure some other para isn't

Left: *Practising all-round observation.*

Below left: *About to make a forward left landing.*

creeping up on you. And if he is, if he's heading straight for your rigging lines, or looks like crashing through them, what do you do then?' Sergeant Hammond waited while his pupils stared at him, nonplussed.

'Well, then you spreadeagle, don't you, arms right out or to the front and to the rear to stop an entanglement, just as – if you find you're heading towards someone – you don't wait till he hits you, you reach up for your lift-webs and start steering away, don't you now? And do it vigorously, as hard as you can. I want to see you really pulling about in the harness, using your big muscles, working at it. OK?'

Then, before you knew where you were, it was time for Panic, the ground was coming up, so parachute position everywhere, knees bent, elbows in, toes up, everything tight, squeeze tight, squeeze everything tight, feet back a bit, toes up now, and crash! you were in, or would have been if you weren't hanging in a harness suspended from the roof of the hangar and waiting for someone to push the aluminium bench back underneath you so you could unbuckle the harness, pull out the leg straps, climb down and let your partner get up and have a go for himself.

It was a tiring business, even for young men as fit as the seventeen from 480 and their eight companions. Different muscles were at work. It was all in the arms and shoulders, in the ankles and thighs. But they weren't complaining. Brize was terrific. The staff were fantastic, the food was marvellous, the Spotlight Club great. No drill, no guards, no being chased about, well, not much anyway, just four of them getting caught walking across the grass by Corporal Baker, who was the NCO in charge for the first week of the course and who was busy finding them some chores to do as a punishment.

How did they like the way the staff treated them? Well it was a bit different from the Depot, wasn't it? Anybody would think they were all officers, the polite way the instructors talked to them. That was a tradition really. All stemming back to mid 1941 when Group Captain Maurice Newnham was made Commandant of the Parachute Training School at Ringway. He was determined that the relationship between the staff and students should be a happy and relaxed one. He also wanted them to live well, have comfortable billets and good food. It was a welcome the troops appreciated and one that the PTS continued to extend, even if the rest of RAF Brize Norton were rather less enthusiastic about the Pongos living temporarily in their midst, finding them brutish, nasty and prone to punch-ups in the Spotlight Club. In consequence, any fighting was now severely punished, instant RTU (Return to Unit) for the offender, which RSM Jim Wilsher of the PCAU – the Parachute Course Administrative Unit – found rather unreasonable. Paras were supposed to be aggressive. What harm could the odd punch-up do? And anyway there was a tendency for some of the blue jobs to run off and complain to the RAF Station Police if someone so much as looked sharply at them.

So far, however, nobody was tempted to get into a fight. It was a pleasure to be there, to walk over to the canteen or the shower-block in the late afternoon sunshine and swop stories with each other and their instructors.

Again 480 were being lucky with the weather. Major John Evans, OC PCAU, explained how critical a factor the weather could be. Four weeks might seem a long while to complete the ground training and then carry out the statutory eight jumps, but sometimes the weather was so bad, the winds so high, that as many as two weeks could be completely lost. In which case the whole programme fell apart and the jumps had to be fitted in at the earliest opportunity. On the other hand, if the weather was good, then the programme was often accelerated as an insurance against bad weather later on. Theoretically, the first week consisted of ground training; in the second the balloon jump and the first aircraft descent took place; then in the third and fourth weeks the other six jumps were fitted in as was most suitable; and the course ended with the Wings Parade on the final Friday. Already the recruits were thinking about that and working out how many pairs of wings they were going to need for their shirts and sweaters and various uniforms. Five? Or was it six? Oho. That'd be the day all right.

The first week passed quickly. More Exits, Flights and Landings. Then still more, until by the end of the week they were beginning to feel ready for the real thing. The Fan had been no problem. They had all leapt off the platform and sailed down on to the mats, their descent controlled by the fan that gave the device its name. A French fairground gadget originally, said Squadron Leader George Sizeland. Spotted by an English parachutist and incorporated permanently into the PTS's training equipment. It was a useful device. Some people found it quite frightening in its way, and it certainly gave the pupil some idea of the sensation of jumping into space – if not quite as forcefully as the two pieces of training equipment out by the perimeter fence.

The second week began with a visit to these – the Tower and the Exit trainer. It was a windy Monday afternoon and the lofty steel frame of the Tower creaked as the pupil parachutists climbed to the top and strapped themselves into the harness. First they leapt into space and hung there doing the flight drills they had been taught. Once those had been accomplished to the staff's satisfaction – and the staff were close enough to observe every single one of their inadequacies – they were then lowered under controlled descent to the ground for a landing, where they sprawled in the dirt under the critical eyes of the rest of the course. The Flight Sergeants compered the proceedings, pointing out to the others where the unfortunate guinea-pig – and they all had a turn at being that – was going wrong. The wind was really quite blustery. So much so that Tattum's eyes were streaming as he swung out high above the ground for his turn.

Opposite:
Top left: *On the tower at Brize Norton. Compare this with the photograph of the Ringway tower on page 138, where a parachute canopy was used.*

Top right: *Stoner prepares to steer away.*

Bottom left: *Going out of the exit trainer, with a man on the tower in the background.*

Bottom right: *Two good exits from the trainer, both with their feet together.*

'Come on, Tattum, all-round observation. Rigging lines! . . . Look at them, look at them, you bounced off. All right, carry on, carry on. He's crying. Stop crying, Tattum, come on, steer away, in your own clear air space, stop crying. Right . . . on the front left, parachute position, elbows in, legs back underneath you, get your knees tight, yellow brake off . . .' The brake came off and Tattum headed for the dirt beneath.

'Do you reckon he was crying there?'

'No. Just wanted to show everyone his teeth . . . who's next then?'

The Exit trainer, or 'Knacker-cracker', was less useful in many respects. Frightening, certainly. Uncomfortable, definitely. But nothing like the

O'Hare practises spreadeagling to stop another parachutist passing through his rigging lines.

actual sensation you got when the slipstream hit you. Once you'd jumped, you bounced up and down like a yo-yo along to the end of the wire where your mates were waiting to leap up and grab your feet and help you down out of the harness. Nobody cared much for the Exit trainer. Though it did bring home one useful point. It taught you the importance of fitting your harness properly – especially the straps between your legs – and took you some of the way towards that moment when you would be stepping into the balloon car on the DZ at Hullavington, ready to be lifted 800 feet above the ground for your first parachute jump.

Ballooning was scheduled for the following day. That night 480 lay in bed psyching themselves up for the next morning – imagining the moment when they would be called forward to the door of the cage, put their arms across their reserve chutes, and be told to go . . .

There was no need to work in the Met Office to see that the wind was too high for jumping that day, so Ballooning was scrubbed and the Course went back into the hangar for more ground training instead of boarding the bus for RAF Hullavington. There was a mixture of disappointment and relief – as always when parachuting is cancelled. But mainly disappointment. Having girded themselves for the ordeal of making their first jump, they wanted to get on with it and get it over.

Also planning to jump that day were Captain Baird, Sergeant Riley and Corporal Slater. Slater had now taken over from Baker the duties of NCO in charge of the platoon while it was at Brize, and had at once made a characteristic impact. Having heard Hunt singing happily in the shower, he had given him one of his famous black scowls and told him he wouldn't be happy for the ten days he was there. Another of his duties – besides tormenting Hunt – was to parachute with the platoon, and to do this he had to bring with him from the Depot a proforma endorsed 'Fit to Parachute'. The platoon commander was also required to make the first balloon and aircraft descent with them, while, as part of his duties, the platoon sergeant was required to visit Brize Norton and take Drill Instruction – at which time he, too, was expected to jump with them.

None of the staff complained about these regulations. Balloon jumps were popular. They were done without equipment and were considered to be in the category of a 'fun' jump. Nothing nicer on a sunny day than to be hoisted 800 feet above the English countryside, with splendid views at all points of the compass, and then hop out of the cage for a pleasant, problem-free descent on to the lush turf below. Or something like that. That was certainly how Baird, Riley and Slater viewed the matter, and they were annoyed to find the proceedings postponed. That Sergeant Riley had made some twenty odd jumps in the previous two weeks did not prevent him from being as annoyed as the others. For those who like parachuting, it is difficult to get enough of it. And Sergeant Riley liked it a

Right: *Landing with simulated lift-webs. Note the mock-up Hercules fuselage in the background.*

Below right: *Stirling hits the dirt beneath the tower.*

great deal. So much so that he had grasped eagerly at the opportunity to go on a fortnight's Adventure/Experience free-fall course at Weston-on-the-Green while 480 were at Brize.

It was normal practice to provide courses for the Platoon staff during their recruits' four weeks' absence. But the free-fall course was a special treat. Staff Parker of P Company had been on it, too. So had a mixed bag of services personnel, ranging from Paras to RAF girl typists. Adventure/Experience courses were available to all ranks of all arms of all the services and included such things as skiing, canoeing and mountaineering, as well as free-falling.

Not all those who signed up for the course found it as attractive as they had imagined. Even Staff Parker, who had made dozens of military jumps, found that sport parachuting required a radical change in his psychology. From being part of a disciplined, organised group he was suddenly thrown onto his own resources. And the move from static-line to free-fall jumping required an even greater psychological shift. The static-line jumper felt he was attached to the balloon or aircraft by his line up to the very last moment when the chute was fully extended and about to open. A free-faller, however, just leapt into space, after which his life was in his own hands and it was all up to him.

Kevin Riley found this exhilarating. As soon as he was down, he was busy repacking his chute so that he could go back up again. He was the course's best student, the only one who had reached the point of doing drops with 15-second delays. And as his orange-clad figure came hurtling from the sky, it was interesting to observe that, just as the Kop sings with a Liverpool accent, so some people whoop with delight in a Geordie one.

But that did not mean Sergeant Riley had not been looking forward to 480's balloon jump, and he was there again next morning when they began boarding the coaches which would take them to Hullavington. This time the forecast was good. Too good in some ways. Hardly a breath of air. No problem from an aircraft, of course, but if there was no wind and the balloon was stationary, there was a danger of a jumper colliding with the cable. The only solution then was to 'crawl the balloon', drive the truck slowly into what wind there was, until the cage had emptied.

At Hullavington the proceedings began with a demonstration drop by the staff. Sergeant Corkish, just to cheer his section up, told them he wanted them lying on the ground underneath the balloon so that if his parachute failed to open he would have the satisfaction of taking a few of them with him. This was normal gallows humour on such occasions and received with an appreciative jeer from Tattum and Co.

For some reason the sight of Sergeant Riley drawing a parachute from the truck inflamed a number of the platoon. Unexpectedly – in view of his absence for the last two weeks – his popularity had reached a new low. Admittedly, on one of the rare occasions he had been spotted at Brize he had shouted at Birrell that he didn't believe he'd got the bottle to jump, but that was only mildly provocative stuff, all part of his declared policy of getting them to hate him and so provoking their aggression. Like it or lump it, he argued, the platoon staff were geared to train a guy for war. If the men didn't do what they had to do straightaway, if they hesitated, they were done for. What he was after was trained soldiers who could do the job and not be a platoon sergeant's nightmare, men who knew how to act with controlled aggression, and by the sound of it he was getting results. Several of them felt very aggressive towards him. A show-off was what he was. A big mouth. A knob. And they dared the author to say so in his book.

Meanwhile, nobody seemed to be paying much attention to the demo drop. Instructors were coming out of the balloon and descending in what looked a very undramatic fashion. In any case it was really rather too late to learn much from watching them. Everybody was more interested in the weasel-like thoughts that were scuttling about the recesses of their own minds – such things as: will I bottle out/shit myself/crumple at the knees/slither over the edge like an alligator going into the swamp? At times like these, the individual has a habit of withdrawing into himself, leaving it to the staff to keep up the cheerful time-filling conversation. 'From 800 feet you've got about thirty-five seconds under the canopy, you know,' said Sergeant Corkish informatively. 'And how long if it doesn't open?' asked Tattum, who had been quietly making an enormous daisy-chain for the last half-hour. 'Seven seconds,' said his sergeant. 'But you're very calm and relaxed this morning with your effing mayor's chain of daisies round your neck. Mind you don't pull *them* out instead of your red handle, if your main chute fails.'

The syndicate flight sergeants organised the balloon-cage manifests and the issue of parachutes. Taff Evans was brusquely efficient. Butch Casey was more relaxed, doing his old-timer turn, applying soothing fatherly words of advice to his pupils: 'Lead on, young Lieutenant Kennett, your merry men round, draw your chutes and then back with this lot.'

There was a last-minute briefing from Flying Officer Chris Simpson, the course officer, who reminded them of their flight drills, took them through their parachute position and warned them to hang on to it right up to and through the landing regardless of ground-rush or panic as the deck suddenly came up to hit them. Then . . .

'Everybody happy?'

Silence.

'IS EVERYBODY HAPPY?'

'YES, SIR!'

Two of 480 were not jumping. Thomas had a stiff neck, got from cracking his head on the top of the opening in the mock-up fuselage while practising exit drills. Butler had an infected knee he had been trying to

Butch Casey gives a few last-minute words of advice.

conceal from his supervisors. With luck they could catch up with the balloon jump the following week on a TA course.

'Up 800 and four men jumping,' rang out the cry.

As the cable paid out, one of the RAF crew hooked a red and white pennant on it at every two hundred feet. Just so everybody would know. Especially the balloon crew. Meanwhile . . . inside the balloon cage . . .

'When I call you forward at 800 feet, walk forward and take hold of both uprights. I'll tell you to look up at the balloon, put both arms across your reserve, and go. Just step off, like you step off a pavement, head back, compulsory count, one thousand, two thousand, three thousand . . .'

They were up to six hundred feet now and still climbing. 'A few landmarks while we're on the way up. You've got the M4 on the other side, and over there, behind the married quarters, is the church. See the church? And just in front of the church is the graveyard. Right, O'Hare. Give me this joke, then. Come on.'

'An Englishman, an Irishman and a Scotsman . . .'

'Can't hear you! Speak up a bit . . .'

A little later, and Pete O'Hare had gone, arms across his reserve, stepping off like you step off a pavement, 800 feet above the road, on to a zebra crossing. Now it was Dean Ward's turn to tell a silly joke, just to keep *his* mind off things.

'One Irishman falls down a manhole and the other one says, "Paddy, is it dark down there?" and Paddy says, "I don't know, I can't see." '

'Is that it? Is that your joke? . . .'

It was dreamlike up there. Really dreamlike.

'And on the other side you can see the Post Office Tower in London, see

One parachutist prepares to land while the other practises steering away.

that? What are you looking for, Tattum, you plank? The Post Office Tower's a hundred and twenty miles away . . .'

And the ground was 800 feet below, with tiny figures dotted about the green baize.

'My stomach went to my mouth, I tell you. It just did, I didn't think I was going to be that scared. My stomach went to my mouth and I just looked up and there was the chute, I just didn't count, just didn't bother . . .'

But underneath him, somebody was bothering. 'OK, Barrett, when you left the balloon, your legs were apart. Remember we want a good tight position, legs tight together, because remember we're going out of an aircraft and an aircraft's got a slipstream . . .'

'My God, this is marvellous. The parachute is open and I'm just hanging here in space!'

'OK, number one, stop steering now. Look down and assess your drift, you are drifting forwards . . .'

'Stay away from the cable, number two . . .'

'Elbows in, number three, feet back underneath you, squeeze it tight, watch the ground now . . .'

'Turn over and get your reserve off, number four. Roll away from it.'

Down. Arrived. Made it. Finding it hard to pay attention to the harness-release and drag drills. Feeling a strong urge to abandon the lot and rush across the DZ and tell your mate who hasn't jumped yet just how marvellous it's going to be. After your knees stop knocking and your ring stops twitching, of course . . .

And suddenly everybody seemed to be talking at once.

'I didn't pull down till ten feet off the ground, I got the wrong lift-webs . . .'

'And your legs went into a banana position. You came down and you were bent, like that . . .'

'I was going to do a forward one but I done a backward one, oscillating I was, that's the word, is it?'

'Did I really do that? Did I really jump out of that thing up there?'

'Don't put your size 10s all over the bloody canopy,' cried Flight Sergeant Casey. 'Come on, move it, move it.'

'And when I'd seen Tattum go out as well, he couldn't show me up, could he? Great it was. But the worst part about it is when you're just jumping out, before your canopy's opened, and you feel you're just dropping, you know . . .'

Then it was all over. They had all jumped. No one had refused. One or two had done a slow-motion alligator slide off the edge of the cage, but no one from 480. They had all stepped out nice and firmly into that big empty space as they had been trained to do whenever they got the order to go. It was just automatic, just another exit from the exit trainer – well, no, not really, not quite, it was pretty scary up there, worse going up in the cage than stepping out, quiet and a bit cold-blooded.

'It's very still, it's very still in the air,' said Sergeant Corkish, 'with no noise at all. You're going up and you can see what you're going to jump into all the time. When you do come to the door you know you're going to jump into the space, and because no one's holding you, you don't feel as though you're supported by anything until the canopy opens. Whereas in an aircraft you're hooked up, you're hanging on to something. And we do get quite a few people in the aircraft, when they get to the door, they will not let go of the strop, because they feel so secure, and they go out of the aircraft still hanging on, and we're pushing the arm off the strop, yes, literally smacking their hand off it . . .'

The following day they all set off in a Hercules heading for Weston-on-the-Green and their first aircraft jump. The weather had changed again, the visibility getting worse all the time, down to a few hundred yards towards the end. So the jump was scrubbed. And what with the turbulence, heat, discomfort, anticipation, disappointment and frustration, a lot of them ended up vomiting into the bags provided. Already their jumps were being postponed. First the balloon and now the aircraft. It was almost the end of week 2 and they had done only one out of the eight jumps needed to qualify. Suddenly the four-week course seemed shorter than they had imagined. So when they woke the next morning, Friday 28 May, to a cloudless dawn, a big orange sun rising through the ground mist, they prayed the weather would stay that way till they got their jump off.

It was the morning 2 Para attacked Darwin and Goose Green on East Falkland Island, though 480 did not know it until the announcement was made by the Ministry of Defence later that day. Sergeant Riley and Corporal Baker both came from 2 Para. They were not pleased at being left behind at the Depot. They appreciated that somebody had to train recruits but they didn't see why it had to be them when their mates were slogging across East Falkland Island en route for the Argies. Bob Baker had tried to talk the Colonel into letting him go, but the Colonel had said it was impossible, he had to draw the line somewhere. Bob Baker suggested Colonel Brewis drew it just behind him, but his pleas were unavailing. Theirs not to reason why. Theirs but to stay at the Depot and get on with the training. But it wasn't much fun. They'd been getting letters through the post from their mates with bits of paper with yellow lines down the middle or little white feathers inside. Only joking, of course. But not much of a joke if you were stuck in Aldershot with a lot of crows, teaching them section in the attack while your mates were actually doing it out on the ground.

It was just as bad for a platoon sergeant. As Kevin Riley said, who would ever take any notice of him and his opinions on the platoon in the attack when in the next room was a guy who'd actually *led* his platoon into the attack against the Argies? Corporal Slater felt much the same and he came from 1 Para, the non-combatant battalion as it was known, so at least he wouldn't feel out of things when he rejoined them. But his battalion wouldn't have the medal, would they? The one they were talking about the other afternoon in the House of Commons. It was the sort of thing that was going to matter in the Regiment in a few years' time. People's military careers were going to be affected by it. If there was Corporal X who'd spent two years at the Depot and Corporal Y who'd been to the Falklands, and you were looking for someone to promote, you'd obviously have to pick Corporal Y, wouldn't you? He was more experienced, he'd done it for real, he hadn't just been playing and training people like the unfortunate Corporal X. It would be the same for the officers, too. The fact that 2nd

Lieutenant So-and-so had led his platoon into battle against the Argies would count for something in the future – and not only when the lamps started swinging in the Mess. That was what soldiering was all about. Not sitting on your backside at the Depot. If Sergeant Riley had had his way, he'd have closed the Depot down altogether and taken everybody out to the Falklands, as he'd suggested to the Colonel.

480 were not thinking about the Falklands just then, however. They had just come back from breakfast and were hoping the wind would not get up before they were due to jump. The morning was often a good time. The evening, too. Steve Birrell was quietly confident they'd make it today, and Graham Robertson hoped he was right. He'd enjoyed the balloon and was looking forward to the aircraft jump. So was Thomas. His neck was much better today. He was hoping the MO would clear him to jump with the others.

They stood around waiting for their bus to come. Scrumpy Barrett was talking about a girl he'd met, a nurse in a nearby hospital. Or rather his mates were teasing him about her. Very bright girl, she was, according to Dean Ward. Knew all the bones of the body, she did, and had told Scrumpy all his, starting from his head and going right down the front of him. And when she got to his . . . Dean paused, with a mischievous grin . . . lower regions, she came out with a word he'd never heard before! Scrumpy delivered a mock punch at Dean's midriff. A bit of wrestling broke out, spotted by Corporal Slater who called them briskly to order.

Twenty miles away at Weston-on-the-Green the airfield staff were getting ready for the drop. Butch Casey and one or two others of the course staff were preparing too. An Alpha had to be laid out marking the front edge of the dropping zone. By day this was a panel of orange fluorescent material in the form of a capital A. At night it was a similarly shaped pattern of fire-lighters. Each arm of the A was some thirty feet long so that it could be clearly seen by the Hercules pilot. On its first run the plane would drop a drifter, one of the PJIs – probably Flying Officer Simpson – whose job it was to indicate which way and at what strength the wind was blowing. The drifter would not attempt to steer his chute at all. He would just go where he was taken, which would indicate what allowance had to be made for the wind when dropping the sticks.

The programme was carefully graded. The first jump, from the balloon, was from 800 feet and the dress was clean fatigue – which meant boots, denim trousers, combat smock and steel helmet, but without weapons or equipment. The first four aircraft jumps were also clean fatigue – starting with single sticks of six, then of ten, then a simultaneous ten, then back to single sixes for the night descent. The final three jumps were with equipment containers, the last with a rifle as well, and again the size of the sticks increased progressively. The fifth aircraft descent was single sixes, the sixth was simultaneous tens, and the last was supposed to be up to sim fourteen, but that was difficult at Weston-on-the-Green. Tens were about enough there, otherwise the last few might end up amongst the administrative buildings or on the hangar. All the aircraft jumps except the last (from 800 feet) were from 1000 feet – a height designed to give plenty of time for a reserve chute to open in the event of a failure, or for a pupil to kick out of bad twists, or free himself from an entanglement with one of his neighbours. Such incidents were rare, but the extra 200 feet was an additional safety factor recently enforced by the RAF, in response to a fatal accident the previous year.

Flight Lieutenant Dave Huggins, one of the School's PJIs, said the Paras found the RAF too cautious. He had just completed a two-year tour of duty at the Para Depot as the RAF liaison officer there. He and his team had been responsible for all parachute continuation training at the Depot, and because of their close contact with the Regiment they had naturally developed a sympathetic understanding of the Paras' needs. Safety before all else was not one of the Regiment's concerns. They were quite prepared to risk casualties in order to maintain realism in their parachute training, just as they, and the other arms of the services, were also prepared to accept that they must take casualties in the Falklands too. They were all proud of the Navy's and Air Force's achievements so far, and given the chance themselves would be glad of the opportunity to demonstrate their skills and their courage in war. That was their job as servicemen, he said, echoing the staff of 480 Platoon, and they were eager to do it.

The drone of the aircraft could be heard. Then it was sighted making its approach run. Standard operational procedure was for the aircraft to fly to its target at 250 feet above the ground, rise to dropping-height just before the DZ, and then return to 250 feet for the flight home. But this procedure was not adopted in training over the sort of built-up areas surrounding Weston-on-the-Green. The drifter and the staff jumped first. Then the aircraft came round to deliver the first stick of six. The wind was about eight to ten knots, not high but much more than the pupils had experienced at Hullavington and enough to give them some idea of what it was like to carry out proper harness-release drill in order to control their canopy.

The sticks were small to begin with for two reasons: so that the staff could speak to individuals through loud-hailers and give them flight instructions; and in order to reduce the risk of collisions and entanglements while the pupils were still inexperienced. The exit rate from the Hercules was one man per second, or one man every sixty yards, and though that might seem a generous distance for each parachutist, the vagaries of weight, wind and angle of entry into the slipstream could all bring them closer together. And when they were jumping simultaneous sticks, the danger of collision was considerably increased, which was why the flight drills were so important. Spreadeagling was designed to stop entanglements. Steering away was a means of avoiding collisions. Kicking out of twists was another simple but urgently necessary procedure if the twists were high up the rigging and the canopy's lift reduced in consequence. In theory twists should not occur if the parachutist makes a clean and symmetrical exit. But they still do on occasions and are one of the few remaining irregularities that can occur with the present British PX parachute.

A development of the original wartime X chute, the PX has two important refinements that make it easier to land and less prone to faulty deployment. The canopy, instead of being the same density of material overall, is now made of fabrics which become more porous from the centre outwards. This cuts down oscillation, the pendulum-like swinging that in combination with the parachutist's rate of fall very much increases the danger of injury. The other improvement is an ingenious strip of gauze around the outside edge of the canopy which helps prevent blown peripheries – dangerous irregularities where the canopy turns partially, or totally, inside out as it is developing, sometimes causing the collapse of the parachute. Twists are less easy to cure. Some are caused by the way in which the rigging lines happen to deploy from the bag and the chance rotatory movements the slipstream gives them – though it is rare for them to be anything other than a minor hazard.

None of these abnormalities took place on 480's first aircraft drop. The Hercules flew round and round in the bright sunshine, dropping its single sticks of six parachutists. If anything, the sense of exhilaration 480 had felt after their balloon drop was even greater this time. For Thomas it was his first jump, and he came off the DZ carrying his bundled-up main chute in a bag over his shoulder, his eyes shining with excitement.

Butch Casey was busy talking the sticks down. 'Steer away, number four, steer away from number five. Chin on your chest, my lovely boy, elbows in, hold everything tight now. Tight, I said, tight, tight! Pillock!'

The aircraft was a very different experience from the balloon. For a start it was noisy, very noisy, like the inside of a truck compared with a coach, thin on padding, and once the door was open deafening. It was a bit frightening at first when you got the order to stand up, hook up, and then started shuffling forward, one behind the other, as close as you could get till you arrived at the door and turned left or right depending on whether you were going out port or starboard. And that was the first you saw of the sky really, unless you were at the front of the stick or caught the odd glimpse as the doors were opened and the other sticks went out.

Frightened? No, not really, didn't have time to be, said one. A bit, said another, sitting down, waiting there, but as soon as he'd got the order to hook up, all the fear left him. And anyway it was difficult to bottle in the aircraft, especially in the middle of a stick. You were out of the door before you had time to think, you left all that to the dispatcher. Sergeant Hammond explained about that. Dispatching from an aircraft was quite physical. If you had a stick that was holding back, not getting out fast enough, you had to whack them through the door. Conversely, if they were rushing, you'd physically got to hold the whole lot of them back. And he always made sure, when he dispatched them, that they got right clear of the aircraft before he came back for the next man. Because they got wobbly legs some-times and collapsed on the sill and sat down and rolled out the door and all sorts of things. But not 480, they all went out like arrows into the sunshine, or at least it felt that way, and they couldn't wait to get on with the rest of their jumps.

That weekend was the May bank holiday and they were all sent home on a 72-hour leave. News of the capture of Darwin and Goose Green by 2 Para, and the casualties suffered there, set in train a sequence of events that culminated unexpectedly for 480 Platoon on the following Wednesday evening. They were due to make their night jump that evening and had assembled in the hangar with the rest of the course where they had drawn and fitted parachutes. Except for Butler and Tattum, that is. Butler had still not recovered completely from his injury and was scheduled to make his first jump, from the balloon, with a TA course the following day. Tattum had an ear infection that had blown up suddenly the previous night and he was not allowed to jump until further notice. The night was unpleasantly muggy. It was hot and uncomfortable waiting about in their chutes. But at least they had got three more jumps in since returning from leave, two on Tuesday and one that afternoon – their first equipment jump, which had been advanced up the programme to take advantage of the calm conditions. Luckily, in fact, because very soon Flying Officer Chris Simpson had to announce that the aircraft was unserviceable, the flight scrubbed and jump no. 6 postponed for twenty-four hours. They were to hand in their parachutes and fall out till midday tomorrow.

As they were dispersing with the usual mixture of irritation and relief, Captain John Baird called the platoon to one side. He had an announce-ment to make, as well. This came as an even bigger shock to them. Their course at Brize Norton, he told them, would not be running the full four weeks. It would be cut short on Saturday, regardless of whether they had completed their jumps. They would be leaving for Brecon on Sunday.

There was a stunned silence. Then somebody said: 'And when are we going to the Falklands, sir?' There was a big roar of laughter followed by a buzz of excited conversation. John Baird refused to be drawn. All he knew was what he'd told them. They were going down to Wales for Advanced Tactical Training a week earlier than expected. That was all. And they'd be leaving on Sunday as he'd said.

Again there was a mixed reaction to the news. Excitement at the thought that they might be getting out to the Falklands and seeing some action. But irritation, too, at the disturbance of the status quo. Many of them had made plans for the rest of their time there. Some of them had found themselves girl friends. They had been looking forward to the free discos, wanted to get their wings, did not want to be rushed into a situation they were not yet ready for. Once again, at a critical moment in their course, there had been one of 480's famous hiccups – though this had to class as the biggest and potentially the most famous. 2 Para had taken casualties. The CO and sixteen others had been killed, according to the reports. Some twenty or more had been wounded. So 480 might be needed as replacements very shortly. Might even be flown out to Ascension Island. And if 2 Para had captured an airstrip at Goose Green, they might even be flown straight to the Falkland Islands from there.

The speculation was intense as they were driven back to their billets in the bus. One thing they all hoped, though. That the weather stayed fine so they'd be able to get the last of their jumps in before Saturday. That bit of arm just below the right shoulder was itching to get a pair of wings on it. In fact, some of them already had a pair sewn on one of their shirts in fate-tempting anticipation. Just their effing luck if the weather turned lousy.

Melvin gets a hand with his harness fitting.

It was just as hot the following evening. Even hotter as they passed through the exhaust from the Hercules' turbo-prop engines and went up the ramp into the body of the aircraft. It was just after sunset, but inside the plane, with the ramp up and only tiny red lights glowing, it was darker than it was outside, more of a dusk than a night-jump but better than no jump at all. The red lights were to acclimatise the jumpers' eyes to the darkness they would find outside. The interior was a maze of steel tubing and webbing straps where the central seating had been installed. Hercules were also used for heavy-load parachute drops, low-level drops, and straightforward cargo-carrying, so the interior seating had to be removable.

The aircraft took off with a strange, wild, screeching sound as the flaps went up. Then a brief climb to a thousand feet and the ten-minute flight to Weston-on-the-Green. The pupils sat silently along both sides of the fuselage and the central structure. It was difficult to be heard above the roar of the engines and there was not much to say in any case. Some had their heads on their arms, which rested in turn on their reserve chutes. Some stared blankly ahead. Some flashed an occasional smile at their neighbour. Then it was time for the drifter to go. The starboard door was opened and the noise doubled.

Boarding the Hercules for their last aircraft jump.

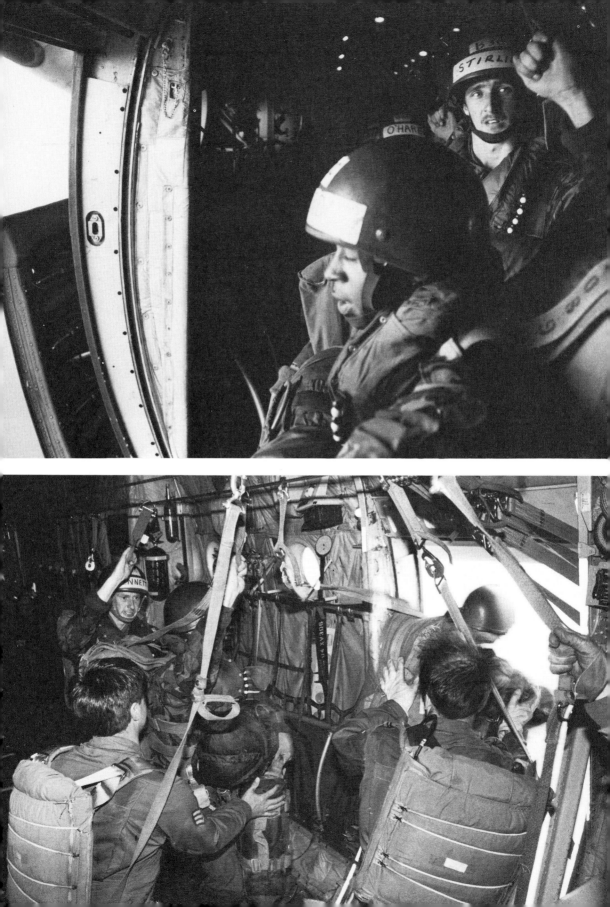

Left: *Ward about to make a port exit.*

Below left: *A dispatcher offers a helping hand.*

Outside, the sky was still pink in the west. Fairy lights shone below, streams of cars moving with long rectangles of light laid out before them. The A43, Bicester, market gardens under glass, all twinkled beneath them as Flying Officer Simpson and three other PJIs went out. Then the dispatchers shut the door and the aircraft began to bank and go round for the next run-in. It was hard-work time for the dispatchers. They were hooking up strops, checking equipment, pulling on hooks and dog-clips. Then the port door was opened, the step folded out, and the first stick got up and went to the door.

Red on, and the stick braced up.

Green on! Go, go, go, go, go, go – a steady rhythmical movement, at one-second intervals, a thump on the shoulder as each man turned hard right and leaped out from nothing into eff-all, as the saying goes for night jumps. The last man had barely disappeared before the dispatcher was on his knee, a quick look out of the door to check they were all away safely, then he was on his feet again, heaving with another PJI on the strops and bags outside the aircraft, pulling them in against the drag on the slipstream, putting a quick boot against the strops as the bags reached the door to kick them clear of the jamb and help them over the threshold. Then the step was folded in, the door closed, and the starboard team got to work opening their door ready for the next stick to go out.

Ten sticks in all, and a group of trainee dispatchers, then the aircraft was empty and could head back to Brize. Down below on the DZ, the last few sticks were packing their parachutes into the bags they carried with them in training. That done, they hoisted main chute and reserve on to their shoulders and headed for the RV point where the bus was waiting to take them back to Brize Norton. No one had been injured. No one had had any hairy experiences. Their luck was holding up. If it continued tomorrow they would get their last two jumps in by teatime and be swaggering around the Spotlight Club with wings on their shirts later that evening.

Their luck did hold up. The weather stayed fine, and the last two jumps took place without incident. Or rather, without any incident leading to injury – though one lad from 480, Payne, a back-squad from 479, went out head first, got twists, had a foot caught up in his rigging lines and was still spiralling when he landed. Thought he was going to die, he did. Hanging upside down like that, nearly had a heart attack, thought he was going to land on his head. Sometimes rigging lines could melt on the boot, stick to the boot from the friction. The only solution if you got a foot caught was to reach up, grab it and pull it out. Good experience really, said Sergeant Hammond, all bound to have some minor mishap sooner or later. The sooner the better, really. When a guy had nothing go wrong all the way through the course, he might start thinking there was nothing to it, and not be ready when some mishap did happen. This course had had it easy.

Left: *PJIs haul in the
strops after a stick
has gone.*

Below left: *A Hercules
makes its run over the
DZ.*

Right: *Landing at
Weston-on-the-Green.
The different-coloured
chutes identify port and
starboard sticks for
training purposes.*

Normally, out of sixty-odd guys, you had some kind of collision and entanglement on the final descent.

The Wings Parade took place on the asphalt in front of the hangar at Weston-on-the-Green. A crop-spraying helicopter swooped up and down over the strips of barley on the edge of the airfield during the first part of the ceremony, but nobody cared about the noise. The course was over. They had done their eight jumps. They were about to receive their wings. First Major John Evans, the Officer Commanding the PCAU, addressed them, thanking them for giving him such an easy ride by behaving themselves so well at Brize Norton. He then went on, like a priest at a wedding, to ask if any of them had any second thoughts about parachuting, and if so to state them now, or else for ever hold their peace. Because, as he read out to them from the official document:

'Once formally awarded your wings, you are deemed to have accepted, as long as you are medically fit to do so, the obligation to serve with a parachute unit on operations, and to carry out parachute descents when ordered or required to do so. For this, parachute pay is awarded. Future failure or refusal to carry out a parachute descent will result in disciplinary action being taken against you. This will almost certainly result in a trial by Court Martial and the withdrawal of the right to wear the qualified parachutist badge with wings. If you are not prepared to accept this obligation, then you should say so now.'

He paused, looked up and waited a moment. The helicopter swooped and snarled in the distance at the bottom of the DZ. No one moved in the assembled congregation. No impediment was about to be revealed. 'Well done,' said Major Evans. 'Welcome to the airborne brotherhood. I salute you all.'

Wing Commander Mervyn Green, Officer Commanding No. 1 PTS, went round with the PJIs and presented the coveted wings. Before that he reminded them all that a safe parachutist was a current parachutist. It was important they should jump as often as they could with their units. He also reminded them that parachuting was a means to an end, not an end in itself. It was a means of getting them down on the ground, either on an exercise or indeed on operations. They must also remember, now that they would be wearing wings, that they would be identified as members of the airborne forces, and linked with all the proud history and traditions that went with that organisation. And, from what had been going on down in the Falkland Islands, they would have seen what a fine bunch of men some of them were now going to join.

He did not necessarily mean at once. Or even in a few weeks time, after the tactical training in Wales. He meant at some time or other, probably after 2 and 3 Para had returned home. But it was certainly possible they might be going sooner than that. 2 Para already needed replacements. If the fighting got worse in the Falklands, they and 3 Para might be needing a lot more. But were the recruits of 480, after the training they had had so far, really ready to go out and fight a war? Tattum reckoned they were – once they'd been to Wales and practised platoon attacks and live firing. The only difference from that and real war was that the enemy would be aiming at them and they would be aiming at him. Obviously they might get killed, but that was what they were there for, wasn't it? As he'd said before, they were trained to accept that, been told from the start they'd always be outnumbered and wouldn't have much chance of surviving once they did go in. But that was the sort of price they had to pay for being in the best regiment, wasn't it?

They were brave words. Considered words. Words many of his predecessors had voiced across the years. They also had had the urge to put their training into practice, do something with what they had learned, get out there and have a go. It was the way our three Arnhem veterans had felt after they finished their training in 1942. John Nicholson was sent out to North Africa as a replacement for the casualties suffered by the 1st Battalion of the 1st Parachute Brigade in February 1943. Ron Holt followed him out to the 2nd Battalion in April. Bill Collard had been sent out much earlier, sailing in December 1942 and reporting on arrival to B Company of the 3rd Battalion camped in a vineyard just outside Algiers.

The Brigade itself had arrived in North Africa during November 1942, partly by air but mainly by sea. Before the month was out each battalion had carried out an operational drop, though quite independently of each other. North Africa – and Tunis in particular – was to see the blooding of the Brigade, and in the course of the next few months all three battalions would take part in some of the fiercest fighting of the war. As a result they would be given the admiring nickname of the 'Red Devils' by their German opponents. The British Airborne Forces had come a long way since that first modest sabotage operation against the Tragino aqueduct.

12 Red Devils

A whole year elapsed between Operation 'Colossus', the attack on the Tragino Aqueduct, and Operation 'Biting' at Bruneval on the coast of north-west France. This attack, carried out on 27 February 1942 by C Company, 2nd Parachute Battalion, commanded by Major John Frost, was a commando-type raid on a German radar station.

General Student had not been in favour of using his airborne forces in small raids or sabotage attacks. The British had no reservations on this score. Such raids were very much part of their history from Drake onwards. The quick descent on an enemy coast, the destruction of his arsenals and fortifications, the carrying-off of his gold and goods – these activities were deeply ingrained in the blood. Nelson's Navy had carried on the tradition, and one of the most famous events of the Great War was a relatively small operation against the Belgian port of Zeebrugge. While very few people can remember exactly what happened at the Battle of Jutland, many know that the attack on Zeebrugge in 1918 was intended to block the entrance to the Bruges canal so as to deny its continued use as a U-Boat base. It was the sort of operation that appealed to the imagination – as did the snatching of parts of the giant Würzburg Radar at Bruneval which had been tracking RAF aircraft crossing the French coast during the latter part of 1941. Admittedly ships were not being used in the attack this time – though they were used to bring off the troops afterwards – but the quality of the earlier raids was maintained. It was daring, well planned, brilliantly executed and totally successful. In some respects it was too successful. It made airborne operations by night seem easier than they in fact were. Certainly one party went astray, though managing to rejoin the others later. And of course there was an exit route by courtesy of the Navy after the operation was completed. That would not always be the case after a parachute drop. Getting back to his own lines would prove rather more difficult for John Frost and the force he was to lead on his next operation.

In November 1942 the 1st Parachute Brigade – made up of the 1st, 2nd and 3rd Battalions – went to North Africa as part of the 1st Army. In a series of operations, each battalion was given an independent task. On 12 November the 3rd Battalion was ordered to seize Bône airfield along the coast from Algiers and some fifty miles from the Tunisian frontier, and since a German parachute battalion stationed at Tunis was thought to be

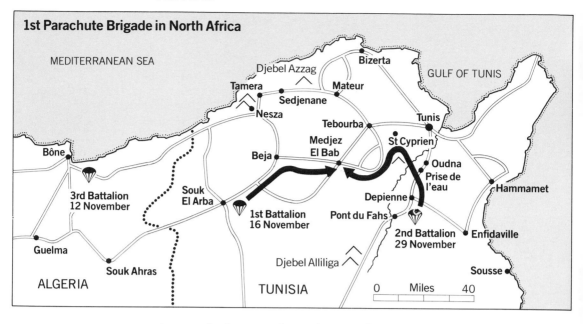

1st Parachute Brigade in North Africa

about to do the same thing, the CO of 3 Para was urged to get a move on. The American pilots of the Dakotas they were using had not dropped parachute troops before, so a night operation was wisely abandoned in favour of a dawn attack on the twelfth. Atmospheric conditions were bad and a number of men were killed and seriously injured on landing, but the airfield was occupied without opposition. Unknown to the British, the German parachute troops had been approaching the airfield at the time in their Ju 52s but, on observing the British drop, had turned round and flown back to Tunis.

It was the 1st Battalion's turn next. Ordered to capture the road junction and airfield at Beja in Tunisia, they dropped unopposed into the Souk el Arba plain on the sixteenth. Then, borrowing a fleet of old buses, the battalion moved up to Beja in comfort, and on the following day persuaded the local Vichy French garrison to join with the Allies against the German and Italian forces.

The 2nd Battalion was not so lucky. Dropped at Depienne, some twenty-five miles south of Tunis, on 29 November, they were given the task of seizing the airfields there and, if possible, at Oudna on the outskirts of Tunis, before linking up with the 1st Army at St Cyprien. John Frost, now the battalion commander, selected the DZ by the simple process of flying low over Depienne until he found a suitable spot, whereupon he jumped. All the other aircraft took their cue from him, but the battalion was widely scattered over a series of ravines and gullies. When they had assembled and marched through the night to Oudna, it was to discover that the so-called airfield was a landing strip empty of the German aircraft they had been sent to destroy. Worse still, the allied attack towards Tunis had been halted and driven back and 2 Para were now stranded fifty miles behind the lines.

For the next four days Frost and his men carried out a fighting withdrawal towards Medjez el Bab. En route they were attacked by tanks, aircraft and German motorised infantry, at one point being totally surrounded. Leaving their wounded in the care of a rear party, they fought their way out, finally making contact with an American column late on 3 December. That evening 180 men marched into Medjez el Bab, a quarter of those who had set off four days before. It had been a useless waste of valuable fighting men and an indication, in John Frost's eyes, of the British Army's lack of understanding of how the new airborne capability should be used.

For the rest of the North African campaign there were no more parachute drops. The 1st Parachute Brigade was put into the line and fought as infantry until the German surrender in May 1943. During that time the Brigade had 1700 casualties out of an original total of 2000 men. They played an important part in the critical battles of that winter and it was here they earned their nickname of the 'Red Devils' from the Germans as a tribute to their courage and tenacity in battle. It was here, too, they acquired their battle cry of 'Waho Mahommed', in imitation of the cries of the local Arabs. Nine out of the Regiment's twenty-eight battle honours recall the North African fighting, and nowhere were the honours more deservedly gained.

Bill Collard fought right through the winter with the 3rd Battalion at Beja, Netza, Tamera Valley and Sedjenane. He claims it was the red clay of the Tamera Valley staining their uniforms that got them their nickname, but whatever the reason there was no doubt in his mind that the troops on both sides   they were up against German parachute regiments much of the time – had a great deal of admiration for each other's fighting abilities. In the spring the 1st Airborne Division was formed – consisting of the 1st, 2nd and 4th Parachute Brigades and the 1st Air-Landing Brigade. Very soon its commander, Major-General Hopkinson, had convinced General Montgomery that it would be needed in Sicily and that his glider-troops should lead the assault.

And so it was. On the night of 9/10 July 1943 the seaborne invasion forces were preceded by British glider-borne landings near Syracuse and American parachute drops near Gela. There were 2000 British troops in the glider battalions of the 1st Air-Landing Brigade and they were carried in 137 American Hadrians, with eight Horsas for the heavier equipment. To ensure surprise the tugs took a roundabout route via Malta, but before Sicily was reached the wind had grown to gale proportions. Many of the gliders broke away prematurely from their tugs. Some of the tugs turned back too soon. Altogether 250 men were drowned, and only twelve of the gliders landed anywhere near their targets. Nevertheless, the men who

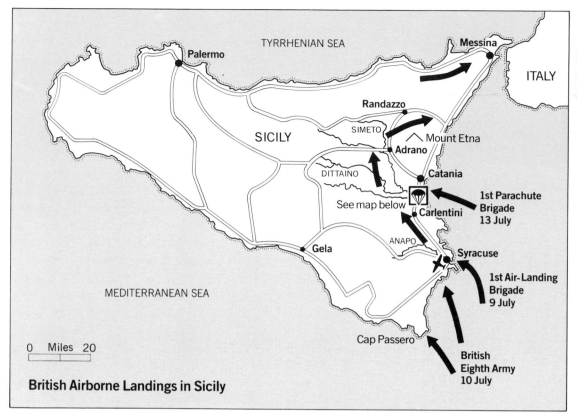

TYRRHENIAN SEA

Palermo

Messina

ITALY

Randazzo

SICILY

SIMETO

Mount Etna

Adrano

DITTAINO

Catania

See map below

Carlentini

1st Parachute
Brigade
13 July

Gela

ANAPO

Syracuse

1st Air-Landing
Brigade
9 July

MEDITERRANEAN SEA

Cap Passero

British
Eighth Army
10 July

0 Miles 20

British Airborne Landings in Sicily

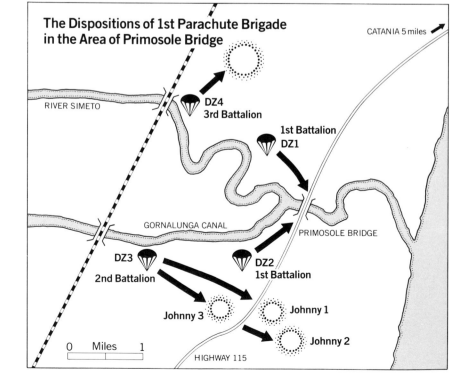

**The Dispositions of 1st Parachute Brigade
in the Area of Primosole Bridge**

CATANIA 5 miles

RIVER SIMETO

DZ4
3rd Battalion

1st Battalion
DZ1

GORNALUNGA CANAL

PRIMOSOLE BRIDGE

DZ3

2nd Battalion

DZ2
1st Battalion

Johnny 3

Johnny 1

Johnny 2

0 Miles 1

HIGHWAY 115

did arrive succeeded in taking their main target, the Ponte Grande canal bridge south of Syracuse, and holding it long enough to prevent its destruction before troops coming up from the beaches recaptured it again.

On the night of 13 July it was the turn of the 1st Parachute Brigade to attack and capture the Primosole Bridge over the River Simeto near Catania. The airborne armada was a mixed fleet: 105 Dakotas and eleven Albemarles carried the parachute troops; eight Hadrian and eleven Horsa gliders carried gunners, sappers, anti-tank guns and field ambulancemen. The plan was to land on four DZs and two LZs to the west of the main Syracuse–Catania Road. The 1st Battalion was to seize the bridge and its environs. The 2nd and 3rd Battalions were to secure the high ground to the north and south of the river. The aircraft followed the same route taken by the Air-Landing Brigade. As they crossed the British invasion fleet off the coast of Sicily, they were fired on by nervous gunners fearing they were German torpedo-bombers. Two Dakotas were shot down and nine, hit by the fire and damaged, turned back. As the remainder came in over the coast the German and Italian gunners opened up on them. Thirty-seven crashed into the sea or on the beaches and ten more turned back. The surviving planes dropped their parachutists or advised the gliders they were towing to cast off wherever they thought best. Out of the 1900 men who had taken off from North Africa, only about 250 reached the Primosole Bridge.

Neither John Nicholson nor Bill Collard were among those who did, but both of them parachuted safely down and did useful work in the areas where they found themselves. Nicholson reckoned his pilot must have been Errol Flynn. He flew round three times before giving them the order to go. The flak was intense and everyone aboard got airsick from the violence of the pilot's manoeuvres. Collard had an equally valiant pilot. Tracer was coming at them from all sides. At one point the plane made a violent turn, but as in Nicholson's case, it was merely an evasive manoeuvre and the pilot came round again for another go. The plane was in a shallow dive as they jumped and crashed shortly after they had all got out.

Ron Holt was one of the few hundred men who did reach their target – 'Johnny 1' in his case, a hill to the south of Primosole Bridge. He too had a pilot whose courage and determination were beyond reproach. After a rough flight from Malta, heavy flak on the run-in and difficulty finding their DZ, they were dropped accurately on to DZ3 as intended. At 'Johnny 1' they got into a fight with the 4th German Parachute Battalion, who had been dropped in their turn to defend the bridge. Finally, after shooting a motor-cyclist, Holt got into a quarry and held out till the Durhams arrived with tanks of the 4th Armoured Brigade on the morning of 16 July. As at Syracuse the target bridge was captured, lost and finally recaptured undamaged.

From the Allied side, the airborne operations in Sicily seemed costly and disappointing. From the German side things looked very different. The targets attacked had been captured; the German defences had been thrown into confusion; small parties of parachutists scattered over the countryside harassed the German rear. Certainly in the eyes of our three veterans it had been a highly successful operation. Ron Holt had reached the target. John Nicholson's group ambushed three German trucks. Bill Collard's seized a bridge further up the Simeto and stopped German and Italian troops from retreating across it. Naturally there had been casualties, but casualties were expected in an airborne landing.

More important, everything that had happened was invaluable experience for the next phase – the allied invasion of Europe, the coming assault on the German forces in France. Until the attack on Sicily no allied airborne force larger than a battalion had gone into battle. In Sicily the 1st Airborne Division had launched two separate attacks of brigade strength – the 1st Air-Landing Brigade at Syracuse, the 1st Parachute Brigade at Catania. The complexities of such operations had been brought home to all involved – the navigational difficulties, the need for intensive training for the pilots of the transport and tug aircraft, the vulnerability of lightly-armed parachute troops against armour and guns. How to circumvent these problems would be the task of airborne planners during the course of the next ten months or so before D-Day in Northern Europe.

Meanwhile 1st Airborne Division, after resting and regrouping in North Africa, took part in the invasion of Italy, sailing from Bizerta and landing at Taranto on 9 September. From then until November, when it returned to England to prepare for the invasion of France, it fought as an infantry division of the line in the gruelling Italian campaign. Yet again the men of the 1st Airborne were being reminded that parachuting was a very small part of an airborne soldier's life. Most of the time he was an infantryman, who could survive only through a mastery of the infantryman's skills. And that state of affairs is, if anything, even more true today. As the recruits of 480 Platoon had been reminded at their Wings Parade, parachuting was just a means to an end, a vehicle for getting them on to the ground.

But a luxury liner could serve the purpose just as well on occasions, as the SS *Canberra* and *QE2* had recently demonstrated in the South Atlantic. Once there, the troops had to know how to fight, how to use cover, how to locate, attack and kill the enemy. Which was why 480's second period of training at Brecon was so important. This time they would be practising all their basic skills under realistic battle conditions. They would be using all their weapons and firing live rounds. They would be completing their training as infantrymen.

13 Back to Brecon

Out of the seventeen original members of 480 Platoon who had gone to Brize Norton, only fourteen received their wings that Friday afternoon. The abscess on Butler's knee and Tattum's ear infection had prevented them from finishing the course. Both of them would have to come back later and complete their jumps. Thomas's case was rather different. Although he had not finished the course either, he would not be coming back again. Unexpectedly, when he came to do the balloon descent he had missed because of injury, he had refused to jump. His mates were very upset about it. Pete O'Hare was convinced that if Tommo had been able to do his first jump with them, instead of with the TA people, it would have been a different story. But amongst strangers, 800 feet up in that horrible little metal box, it wasn't surprising he didn't fancy it very much. He'd already done three aircraft jumps, don't forget. It was that effing balloon that caused the trouble. It was much too quiet. Unnatural.

Tattum and Butler were relieved to hear they weren't going to be back-squadded. Their superiors had had a much better idea. They were very kindly going to let them finish their parachute course while the rest of 480 were on leave after passing out. Provided they all got through the training at Advanced Wales, of course. They must not imagine it was a foregone conclusion. Plenty of people had fallen at that particular hurdle in the past. It was a tough course. It wasn't designed for wimps and wankers.

Barrett and Robertson set off for Brecon with modest feathers in their caps. Each had been declared best student in his syndicate. So out of a course of sixty-two men, the Paras had won both the awards. Now they must get back to the realities of the infantry soldier's life in Wales.

The exercises 480 Platoon had carried out in week 7 of their course had been designed to introduce them to the elements of infantry tactics in the field. They had done navigational exercises, section attacks and fighting patrols, both by day and by night. Advanced Wales would take all these things a step further – and would add one very important new ingredient: many of the exercises would involve the firing of live rounds.

But as always with army instruction techniques, the subject to be taught was introduced methodically and gradually. The recruits were taken through the various processes stage by stage. First they went individually down the Battle Range, then in pairs, then in groups of four, until they were capable of carrying out a full section attack and could work efficiently in the basic unit that went to make up an infantry battalion. They had fired live rounds often enough on the ranges at Aldershot. They had learnt to watch and shoot as snap targets were presented for brief periods in front of them. Now they would make the slight transition to the IBSR – the Individual Battle Shooting Range – as a preparation for the more realistic battle ranges they would be moving on to very soon. But first they had to practise their individual skills.

Each recruit would have one of the staff close behind him, whose job it was to ensure safety procedures while coaching the man he was with. 'Keep your weapon pointing down the range!' was a familiar cry. Understandably. While a recruit was busy undergoing this new experience – taking in a mass of new information – he sometimes tended to forget he had live bullets in his weapon. It was at times like these that the automatic drills that had been dinned into him over the months stopped him from being a danger to himself or others. He kept his SLR pointing at the ground. He applied his safety catch when changing position on the firing-point. And if he did not do it fast enough, his coach was quick to tell him. 'Stop. Move right. Quickly. The safety catch. Quickly. Into the trench. Watch and shoot. Watch and shoot . . .'

The firing point on the IBS range provided a variety of positions to shoot from. First there was a low mound of earth with a dip in the middle. Then a post, with a log at right angles to it. Next came a fire trench, six feet by two by four deep, followed by a five-barred gate, a low wall, a sloping wooden surface simulating a roof, and a window set in brick. All these represented the kind of cover the soldier might use in action. And wherever possible he was expected to fire round, rather than over, his cover. Best of all was to fire through it, but that was difficult, and the kind of cover that made it possible was in fairly short supply at Brecon. As indeed it was in the Falkland Islands, where the ground had a lot in common with the ground they would be training over in the next few weeks. This was a point to bear in mind. It gave added piquancy to the exercise and added urgency to the need to learn how to make the best possible use of the cover available. Watch and shoot, watch and shoot . . .

Four at a time could use the range. Once they had fired from the fixed positions, they moved out in front of these and advanced down the range for the second part of the exercise. The shooting they had been doing at the firing point was defensive shooting. Now they would have to advance to the attack, independently, some fifty yards apart, against their individual enemy. He was a plywood figure – head, shoulders and chest – and he flipped up to right and to left of the advancing recruit within a fairly narrow arc. The controls for these figures were installed in a brick hut behind the firing points. One of the staff sat at the console and operated each figure as required. Once it flipped up, the recruit had to get off two shots rapid fire at it before throwing himself down behind the nearest piece of cover. Two shots. Double tapping, as it was called. Designed to make the enemy get his head down, if not actually kill him. You could kill him later, from cover, as he cautiously put his head up again to see where you'd got to.

'You nearly got him there. Well done, lad. Your shots were definitely in a much closer, tighter area around the target. Still more practice though, on the quick reaction technique. Practise swinging up, all right? Fire off two shots, then go quickly to ground.' They all took their turn and some of them were lucky enough to get Kevin Riley as their coach. Ward did. So did Hooper. And they set off down the range with 480's keenest critic behind them. 'Come on. Down, down. Don't wave the rifle around like a flag, son! Watch and shoot, watch and shoot . . .'

The staff wore berets and yellow ear-defenders. The recruits were in combat gear, steel helmets, smocks, cam cream, webbing. Sergeant Riley stayed close to them, watched every move, advised, checked, criticised, nagged, congratulated. 'Aim. Wait. Up. Down. Watch your arc. Bang-bang. Stay put. Relax. Forget about that. Keep in the aim. Walk a bit faster. Down on your belly. Don't drag your weapon. Up. Down. Bang-bang. Good lad. Good shooting. Well done, son. Don't look at me. Look for the enemy. Keep your weapon in your shoulder. It should be keeping you alive!'

'It should be keeping you alive.' In various forms, this was a sentence that recurred frequently in the next two weeks. Killing the enemy was something that figured less prominently, less immediately, than this business of staying alive. And the way you stayed alive, en route to your objective, was by putting down fire on the enemy – bang-bang, double-tapping at him whenever he appeared. If he couldn't get his head up, he couldn't get his weapon up. So bang-bang, and dive for cover, then watch until his head came up again, and shoot. It was simple but not obvious. Vital but not instinctive. Fundamental but needed to be learnt. It also had to be practised over and over and over again. Watch and shoot, watch and shoot. And hope to God you didn't actually end up in real life like the guy in the next exercise, CQB, or Close Quarter Battle, where he had to go it alone up this stream, just him and an SMG, through an enemy ambush back to his company position way up on top of the hill.

Captain Dave Allen, the Range Officer, was in charge of these Fire and Manoeuvre exercises as they were called, and he briefed 480 carefully before they began. They had all been on the Individual Battle Range twice. They had practised the elements of the advance through enemy-held territory. They had learnt quick-reaction shooting, engaging a fleeting target – initially with two rounds – then going for cover. Today they would use the same technique under more realistic conditions on a live firing range. It would be difficult, extremely knackering. The ground was uphill, rough, there wasn't much cover, but the principles were exactly the same as yesterday.

'Every time an enemy appears, engage him with two rounds – it's more accurate, double-tap, all right? Just one thing different today. There will be somebody with an effects weapon firing on the flank, into the water or the bushes – to add a touch of realism. All right? You've got two magazines and you've got to get back up to the top of the hill as quick as you can.'

The IBSR had been a doddle compared with this. There you had a bit of time to look round and get yourself sorted out so that, when the target flipped up, you just dropped yourself down behind the handy bits of log or fencing the staff had thoughtfully provided you with. Different here, it was. The only cover available was what nature had left lying around – a pile of rocks, the bank of a stream, or a scrubby old bit of bush that wouldn't have kept a mosquito off you, let alone an enemy bullet. Luckily, mind, there weren't any enemy bullets about just yet. Only flip-up cutouts and one of the staff banging away behind you with an SLR. Hard work, that was. Put a foot wrong up that effing stream, and you'd be arse over tit among the boulders taking your effing knee-cap off.

'There he is! Look, there he is!'

Bang-bang!

'Come on, quicker, quicker! And when the enemy shows himself I want that weapon in the shoulder, right? You'll hit nobody from down there. Right. Push on, push on. Keep low, good footholds, and keep looking ahead as well.'

Up came another cutout. Bang-bang, and down you went behind a bush. No effing good there. Captain Allen didn't like it. So he started putting the boot in, he did, kicking you into the stream, down behind the bank. 'Get down, down! You're out in the open up there. I'm trying to save your life, son, remember? No point lying on top of cover like that. Because all you're doing is giving him a chance to get the medal you're after, understand?'

One after the other, Captain Allen took them up the stream, with the SMG, patient, encouraging, driving, coaxing. 'Bear those points in mind, son. That was a good exercise. You did well.'

Apart from when you were up on that bank, and hearing the dead man's click, as they called it, when the magazine ran out. Nasty feeling, that. Even nastier for your mate if he was out in the open doing a leg while you were supposed to be giving him covering fire. Click, click. And suddenly a deadly hush. Deadly for your mate at any rate, if he didn't hit cover fast enough.

That was the next exercise. Live pairs. Two by two, up another bit of river where the cover was thicker. Leap-frogging forward, one giving covering fire while the other moved. But still the same principle, shooting

Captain Baird debriefs a section after an attack.

at the enemy to keep his head down. That was enough for the time being, anything else was a bonus. The vital thing was never to get a dead man's click while your mate was out in the open. And how could you stop that happening? How could you be sure your magazine wasn't empty? By counting the shots you'd let off, of course!

By counting the shots. It sounded all right. An SLR magazine held twenty rounds. If every time you fired you fired twice, then all you had to do was count up to ten and there was no problem. Except – as Scrumpy Barrett said – he'd got it all in his mind what he was going to do when he got out there, then all of a sudden he forgot it all. He was just running, and he didn't know what he was doing. Counting rounds was the last thing to cross his mind – until, at the very end, he ran out of ammo altogether and the officer said:

'What are you going to do?'

Bang-bang, went Scrumpy's mate.

'Think, think!'

Barrett dug down hard into what he'd been told.

'Think, think! What are you going to do?'

Suddenly, amazingly, he came up with something. 'Bayonets . . .'

Above: A Fire and
Manoeuvre exercise.

'Bayonets! Good idea, get it out! When he starts firing make a beeline
for that tree, all right? That one.' Bang-bang! 'Come on. Let's go.'

Scrumpy had been congratulated. He had done well. If you were out of
ammo, you had to do something about it. Like fix a bayonet, pick up a
brick, your shovel, anything. OK. That was good thinking. Except for one
thing, said Taff Hunt with a grin. When he fixed bayonets, he forgot his
barrel was boiling hot . . . 'Show 'im your skin on the end of it, Scrump!'

Well, these things happened. What you weren't supposed to do on any
account, at that particular stage of the proceedings, was what Fleming and
Tattum and one or two others did when they were advancing up the range
with the GPMG. Captain Allen was with them as they ran forward – could
easily have been in front of them at the time. On this exercise, when you
were running, it was your mate who was supposed to do the firing, not you.
'Stop, stop! Don't you ever, ever fire on the run again. I have not taught
you that, you have not been taught it these last three days, so don't do it, all
right?'

Captain Allen's anxiety was only too understandable. There were times
when you all felt frightened that your mate's covering fire was coming too
close, cutting across you as you ran. In his case, said Hunt with a teasing
grin, he just jumped over the bullets – well no, not really, the other guy's

Left: Craddock gives
covering fire with the
GPMG.

instructor was watching him, telling him when to stop, but all the same you hoped the other bloke was switched on, that was all, so that all of a sudden you didn't run into a volley of shots.

That was what worried you on exercise. In action, the opposite was likely to be even more worrying. Your mate's empty magazine, his stoppage, could mean you were out in the open when the enemy got their heads up. And vice versa. So if you had a stoppage, you shouted 'Stoppage!' at the top of your voice. And if you had an empty magazine, you shouted 'Magazine!' to warn your mate not to move until you'd cleared that stoppage or changed that magazine just as fast as you could.

'We want that magazine out and on the weapon straight away, and the weapon back in action. Because his life depends on it. You understand that?'

'Sir.'

'You do understand that, don't you?' said Captain Allen quietly. 'We're not just playing a game.'

That was on 9 June, the day before 3 Para began their attack on Mount Longdon. But it was still a bit hard for 480 Platoon to haul in such thoughts – as the jargon had it – and actually grasp the fact that in a few weeks' time they might be doing this for real. In any case, the present was so action-packed, they were working so hard, they had no energy to spare for thinking about the future. They got up at six, worked all day till nine or ten at night, then when they got back to camp they had their boots and trousers and kit to clean – it could take half an hour just getting that cam cream off – and it was usually a good twelve o'clock before they finally got their heads down. Mind you, they weren't complaining. They were enjoying it here, they felt they were achieving something, even if it was all a bit compressed. But then, everything other platoons did in three weeks they were having to do in two, so it wasn't surprising they were doing the extra in the time they would normally have had free at night.

The Fire and Manoeuvre exercises went on for most of the week. Then came FIBUA – or Fighting in Built-up Areas. This was not a live exercise. The kind of close-quarter shooting involved ruled that out. The ricochets were too dangerous for a start. But the realism of this exercise was added to by the use of thunderflashes to simulate hand-grenades.

They attacked in sections, one half putting down covering fire while the other half went up to the house and flattened themselves against the outside walls. Then grenades went in through the windows and, once they had exploded, the section stormed in. That was the theory anyway. Corporal Slater had to stop some of his men bursting through the front door before the bomber had done his work. It was always the same principle, though. Part of the section put down covering fire while the others moved. Inside a house, this principle was harder to apply as there was less room for manoeuvre. So the grenade was a kind of advance covering fire. It killed any enemy exposed to it, and drove the less determined out into the open where those of the section covering the house were ready to deal with them.

Once inside the house, getting on to the landing was the next major problem. Especially if someone had left what looked like a corrugated-iron deep-freeze half-way up the stairs. And though your section commander, Corporal Priestley, might be urging you to get it effing moving, it was all very well for him to talk, as he wasn't the one actually tangling with this lump of jagged metal! More bursts from the SMG. Figures silhouetted in the doorway that led to the back kitchen. Smoke, flame, the crackle of fire, and they were up the stairs, the whole lot of them, blasting their way into the master bedroom.

Now they had to be ready for the counterattack. That was the time when you could get caught off guard, just after you'd cleared the house. There was the temptation to relax, have a fag, take it easy for a moment. That was when the enemy grenades could start coming in through the windows, followed by bursts from his SMGs. So you had to catch him as he was forming up down a side street, or coming at you over the fence and up the garden path.

'Stay away from the windows till you're given rapid fire! Right? And I want effing everything you've got left, the lot – OK?' Those that still had some, clipped on fresh magazines. 'Rapiiiiiiiiiid . . . fire! Come on. Come on. Keep it going.'

This exercise was part of their CRO training: Counter Revolutionary Operations. But though its most likely application might be against urban guerillas, it was also preparation for the kind of bloody house-to-house fighting 1st Airborne Division got engaged in at Arnhem. The sort of thing everyone was hoping would not be necessary in Port Stanley. When the bullets were live and the thunderflashes high-explosive grenades, the casualties could be very high.

That weekend 480 went up on to a plateau in the Beacons and began to dig in for a defensive exercise. But first the sections had to be sited and shown their place in the scheme of things. A defensive position is carefully designed to bring maximum fire to bear on any attacking enemy force, but in order not to endanger your own troops each formation has to have its arcs of fire, as they are called, clearly indicated. So the Captain told the Corporals and the Corporals told the men.

'Directly to our front, there is a small copse on the top of the spur, see? The right-hand edge of that is your left of arc . . .'

Corporal Slater passed the information on to his men and warned them they'd better get it clear in their heads because the platoon commander was coming round in a minute and would be wanting them to tell him exactly where their arcs were. And Stirling was having a bit of trouble sorting it all out.

'What's your right of arc, Stirling?'

'The flagpole, Corporal?'

'Bollocks. You're not paying attention. It's your job to listen when I'm explaining things to you.'

Stirling stared glumly into the distance. Bushy-top trees. Three o'clock from the flagpole. Right-angle drive between two banks, leading down to that triangular wood, bottom left. It was true. He didn't know his arcs. He didn't know his arcs from his elbows. But Nick Moy did. Moy had been listening. He could explain their arcs to the platoon commander with a bit of confidence instead of humming and hawing about it . . .

That first night was spent mainly digging in. In theory a fire trench should be dug whenever they were close to the enemy and not moving for at least two hours. Its vital statistics were six feet long by two feet wide by four feet deep, and it would hold two men. Bigger ones could be dug as well, of course. Sergeant Riley felt all trenches should hold at least three men. In his eyes, the trouble with a two-man trench was that, if one man got his head blown off, the other tended to lose interest in the proceedings and cease to be of any military use to the rest of the section. So it was better to start off with three men in order to counter such an eventuality.

The kind of job that is only done in training – filling in trenches after the defensive exercise.

They were also expected to dig a shelter – which meant covering one end of the trench with logs and putting some of the earth on top to give overhead cover and a place for a man to sleep when off-duty. Some of the turf was then put back on as part of the camouflage. Which was why they had to be so careful cutting the turf before they started digging their fire-trench.

It was very hard work. The ground was stony and they needed a pick to break it up before setting to work with the spade. But everybody understood the importance of getting below ground level if they wanted to stay alive in battle, so there was no griping. There was no award for digging trenches, but everyone agreed that, if there had been one, there would have been no argument about who should have had it. Butler's work-rate was astonishing. He might not have been very well up on MBEs when the adjutant quizzed him on the subject but he certainly knew what to do with a pick and spade. Even the moles would have been impressed. Alternately hacking and shovelling, he sank steadily below the surface of the plateau they were on.

At last the work was done. Their bodies aching from the labour and grimed with dirt, it was time for some to watch while others slept. SLRs and GPMGs resting on the parapet in front of them, the sentries stared out into the summer night. Dark clumps of cloud were piled high on the horizon. The moon shone palely through. Owl hoots gave way gradually to the first twitterings of the dawn chorus. 480 Platoon were well dug in and ready to meet an enemy attack. But none came. The digging was the point of that particular exercise. Just as practising a withdrawal was the point of the one they did the following night.

As dawn broke twenty-four hours later, Corporal Baker's section were making their way up a track beside a stream. One, two, three men – then a break. Four, five, six – and that was all. The other three had lost touch, been left behind in the dark somewhere during the withdrawal.

Corporal Baker got the remnants of his section down into a ditch. They were doing a withdrawal out of contact with the enemy, as this particular exercise was called, but if they hung about much longer for the others it would turn into a withdrawal *in* contact, because the enemy were pushing right on their tails now, and if they weren't careful they were going to get bumped. What was happening now, he told them, was all down to the laziness of a particular person in the rifle group, there in the ditch. As a result the gun team had been lost, hadn't they, Butler?

The dawn chorus was getting stronger. Blackbirds and thrushes were in full throat now. A cuckoo joined in. Butler hung his head in shame as the odd sheep began to bleat. 'Right,' said Corporal Baker, 'same order of march. Let's go.' With a soft creak of equipment, a faint clump of boots, they moved off up the road, the sun just starting to rise behind them. Sights at 300, weapons in the shoulder, observing their arcs. They should be able to keep that pace up all day. Not just for a couple of miles in the morning,

Left: *Craddock, Fleming and Ward listen to a briefing before an attack.*

Right: *Some of Corporal Baker's section who didn't get left behind.*

Below: *Corporal Priestley points the way.*

but all day – just a steady shuffle. The withdrawal exercise had gone off very well, apart from that bit where they had lost the gun team.

But when they got back for the debriefing and Butler tried to take the blame, Captain Allen wasn't interested. He didn't care who was to blame. He just wanted to ram home the lesson, that was all. It was the responsibility of everybody within the section to know where everybody else was. Nevertheless Corporal Baker felt it was more Butler's fault than anybody else's. Butler hadn't got left behind, had he? The person who was link man between the rifle section and the gun group was always telling Butler to come up, wasn't he?

The three missing members of the section were found eventually. Hunt, Ward and Craddock. Corporal Baker allocated ten per cent of the blame to Ward. He had been second-in-command of the section in that particular phase and should have kept in touch with Butler too. He couldn't just expect to lay there and forget about everybody else. Even if he did have his arcs to face, it was his job to keep looking out to see if the rest of the section was still there.

Hunt was grinning while Corporal Baker was ticking Ward off. The missing trio had already had their own inquest into what had happened. Ward reckoned he hadn't fallen asleep, but Taff reckoned he must have done. And what did the rest of the section think had happened to them? Taff grinned. Thought they'd sold the GPMG for transport, they did, and legged it back to Brize. All right at Brize. You got a lot of NAAFI breaks.

The second week of Advanced Wales was mainly section-in-the-attack. First, dry runs to practise it, then with live rounds up on the range. Again the principle remained the same. Some fired while the others ran. Two at a time, a quick dash forward and into cover, until the section had leapfrogged close enough to put in the assault on the enemy position. Fighting through, that was called – and the assault group had to fix bayonets for it. They also had to remember to take them off afterwards – didn't they, Hooper? – in case they were counterattacked or came under fire from an enemy position some distance away. The SLR was less accurate with the bayonet fixed.

But suddenly such details became less urgent. The Argentines had surrendered. With Paras, Marines, Guards and Gurkhas closing in on them, they had very sensibly decided to call it a day. So even if 480 did get out there they would have missed all the fighting. Advanced Wales had become an exercise once more, interesting, necessary, but not the final dress rehearsal for the real thing they had been psyching themselves up for. They finished the week with platoon attacks. Lots of smoke going down from the two-inch mortar, lots of blanks blazing as they closed in on their target. Before that, however – at some point during the defence exercise – Andy Cunningham was unfortunate enough to have another Negligent Discharge. On the GPMG for a change.

Bang-bang-bang-bang! 'Cunningham! What are you doing, Cunningham? What do you think you're doing?'

It did not help him a great deal at the course assessment. According to his section commander, Corporal Slater, it made people very wary about moving behind him when he had a round up the spout. He was a nice lad, keen, interested and tried hard, but he did have this unfortunate habit where his weapon-handling was concerned. And his fitness still let him down from time to time. He really needed to do another week of revision before he'd be ready to go to the battalion. He was all right on defence. He had dug his trench well, and he'd had a hard one to dig. But it was more weapon-handling he needed. More live firing to build up his confidence.

So Cunningham was given another week at Brecon with 482 Platoon. He wasn't the only one either. Four of the back-squads went with him, plus Birrell and Hooper. In Birrell's case it was the defence phase that had let him down. It was too much for him, he couldn't cope and he got a bit demoralised. As for Hooper . . .

'That's mine, sir,' said Corporal Slater, like Prospero claiming Caliban.

It seemed to Captain John Baird as if his corporal was a bit depressed about it. Corporal Slater explained why. Hooper's reaction to any order given him was non-existent. His fitness was atrocious. His idea of standing-to was to rest his rifle on the bullet-stop and stand in the trench with his hands in his pockets. To send him to the battalion until he'd done some additional training would be very unfair to the section commander who got him.

John Baird did not disagree with this judgement. What did the others think? Well, some thought he could be described as plant life. Others felt that was going too far. He was some kind of animal all right, but possibly extinct. The brain certainly was. At the same time, they mustn't forget he had been one of the best on the SMG range. Also on the CQB range with the SLR. Well, to start with at any rate. But once he'd got that stoppage he had gone to pieces. He couldn't adapt, said Baird. Simply couldn't adapt. He'd have to go back with Birrell and the rest.

Of the others, Stirling was a scrape pass only. He was still suspected of being fly, and from that unfortunate impression all evil seemed to stem. For instance, his exemplary speed in getting to the washroom or to the head of the scoff-queue was seen as a vice instead of a virtue. The cooperative way in which he was quick to produce boot polish if an NCO needed some was seen as toadying. And even the expression on his face was thought to reveal resentment at being given an order. Whereas a wide-eyed look in most people would be considered a mark of enthusiasm, in Stirling's case it meant: 'Why me? Why ask me?' There was a general question-mark over his whole attitude and personality, and it was decided that another talking-to was in order for Private Stirling. Luckily for him, nobody mentioned the fact that he had also been in the TA. Had they done so, that would probably have knocked his E down to an F and meant temporary back-squadding with Birrell and Hooper.

Most of the others got a C. Barrett and Tattum got C plus. Melvin got B minus. O'Hare and Fleming got B, and Stoner did best of all and got B plus. Fleming might have got B plus too, but it was felt his previous military experience in the TA gave him an advantage over Stoner, and therefore Stoner deserved to score a little higher.

Corporal Priestley, their section commander, was very enthusiastic about both Fleming and Stoner. Fleming was the perfect soldier who passed on everything he knew to the others and deserved a big pat on the back for it. As for Stoner, he picked up things so fast, he seemed to be reading his corporal's mind. And when he'd been acting second-in-command of the section he'd anticipated every need and command. Really keen, he was. Really wanted to be a soldier.

They were also very impressed with O'Hare's performance. Not only had he taken everything in and worked very hard, but he actually enjoyed soldiering, said Corporal Baker, his section commander. There weren't many recruits you could say that for – not when they were doing their basic training anyway. Corporal Baker said he'd have O'Hare in his section in the battalion, if it was next week – and everyone had to agree that was the acid test, really.

So that left Fleming, O'Hare and Stoner as candidates for Best Recruit. What happened in the next few weeks might tip the scale in one or other's direction. The staff were now left with the job of deciding who was to be awarded the Spender Trophy for Most Improved Recruit. Borland had won it on Basic Wales. Who did they want to give it to this time?

14 Normandy and After

They decided to give the award to Barrett. He was a bit slow, sometimes, but he had grafted hard on defence, he understood more of the section work than he used to, and he was improving all the time. That was what the Trophy was all about.

With that, the assessments were at an end. All they had to do was announce the results and they could pack their bags and be back in Aldershot for the weekend. It was then that they got an order that changed these plans. They were all to stay down at Brecon for a third week. 480 would not be going to the Falklands now. The 2nd and 3rd Battalions would soon be home. So those recruits who had been temporarily back-squadded proceeded to join 482 as planned, while the rest brushed up on section and platoon attacks and anything else they had previously had to skimp. Then, at the end of the week, Cunningham and Birrell rejoined the platoon and they all returned to Aldershot, leaving Hooper to follow on later.

With the conflict at an end in the South Atlantic, 480's future postings were yet to be decided. Would they go to the 2nd and 3rd Battalions as replacements regardless of the preferences they had expressed? Or would some be going to 1 Para as well? For the time being that decision was left in abeyance. There was plenty of time before they passed out. Another three weeks. All the loose ends could be tidied up by then, including such things as what was to happen to Cunningham as a result of his second Negligent Discharge. This time the offence could not be left to his company commander to deal with. He would have to go before the CO of the Depot, Lieutenant-Colonel Brewis.

The Colonel tempered judgement with mercy and fined him £150. The last time he had done it, he had been warned that something much worse might happen if he repeated the offence. What exactly passed between Cunningham and his Colonel was not revealed, but no doubt it was made very clear to him that third time would not be lucky in his case.

Meanwhile, the platoon had been catching up with some of the skills that had been allowed to go rusty during their six weeks at Brize and at Brecon. For a start their drill had lost its sharpness and their barrack-blocks had a dowdy air. Sergeant Riley felt the time had come to stop the rot. It was clearly time he applied his technique for developing their aggressive fighting spirit. As a result they were all soon hating him even more than usual, as they attacked the washrooms, dustbin, floors and windows with mops, brushes and wire-wool. Had to make the place fit to live in, didn't they? Had to get their drill up to scratch if they were hoping to pass out in three weeks' time. Because – as he had told them before – not only did Bullshit Baffle Brains, but Prior Preparation and Planning Prevented Piss-Poor Performance. And the last thing they wanted on their Pass-Out Parade was a Piss-Poor Performance, wasn't it?

Nobody would have dreamed of disagreeing with him, even if they had been allowed to. The Pass-Out Parade was something they were all looking forward to. Their parents, their relatives, their friends and their girls were coming to that. It was their big day. The band would be playing. The Red Devils free-fall team would put on a show for them. There would be ballooning on Queen's Parade. There would be drinks and a meal in the canteen for all who wanted it. About nine in Birrell's party, he'd calculated, though he didn't plan to pay for more than six!

Before that there was another formal event taking place. Airborne Forces Day fell on 4 July, but with two of the battalions still in the Falklands, and the Regiment and the relatives mourning their dead, it was not considered the moment for a full-scale celebration of the Regiment's forty-second anniversary. There would therefore be no parade or march-past of members of the Parachute Regimental Association as was usually the case. The day's events would be restricted to sideshows and static displays in the sports field at Browning Barracks, and would conclude with the band and drums of the Junior Company, The Parachute Regiment, Beating Retreat.

480 Platoon's part in the proceedings was to provide waiters for the Regimental Association's Social that evening. The walls of the Gym had been draped with old parachute canopies to give it a suitably festive air. Those celebrating the occasion would be the veterans and their relatives and friends; and before the proceedings began, Sergeant Major McNally briefed the recruits on their duties. The veterans, he said, were not all paragons of virtue, but made up – like the rest of the human race – of a variety of personalities. Some were extremely nice and polite, whereas others could be cantankerous. 480, however, would remain nice and polite whatever the provocation, would on no account drink any intoxicating liquor, and would come off duty whenever the veterans decided they had had enough and wanted to go home to bed. Any questions? Then draw a tray and a napkin and a ten-pound float from the table over there and get stuck in.

480 were not thrilled to be acting as waiters. It was not the kind of role they had envisaged while pumping bursts of GPMG fire into snap-up enemy figures down at Brecon. But they got on with it without much complaint – even Scrumpy Barrett, who had taken part in the Battle of

Woking Disco some nights before in the company of Hunt, O'Hare and Birrell and was still looking and feeling rather the worse for wear. It had all begun when Pete O'Hare suspected someone of deliberately throwing beer over his back. On being quizzed about this the youth in question had gathered together some of his friends, and in the ensuing mêlée Scrumpy had got a beer-glass laid across the bridge of his nose while Taff Hunt had been thrown through a plate-glass window. Amazingly, he had stepped back through it again without having suffered any great damage, and though one of Scrumpy's eyes was still very bloodshot, it was apparently looking a great deal better than it had done earlier in the week. Taff claimed they were all absolutely guiltless. They had been picked on by a gang of yobbos. But since Sergeant Major Lucey had warned them of the unpopularity of squaddies in the nearby towns, nobody offered very much sympathy.

The veterans appreciated that 480 were not exactly over the moon at having to act as waiters, but they tried not to let it spoil their evening. After all, how to make the best use of airborne forces was a problem that had never been satisfactorily resolved in World War 2. And most of the older men who had come down to Aldershot that day on their annual pilgrimage had sometimes wondered whether the best use had always been made of them and the valuable aircraft and gliders that were needed to take them into battle.

The invention of a new weapon does not necessarily coincide with the new military thinking required to make proper use of it. The tank was invented in 1916 but twenty-three years elapsed before Liddell Hart's ideas about the use of mass armoured formations were put into effect by the Germans. By chance the Germans were also successful in their initial airborne attacks, but their near-failure in Crete demonstrated that a great deal more thinking was needed before the use of airborne forces was properly understood and became an integral part of military tactics.

In 1944, when the Allies were planning their forthcoming invasion of Europe, there was considerable argument about how the allied airborne forces should be used in France. The RAF air commander, Air Chief Marshal Leigh-Mallory, had advised against their being used at all on the grounds that they would suffer at least eighty per cent casualties. On the other hand, General Marshall, the US Army Chief of Staff, wanted all three airborne divisions – the 82nd and 101st American and 6th British – dropped *en masse* near Paris at the same time as the seaborne landings took place in Normandy. Fortunately less ambitious plans than his prevailed, and it was decided to use them in a close-support role near the Normandy shoreline – with specific targets like coastal batteries, bridges and road junctions to seize and, where necessary, destroy.

In December 1943 the British 1st Airborne Division had been brought back to England in order to take part in the invasion. It was subsequently decided to give the task to the newly-formed 6th Airborne Division, and keep the 1st in reserve for any follow-up drops that might be necessary in the days and weeks following the invasion. When, on 6 June 1944, this became apparent, 1st Airborne Division were not at all pleased about it. They had not volunteered to join the airborne forces in order to spend their time hanging about Lincolnshire – however welcoming and friendly the local population might be. But they had to admit 6th Airborne Division seemed to have made a pretty good job of things – especially as it was the first time they had been in action as airborne troops.

They had, however, profited from the experience of others. Their commander, Major-General Richard Gale, had made a careful study of all previous German and British airborne operations and learnt the lessons offered by all of them. The attack on Eben Emael, for instance, was a classic example of a glider 'coup de main' assault on a fortress. The German seizure of the bridge over the Corinth Canal had demonstrated how parachute and glider troops could be used in combination to seize a vital crossing-point. And the disastrous inaccuracy of the Sicily drops convinced 6th Airborne of the need to evolve a path-finding unit whose job it would be to mark out the DZs and LZs on which the rest of the aircraft could home.

HRH Princess Elizabeth watches a training drop near the wing of a Hamilcar glider, May 1944.

Eventually 6th Airborne Division were given all the tasks they had anticipated in their training. In order to secure the left flank of the British seaborne landings north of Caen, they were asked to capture and destroy a gun battery and a number of bridges; seize undamaged several more bridges; and prevent the movement of enemy reserves into the area until the seaborne divisions had reached their objectives.

Inevitably there were not enough aircraft available to deliver the whole division in one wave. Since the Americans had two divisions of their own to drop on the right flank of their beachheads, all their transport squadrons were fully occupied. So it was decided that the two Parachute Brigades would fly in during the night before the invasion, and the Air-Landing Brigade would be taken in on the afternoon of D-Day. There was one hitch in the preparations. A few weeks before the operation began the Germans started erecting stakes, made from tree-trunks, in every conceivable spot in northern France that gliders or parachutists might choose to land. To counter this the planners decided that the first gliders in would carry sappers whose job it would be to demolish the stakes and clear the LZs for those who came after them. The problem was irritating but not insuperable.

The bridge over the Caen Canal seized in the early hours of 6 June. The 5th Parachute Brigade was given the task of capturing and holding the bridges over the Caen Canal and the River Orne. Just after 2300 hours on 5 June the force that was to seize the bridges set off in six Horsa gliders,

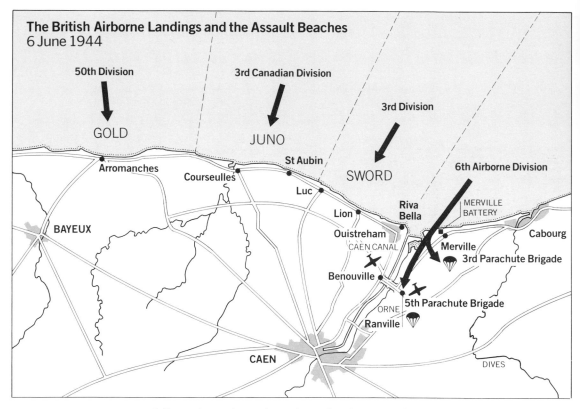

**The British Airborne Landings and the Assault Beaches
6 June 1944**

followed nearly an hour later by the rest of the brigade. After a bumpy passage across the Channel, the gliders released their tow-ropes 5000 feet above the mouth of the Orne and began to descend silently towards their targets. The bridge over the Orne was taken unopposed. At the Canal bridge German troops opened up with submachine-guns as the assault party leapt from the Horsas and sprinted towards their objective. After a brief battle the few German survivors fled to raise the alarm, but without destroying the bridge. Meanwhile the rest of the brigade were parachuting in on the DZ near Ranville, ready to defend themselves and the bridges from the inevitable counterattacks.

The 3rd Parachute Brigade had a more destructive mission, with two separate tasks. One was to blow four rail and road bridges over the River Dives on their eastern flank and so prevent enemy reinforcements from passing to the south of their positions and driving on towards Caen. The other was to destroy the coastal battery at Merville no later than thirty minutes before daylight, by which time the invasion fleet would be off the beaches and exposed to the battery's guns. The 9th Parachute Battalion had been given this target and had carefully rehearsed the attack in great secrecy near Newbury, where a mock-up of the battery area had been built. But when the time came for the attack proper, many things went wrong. Only a quarter of the battalion reached the target. The gliders

Horsa gliders on an LZ in Normandy.

carrying the sappers with the breaching and demolition equipment crashed or landed elsewhere. But the main party blew lanes in the minefields with Bangalore torpedoes and stormed the gun emplacements. Out of the 130 defenders, more than a hundred were killed or wounded. The guns were then spiked as planned with Gammon bombs and the triumphant victors lit yellow flares to announce their success.

The rest of the brigade reached their objectives too, though again, like the 9th Battalion, the 1st Canadian was widely scattered. Not all the bridges were blown, due to a shortage of explosives at the critical point, but the battalions dug in and prevented enemy penetration.

A feature of the Normandy attack was the use of the Hamilcar for the first time. A huge glider, with a wing-span of 110 feet, it could carry a load of $7\frac{1}{2}$ tons, which usually meant in practice either a light Tetrarch or Locust tank, or an anti-tank gun together with its towing vehicle. The anti-tank guns would be essential equipment to fight off enemy counterattacks, and plans had been made to fly in additional guns if necessary and drop them by parachute. When daylight came, the counterattacks began, but by early afternoon No. 1 Commando, the first of the seaborne troops, reached the bridges led by a solitary piper. A few hours later the Air-Landing Brigade arrived in 250 gliders, bringing valuable heavy equipment, transport and guns.

By D-Day plus 1 the whole of the division was deployed and in action against the Germans, forming a determined, if sometimes precarious, barrier between the enemy and the invasion beaches. Its total casualties in Normandy came to nearly 4500, out of whom 821 were killed. But there was no doubt of the importance of the division's contribution to the invasion. Every objective it was given it took. The shield it put up on the British flank was never broken.

In many respects the attack carried out by 6th Airborne Division in Normandy was the most successful of World War 2. Even the German attack of May 1940 – in spite of its brilliant achievements at Eben Emael – could not be counted so successful overall. The attack on the Dutch airfields did not go according to plan, and generally the casualties in Holland were extremely heavy. This was not the case in Normandy. Although some of the troops went astray, the accuracy of the drop on the whole was extraordinarily good, and the manoeuvring of the gliders by night to land within a few yards of their targets was quite exceptional. If only for the part they played in the success of the Normandy landings, the British airborne forces totally justified their existence and the heavy demand they made on resources.

Glider troops dug in at their LZ in Normandy.

Bill Collard of the 3rd Battalion was in hospital in Lincoln with malaria on D-Day, 6 June, and it was not until quite late in the day that he discovered the invasion had begun. At first he was furious, imagining that 1st Airborne had left without him. So it was something of a relief when he found that 6th Airborne had been given the job instead. It was also faintly irritating, as it was for the rest of the division. They had been back in England six months and had been training hard for this moment. It was rather irksome to discover that they, the veterans of North Africa, Sicily and Italy, had been passed over in favour of a division in which many of the troops had not heard a shot fired in anger until they landed in Normandy. However, since the Germans would clearly make the invasion of Fortress Europe a difficult operation, Bill and his comrades assumed it would not be long before 1st Airborne followed 6th Airborne into France on some other mission.

The airborne invasion of the South of France in August 1944 by units of the US 13th Airborne Division and the British 2nd Parachute Brigade Group.

Between 6 June and 10 September 1944 1st Airborne Division was briefed for sixteen different operations. But each of these was cancelled before take-off – usually because the target the operation was planned to seize was overrun by the unexpectedly rapid advance of the British and American ground forces. As a result many of the men in 1st Airborne

Division wrote to their COs asking for a transfer to a fighting unit, as they feared the war would be over before they got back into action. Their letters were received unsympathetically. They would see action, all right. It was just a matter of time, that was all. And when the sixteenth operation, labelled 'Comet', was programmed to take place for 8 September it looked as though this one would not be cancelled.

The final target of 'Comet' lay sixty miles behind the German lines. It was the bridge at Arnhem. Between it and the British lines lay several subsidiary targets, including the bridges at Grave and Nijmegen. The plan was daring and imaginative, and intended to end the war rapidly by funnelling the Allied armies across the bridges of the lower Rhine and out into the North German Plain, where British and American armoured divisions would be able to manoeuvre freely. 'Comet' planned to use the British 1st Airborne Division together with the 1st Polish Parachute Brigade to capture the various bridges between the British front line and Arnhem, but it very soon became clear that larger forces would be necessary to carve such a long corridor through German-occupied territory. It was therefore decided that two American Airborne Divisions would be used as well, the 82nd and 101st, who had fought in Normandy and were now waiting in reserve in their bases in England. Their task would be to seize the bridges at Eindhoven, Veghel, Grave and Nijmegen, while the British and the Poles concentrated on Arnhem. So when, after the cancellation of 'Comet', Bill Collard and his mates were once again sealed into their camp on Wednesday 13 September, and summoned on the Saturday to a briefing in the Town Hall at Spalding, they had a feeling it was going to be Arnhem again. It had to be Arnhem again. It was so far behind the British front line, there was no danger of it being overrun by Allied ground forces this time.

The new code-name for the attack on the bridges was 'Market Garden'. And though anxieties were already being expressed by some of the commanders about the difficulty of the operation, the men set off full of optimism. They had not heard of Lieutenant-General Browning's fear that they might be going a bridge too far. They were not aware that the Polish commander, Major-General Sosabowski, appalled by the complacency being shown at the briefings, felt sure they were heading for disaster. And as Bill Collard got ready to jump that sunny Sunday afternoon in September 1944, he was more concerned about getting out of the door before the aircraft got too low than he was about any potential opposition from the Germans. He was the last one out, he discovered later. His Dakota was too near the ground for any more to jump. His parachute opened, he released his equipment, and a moment later he was touching down. He sensed that somebody was firing, but knew it wasn't directed at him, and it was, to all intents and purposes, an unopposed landing. All round him the men of the 1st Parachute Brigade were getting clear of their chutes, opening con-

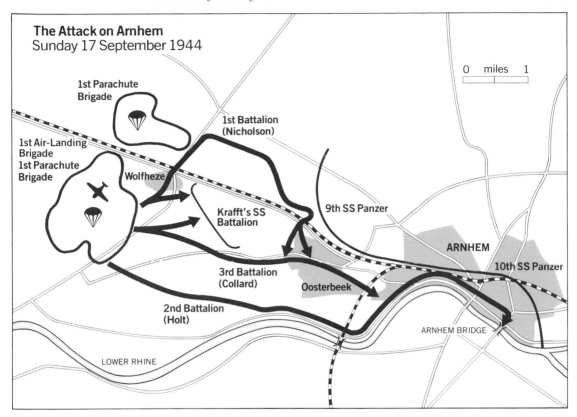

The Attack on Arnhem
Sunday 17 September 1944

0 miles 1

1st Parachute
Brigade

1st Battalion
(Nicholson)

1st Air-Landing
Brigade
1st Parachute
Brigade

Wolfheze

Krafft's SS
Battalion

9th SS Panzer

ARNHEM

10th SS Panzer

3rd Battalion
(Collard)

Oosterbeek

2nd Battalion
(Holt)

ARNHEM BRIDGE

LOWER RHINE

tainers, moving to their RV points. He could hear Frost's horn blowing, summoning the 2nd Battalion towards the yellow smoke. He headed for the 3rd Battalion's red smoke, filled as most men are after a successful parachute descent with the sense of euphoria that in his particular case made him feel he could take on a dozen German soldiers and beat them.

John Nicholson's landing was trouble-free too. The only hitch in his case was the disappearance of his bicycle, last seen floating away towards the river. But very soon he came across a Dutch lad prepared to lend him his own bicycle, so he was a fully-equipped runner once more. He loaded his gear on to the bike and set off on foot with the rest of the 1st Battalion towards their objective – the high ground on the northern outskirts of Arnhem, where they were to act as a protective screen against enemy counterattacks.

Bill Collard, meanwhile, had already been engaged in what was one of the earliest encounters with the Germans, the destruction of the occupants of a staff-car driving straight down the Arnhem–Utrecht road. In it was Major-General Kussin, the Arnhem town commander. It was first blood to the 3rd Battalion, but it wasn't long before Bill's section came under fire from the Germans who began to put up a fierce and unexpected resistance, slowing the battalion's advance to a crawl.

*Above: The 1st Airborne
Division drops at
Arnhem.*

*Right: Reinforcements
of men and supplies are
parachuted in.*

The same thing was now happening to the 1st Battalion on the northern route. They had run head-on into part of an armoured division, and in spite of their efforts they never succeeded in getting past or round the Germans in front of them. John Nicholson did not eat properly for a week. It was too much trouble to take his pack off, and it was largely the Benzedrine tablets that kept him going. Finally, after four days' bitter fighting in the forest, there were only eighteen men left in his company, and the 1st Battalion had given up all hope of reaching its objective. Now it was bent on hanging on to its positions in the north of Oosterbeek as best it could. And it was there that John was hit by a splinter from a mortar bomb in the small of the back. It felt, he said, as if one of those steel balls that demolition men use had smashed down on top of him – and that was the end of his part in the battle for Arnhem.

Bill Collard had been put out of action much sooner – early on the Monday afternoon, he thought, though it was difficult to be precise as all sense of time had long since gone. And he had got nearer the bridge than John Nicholson, marching on a direct line through Oosterbeek and fighting all the way. But as he turned a street corner, a German machine-gunner opened up on him and he went down, hit – as he discovered later – in the knee, though at the time he thought he had merely stumbled. It was only when he tried to get up that he realised he had been wounded, and like John was now out of the battle.

Ron Holt landed safely with the 2nd Battalion and moved quickly along the lower road into Arnhem and towards the bridge. On the way in, his platoon peeled off temporarily to fend off a German attack on the battalion's

A PIAT in position on the outskirts of Arnhem.

The bridge at Arnhem, showing the wreckage of the German armoured vehicles in the middle of the British positions on the north bank of the river.

left flank, then followed the others to the bridge. There he helped fight off the German armoured attack, before digging in on the embankment to the north of the bridge where he was eventually taken prisoner. His platoon commander, Lieutenant John Grayburn, was awarded one of the two Victoria Crosses won by the Parachute Regiment in World War 2. The other was also won at Arnhem by Captain Lionel Queripel of the 10th Battalion. Recently, two more VCs – also posthumous – have been awarded to men of the Regiment for acts of valour in the Falkland Islands campaign. Lieutenant-Colonel Herbert 'H' Jones, CO of 2 Para, won his when he led a frontal attack on two Argentinian machine-gun positions at Goose Green. Sergeant Ian McKay, of 3 Para, gained his on Mount Longdon when he went forward to knock out three Argentian trench positions with grenades.

The 1st Airborne Division had been asked to hold out at Arnhem for two days. Lieutenant-General Browning thought they might manage it for four. In the event they held out for nine. Of the 10,000 men who went into the battle, fewer than 3000 came out; 5000 – including 3000 wounded – were taken into captivity in Germany. John Nicholson, Bill Collard and Ron Holt were amongst these.

The fact that the operation did not achieve what its planners intended was no fault of either the 1st British Airborne Division or of the 1st Polish Parachute Brigade. They fought with outstanding gallantry. And, as is often the case with such defeats, it is Arnhem that is remembered as the greatest airborne assault of all time, rather than the Normandy landings or the successful Allied crossing of the Rhine on 24 March 1945.

That assault, Operation 'Varsity', involved the lifting of the British 6th and the US 17th Divisions in one single wave. Nearly 1700 planes and 1350 gliders carried more than 21,000 Allied troops over the Rhine in a fly-in that took two hours forty minutes. The German flak did great damage to the attacking formations, but by late afternoon all the objectives had been taken and the 2nd Army was streaming across the river. It was the last mass airborne attack of World War 2. And no airborne operation since then has ever involved anything like the same numbers.

Tugs with their Hadrian gliders ready to take off for the crossing of the Rhine, 24 March 1945.

Left: *US parachute troops land east of the Rhine.*

Right: *A Horsa glider comes in to land while US parachute troops clear the bushes for snipers. Both pictures were taken by Frank Capa.*

Left: *US parachute troops land east of the Rhine.*

Right: *A Horsa glider comes in to land while US parachute troops clear the bushes for snipers. Both pictures were taken by Frank Capa.*

Since 1945, British airborne forces have had a chequered career. From a strength of two divisions and one brigade in 1945, they have declined in numbers to the present three battalions of the Parachute Regiment, together with their supporting units from other arms. What the Regiment's future is likely to be after the distinguished and important role the 2nd and 3rd Battalions played in the Falklands remains to be seen. There are certainly some who would like to see its battalions re-formed as a brigade and kept intact as a rapid deployment force for use in NATO and other roles.

At the same time, the precise role of airborne forces in modern war has yet to be tested. A large-scale parachute attack against a sophisticated enemy – even by night – would seem to be an operation fraught with considerable difficulty. Nevertheless, virtually every nation in the world has seen fit to include some kind of parachute element in its armed forces – although very few of these troops have ever been used in their proper airborne role.

One exception to this – at least in the immediate postwar years – was the French army. While the British were cutting back their airborne forces in the late 1940s, the French were expanding theirs. On 16 September 1945 a French reoccupation force was parachuted into Laos as part of France's campaign to repossess her Indo-Chinese colonial territories. During the next nine years French parachute troops made more than 150 combat jumps into those territories. Some of the drops were small – a few dozen men parachuted in as an advance guard or in order to establish a base. Many drops, however, were of near-battalion strength, and as the war against the Vietminh forces approached its climax in 1953 the French had some sixteen battalions of parachute troops at their disposal.

Most of the drops were part of seek-and-destroy missions, usually

*French and Vietnamese
troops parachute in to
Dien Bien Phu,
November 1953.*

*French Paras inside the
perimeter of their base
at Dien Bien Phu two
weeks before the end.*

carried out in support of their ground forces. But in the autumn of 1953 the French decided to try a new tactic. They would stop the Vietminh offensive on Laos by establishing a large airborne base across their enemy's lines of communication, and so force him to the pitched battle the French believed they could win. On 20 November 1953, 4525 troops were parachuted into the area around Dien Bien Phu, and the battle began. What, however, had been intended as a trap for the Vietminh finally became a trap for the French. After a winter of bitter fighting, Ho Chi Minh's forces began their final assault on 12 March 1954. By this time the French were no longer able to use their airstrip to fly in reinforcements and supplies. So, on the following day – in a last desperate effort to counter the Vietminh attack – another 3500 troops were parachuted into Dien Bien Phu. To no avail. On 7 May the garrison was overwhelmed, and two months later the French left Indo-China for good.

While this colonial conflict was taking place, another war even more threatening to the peace of the world had come and gone. On 25 June 1950 North Korean forces crossed the 38th Parallel into South Korea, precipitating an East-West crisis. As an advanced guard to what would later become an international army, US forces landed at Inchon in support of the hard-pressed South Koreans. That October, as the Americans fought their way north, some 3000 troops of the US 187th Airborne Regimental Combat Team were dropped into the Sukchon district as part of an attempted cut-off operation. It was the first time in airborne history that large quantities of heavy equipment had been successfully dropped by parachute. Some months later, in March 1951, the 187th ARCT carried out a further large-scale operation, when some 3500 troops were dropped at Munsan. But a shortage of transport aircraft together with a shift to the use of helicopters for moving men about the battlefield put an end to further parachute operations in Korea.

A helicopter lift of US troops in Korea.

Since 1945, British airborne forces have carried out only one major parachute attack. In July 1956 President Nasser of Egypt announced his intention to nationalise the Suez Canal. As part of the Anglo-French response, on 5 November 1956 3 Para was dropped on to Gamil airfield near Port Said. The battalion flew in from Cyprus in Hastings and Valetta aircraft. None of these was shot down, though some were damaged by scattered anti-aircraft fire. Resistance on the ground was equally scattered – some units having little difficulty in seizing their objectives, while others had fierce, if usually brief, battles with determined Egyptian gunners. The following day the amphibious forces landed, and after the enforced cease-fire of 7 November the British airborne troops were withdrawn. Though the Suez campaign itself proved a political fiasco, there is no doubt that the Anglo-French parachute attack was a highly effective operation, demonstrating that – properly used – airborne forces could still play an important role in a modern army.

Men of A Company 3 Para land on El Gamil airfield, Port Said, 5 November 1956.

Certainly today's great powers think so. The Soviets have eight airborne divisions, the Chinese an estimated six, and the Americans one – which is maintained as part of a rapid deployment force. The role the Soviets have assigned to their airborne forces is reputedly disruptive and sacrificial – that is, they would be dropped on rear headquarters in order to disorganise their enemy's command centres. Otherwise they would be used as the British used them in the Falklands – as élite shock troops.

In Vietnam the Americans preferred to use helicopters to put their airborne troops into position. They were more manoeuvrable, less vulnerable and more adaptable than heavy transport planes like the C130 Hercules. That does not, however, rule out the employment of parachute troops in certain situations, where limited numbers of highly-trained men need to be put down at distances too great for helicopters, carry out their mission and then be evacuated, possibly by pick-up from an airstrip, or by ship-borne helicopters brought in as a follow-up. An example frequently quoted is the drop at Kolwezi in Zaire in May 1978 when a parachute regiment of the French Foreign Legion was sent in to rescue civilians.

Vietnamese parachute troops jump from US Air Force C123s during an operation against the Viet Cong, June 1963.

US Marines land from a C46 Sea Knight helicopter during an action against the Viet Cong, November 1966.

It is this sort of operation that is uppermost in the modern parachute officer's mind when he is asked how he envisages himself and his men being used. It certainly seemed to play a part in the planning of the exercise 480 Platoon were scheduled to carry out on their return from Brecon and after they had brushed up on one or two of their recently neglected skills.

It was the penultimate week of their course. Both 2 and 3 Para were due to fly in to Brize Norton on the following Tuesday. 480 Platoon would certainly not be needed in the Falklands as replacements now. A sense of anti-climax was in the air. Exercise Last Fence, as it was called, would help dissipate that feeling. It would also get them away from the cramping environment of the Depot for a few days and out in the fresh air. 480 Platoon were looking forward to it.

15 Crows into Toms

Captain Baird's Order to the Platoon informed them that they would be inserted by parachute drop into the islands of Snadlakfan. They would then march on their objective, and after the attack be extracted, first by helicopter and subsequently by a Hercules pick-up on a nearby airstrip.

As was customary with such exercises, it was the platoon commander's job to devise it, write the Narrative – as the background story was called – and issue all the necessary orders. As was also customary, approximate anagrams were popular and any similarities between places, people or events in real life were completely intentional. So when the Snadlakfans found themselves invaded without apparent warning by the Tengarans who lived in Southern Greenland, it was not unreasonable that a British Task Force should have been sent north to liberate the islands and islanders who bitterly resented the occupation of their home.

However, that was not the only thing at stake in Exercise Last Fence. The Tengarans had occupied the radar installation. It was 480's job to recover or destroy the highly secret and sensitive equipment it housed before the Tengarans realised exactly what they had in their possession and used it as a bargaining tool for the islands or, worse, sold the equipment to the Eastern Bloc.

Everything went according to plan. No one was hurt on the night jump. The attack on the objective was successful. The Tengarans – impersonated by 6 Platoon of the Junior Parachute Company – were driven off. Then, after repulsing a not entirely unexpected counterattack, 480 were eventually extracted by Chinook and whisked across the Downs to the Hercules pick-up point.

That night they slept in a nearby wood. Next morning they were taken off to the ranges for a practice anti-aircraft shoot with their GPMGs. The target aircraft were radio-controlled models which travelled at 100mph and proved disconcertingly difficult to hit. The guns were mounted on steel poles – as used in the Falklands, where they had been welded to the ships' decks – which helped to steady them. In spite of this, only one of the aircraft was shot down all morning – and that, to Tattum's horror, by a Marine of all people. As they were collecting up the spent cases, he took out some of his understandable irritation on his fellow Welshman, Taff Hunt. Trouble with these South Wales people, he jibed, was that they couldn't even speak Welsh properly. Taff retaliated by pointing out that at least he *sounded* Welsh. Tattum's accent owed more to Liverpool than to Snowdonia. But whether they came from north or south, the Welsh were doing a great deal better, said Taff, than the other nationalities in the platoon. According to his reckonings, two-thirds of them had stayed the course. The only Welshman to drop out so far was Healey, the guy who'd left in the first week. Others disagreed. What about Price and Woodcock? What about them? said Taff. Price came from Hereford and Woodcock lived in London, so no problem there.

While that argument raged, Scrumpy Barrett, who came from Somerset, could be heard maintaining that there was a hundred per cent pass rate for people from Somerset – just as there was for Whitehaven people, too, according to Pete O'Hare who came from Whitehaven. And what about the Scots? said a Scot. They were no doing so bad themselves, were they? Six out of the original ten still left. That was much better scoring than the English. True. True. But then, as one of the Englishmen pointed out, the Jocks had a pretty big incentive to stay the course. Look what happened to them if they failed. They had to go back to effing Jockland!

The banter went on. But Rod Stoner was not paying very much attention to it. He was getting married in Aldershot the following Saturday and was hoping he would not break any bones on the NBC jump that was taking place next day. It was their eleventh jump, and a most uncomfortable one. Wearing one of the Nuclear/Biological/Chemical protective suits on the ground was bad enough. Wearing it in the stuffy, cramped interior of a Hercules on one of the hottest days of the year was almost unendurable.

It was the first time any of the staff or a recruit platoon had done an NBC jump. So the procedures were new to all of them. But everything went off without a hitch. The distorted vision caused by the respirators they wore might make for bad landings, but Stoner's turned out perfectly all right. His fear of having to limp up the aisle with a leg in plaster had proved unfounded.

As a result of the wedding, 480's end-of-course Disco that Saturday night started quietly. But by the time the wedding party arrived to swell the numbers, everything was in full swing. During their six months in the army 480 Platoon had accumulated some £400 in the kitty so there was no shortage of food and drink. And though in some ways it was a pity to have the party almost a week before their pass-out, since they would be going straight on leave the following Friday there would be no time to have it then. Some had suggested having it on the Thursday evening. But the thought of still being legless on parade next morning soon put an end to that. Tonight was better. It was Sunday tomorrow. Those who got a skinful would have plenty of time to sleep it off.

Most of the final week was taken up with preparations for their pass-out parade, with a last brushing-up on the skills that would be required of them when they got to their battalions. As with every other stage of 480's course, the usually straightforward process of posting the trained recruits to their battalions had also run into snags. In view of the exceptional circumstances, various contradictory plans had been put forward. First that they would all be posted to the 1st Battalion in Northern Ireland. Then that they would all be going to the 2nd and 3rd Battalions. Now it had been decided that most of them would go to 3 Para, and a few to 2 Para. But meanwhile all of them would be temporarily attached to 1 Para, and spend their first few months as trained soldiers on active service in Northern Ireland. It was thought far better they should get a taste of life in an active battalion than spend their time as rear parties at the Depot while waiting for their own battalions to come back off their extended postwar leave.

During the final week they were put through a series of test exercises covering the whole range of their training. In theory it was still possible for someone to be back-squadded at this late stage and fail to pass out with the others. But it was rare for this to happen, and although there were some weaknesses in the weapon-handling skills, it was felt that as they concerned the whole platoon and not just individuals, revision in those areas could take place after 480 returned from leave and before going to Northern Ireland. Even the sluggish Hooper had been allowed back into the fold. And a temporarily blind eye was turned to Nick Moy's failure to complete an eight-mile battle march. Sergeant Riley wasn't too happy about that. Fitness was something you couldn't afford to let slacken off. It was a personal thing, a matter of self-discipline, and though Moy had some excuse – being only eighteen and one of the youngest in the platoon – Sergeant Riley felt he would still have to do something about it, because battle marches were a regular and important thing in the battalion. That was something the Falklands campaign had demonstrated only too well.

Suddenly it was Friday 16 July and 480 Platoon were about to march on to the Square for their Pass-Out Parade. They stood at ease behind the HQ block in their Suits, No. 2 Dress, wearing their Shirts Khaki and their Ties Khaki Braid. The slings on their SLRs were the new white plastic issue and gleamed brightly in the morning sunshine. Once again 480 were lucky with the weather. Back in the seventies, when Corporal Baker's platoon had passed out, it was raining so heavily they'd had to parade in the Gym. A right let-down that had been. Weren't even allowed to stamp their feet. And that was no good on your pass-out parade, where you wanted to be able to put a bit of swank into things. Or, as Company Sergeant Major Lucey explained: 'What we're looking for is style, a certain amount of panache, and confidence. Lock the arms at the elbow, swing those arms shoulder-high, pull them fully to the rear and brace the knee as the heel strikes the ground. Chins off the chest now. Right. Stand easy, we're going on . . .'

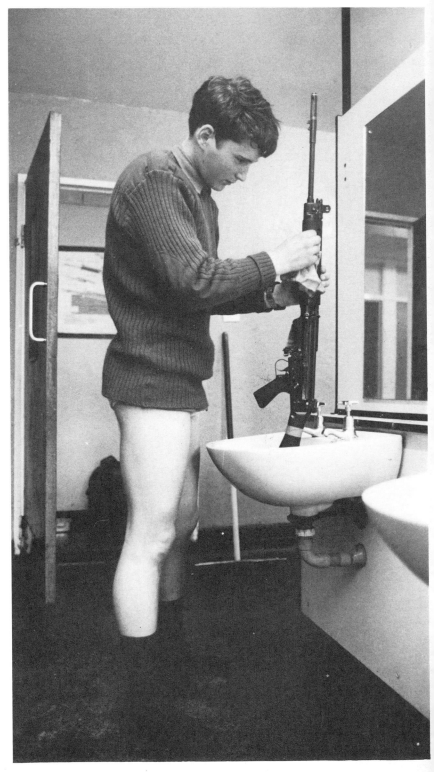

Preparing for the Pass-Out Parade.

Right: Robertson.

Opposite: O'Hare.

Page 220, top: Tattum (foreground) and Moy.

Page 220, bottom: Formed up ready to go on parade. Front rank, from left: Witton, Melvin, Hooper, Payne, Day, Ward, Copley, Tattum.

Page 221: Corporal Baker checks the turnout. Front rank, left to right: O'Hare, Moy, Mincher, Craddock, Hunt, Robertson.

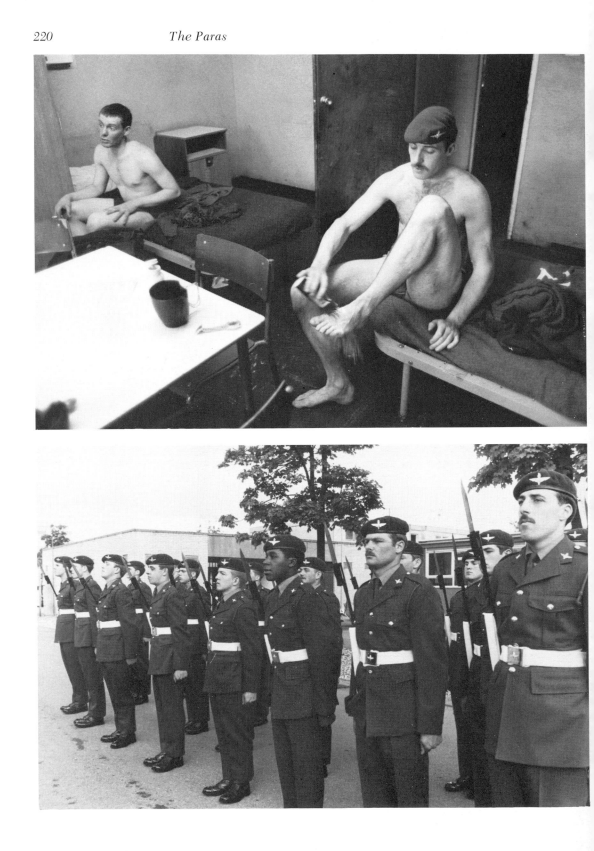

Opposite:
Top: *480 wheel to the left behind Captain Baird.*

Bottom: *Marching past the saluting base, giving the General the eyes right. Front rank, left to right: Sgt Riley, Stirling, Stoner, Birrell, Galasso, Barrett, Butler, Melvin, Cunningham, Cpl Baker.*

Above: *Major-General G.H.W. Howlett, OBE, MC, presents the awards for Champion Recruit and Champion Shots SLR and GPMG to (left to right) Stoner, Birrell and Butler.*

A moment later they came to attention. Then the Band of the 2nd Battalion the Parachute Regiment struck up a stirring march and 480 Platoon stepped out along the road towards the Square.

Since something had gone wrong at every critical moment in the course it seemed unlikely that 480 Platoon would get through anything as hazardous as the Pass-Out Parade without some disaster befalling them. But as time went on it began to look as if their bad luck had finally deserted them. They came to a satisfactory halt in the middle of the Square. They moved into review order with reasonable precision. They answered the General's questions with soldierly politeness. They marched past in moderately straight ranks, giving him the eyes-right almost as one man. And only a churl or a drill sergeant would have wanted to fault the smartness with which they presented arms for the General Salute. Indeed, Major-General Howlett, OBE, MC, who was taking the parade, congratulated them on the standard of their drill and turnout, saying that, as the present Commandant of Sandhurst, he spoke with a certain experience and knowledge of such things. Then – after presenting the awards for Champion Recruit to Stoner and Champion shots SLR and GPMG to Birrell and Butler respectively – he reminded 480 that they had now gone through three milestones: they had been awarded their red berets, they had got their wings, and they now proudly wore the lanyards of the 2nd and 3rd Battalions. Living up to the standards of such fine battalions was going to

Left: *Sergeant Riley and Cunningham's faulty tailoring.*

Below: *Ward tells his family and next-door neighbour all about it.*

test them, but he wished them all luck and hoped they would be able to reach those standards. And if, while he was addressing them, he knew that the inside seam of Andy Cunningham's right trouser-leg had been split from crotch to knee for the previous ten minutes, he certainly gave no sign of it.

Afterwards Cunningham claimed it was sabotage. There was no way those threads could have come undone of their own accord. Nobody else believed this theory, of course. Cunningham's trousers – like their owner – were capable of anything. Anyway, the rest of the platoon didn't mind. The sight of his bare flesh flashing in the sunshine had given a lot of innocent pleasure to friends and families alike. ASLEF were on strike that day, and getting to Aldershot had been a very difficult business for some of them. It was generous of Andy to provide this unexpected treat. After all, it wasn't meant to be a solemn occasion, but a pleasant day out – a day when parents, sisters, brothers, aunties, uncles, grans and girl-friends could meet your mates and your corporal and Sergeant Riley and Captain Baird and see what sort of a life you led as a soldier in the Parachute Regiment in 1982.

Above: *Mr and Mrs Stoner going on leave.*

Opposite: *Flight-Lieutenant Mellor uses Butler to demonstrate the workings of the PX parachute to 480's families and friends.*

The staff enjoyed it too. The biggest pat on the back Kevin Riley had ever had was when one of the fathers in the last platoon he'd trained had come over and thanked him for making a man out of his son. And if that was what the staff were doing, he said, then they couldn't ask for any greater satisfaction.

Another traditional event on Pass-Out Day – after the Red Devils had done their brilliant free-fall stuff – was for the recruits to do a rather more modest jump out of a balloon cage on to Queen's Parade for the benefit of their friends and relatives. Conditions were perfect. Just enough breeze for the balloon not to be obliged to crawl. While 480 got ready to jump, the current RAF liaison team at the Depot prepared for their part in the proceedings. Sergeant Sid Daccus was going to dispatch. Warrant Officer Snowy Robertson was organising the balloon-cage manifests. Flight Lieutenant Derek Mellor (Dave Huggins' successor) was about to demonstrate each stage of the opening sequence of the PX5 parachute – the one used when jumping from balloons. Two Paras from HQ company did the pulling while he did the talking. Friends and relatives gathered round to watch as this very unmilitary-looking bundle of nylon lines and billowing underwear was pulled out bit by bit across the grass.

'All we ask him to do is step out,' said Derek Mellor. 'A quick tap on his shoulder, a boot on his backside if he's a little hesitant, and away he goes . . .'

Right: *Watching the balloon go up on Queen's Parade.*

Opposite: *Lt-Col. Brewis talks to the next cage to jump. Left to right: Copley, Payne, Mincher and Birrell.*

Most of 480 loved it. No equipment, no bumpy flight, no gasmask, no formal exit drill. Just a two- or three-minute ride up into the sunshine over the places they had grown to know so well in the last six months. As they rose steadily above their earthbound friends and relatives, they could see Browning Barracks a few hundred yards to the south of them. Long Valley and Flagstaff Hill of P Company fame lay a bit further off to the south-west. And just over the other side of the canal was their own barrack-block, Ridgway and Blyth. Been their home for six months, that had. Put in a lot of hard work, cleaning it. And they'd had a lot of fun there, too.

'Go when you're ready,' said Sergeant Daccus. Down below were proud parents, envious mates and admiring girl-friends – all waiting to watch them make their daredevil leap into space. Just the sort of reason they weren't supposed to join the Paras for, according to Lieutenant-Colonel Brewis. He preferred more serious qualities, like true grit and determination, and probably he was right. But soon they would be in Northern Ireland. So surely they were entitled to show off just once in a while? Didn't have these wings on their shoulders for nothing now, did they?

'Come on,' said Sergeant Daccus. 'We haven't got all day.'

Just like stepping off a pavement . . .

16 A Regiment for all Seasons

Although the Platoon section commanders sympathised with their CO's point of view, they also felt that parachuting had an important part to play in forming the Regiment's esprit de corps. Jumping from an aircraft was a risk they all shared together, said Sergeant Slater – whose promotion had come through shortly after 480's return from Brecon. In Corporal Priestley's eyes the act of parachuting forged a bond between them. They all jumped together, fought together, drank together and stuck together. And with the feeling of solidarity that parachuting gave, it was easier for them to get on with the job.

480's immediate job was a spell of service in Northern Ireland. They were now trained soldiers – Toms instead of Crows – and the temporary attachment to 1 Para was an excellent opportunity for them to get a taste of one of the British Army's regular postings. Since 1969, when the Army had first gone into Northern Ireland to protect the Catholic population from Protestant harassment, the Parachute Regiment had played a noteworthy part in helping to maintain the security of the Province. During those years it had also been involved in two of the major tragedies – Bloody Sunday, as it was called, in 1972, and the ambush at Warrenpoint in 1979. In the first, 1 Para had killed thirteen Catholic civilians while dispersing a forbidden civil rights march. In the second, the IRA had blown up and killed eighteen British soldiers – sixteen of them from 2 Para. And although things had been a great deal quieter in Northern Ireland during this recent tour, it was incidents like these that stuck in the mind and influenced 480's thinking about the situation they would find when they arrived there.

Many expected they would be patrolling the towns, dealing with riots. Others imagined there would be a gunman behind every bush waiting to shoot them in the back. At the very least they expected to be stoned by the local population every time they went down the street. In fact, as they very soon discovered, a soldier's life in County Fermanagh where 1 Para was stationed at the time was very different from that. To start with, the towns were few, small and to a large extent the responsibility of the Royal Ulster Constabulary who were now in charge of Northern Ireland's security operations. The Army was out in the country, down on the border between the Province and the Republic, amidst the islands and peninsulas of Lough Erne and its neighbouring smaller loughs and rivers. There were no riots to be dealt with in the hamlets and lanes of South Fermanagh. The work there was far less dramatic and consisted largely of manning the VCPs (Vehicle Check-Points) which had been set up on most of the roads coming into the north from the south.

These check-points were usually on bridges or at road junctions and varied considerably in size and comfort. But all had certain basic ingredients, even though some were more rudimentary than others. There would be concrete blocks barring the road; a pillbox of some kind to give protection to a sentry; an area nearby in which to eat, sleep and watch TV when off duty; and a walled compound, usually topped off with steel-mesh fencing, surrounding the living accommodation. It was frontier life of the most unexpected kind, and although 480 had been told in their briefing that operating check-points would be one of their duties, they had not realised that some of them would be doing very little else while they were there. Nor had they realised quite what these check-points would be like. The fact that they would be holed up in breeze-block forts – like a US cavalry detachment in Indian country – was something that had not really got through to them.

The VCP at Lady Craigavon Bridge in South Fermanagh where Stoner and Stirling spent much of their time while with 1 Para.

The new boys were spread evenly around the battalion – some half-dozen or so to a company. Stoner and Stirling, for instance, were posted to the same platoon of C Company and spent almost all their time in Northern Ireland at two VCPs. It was like being on permanent guard duty, six hours on and twelve hours off turn and turn about. Half the time they were on

Stirling looks through the weapon-slit of one of the Sangers. Note the cord used for pulling the caltrops into the road.

duty they spent in one of the Sangers, as the pillboxes were called, peering out through a steel-framed weapon-slit at the countryside beyond. They found that part of the job boring. Very boring. As a result the remaining three hours they did on the road-block seemed positively entertaining by contrast. There they stopped vehicles, checked driving-licences and identities and – when it was thought necessary – looked into the boots of cars and the backs of lorries. Some of the lorries had gravel in them, some had furniture. Some were carrying pigs or sheep to market across the border. But however innocent the load might seem, it was still a potential hiding-place for arms and explosives and therefore liable to be searched.

Stoner found it difficult to talk firmly to the drivers at first. He started out by saying things like: 'Oh, excuse me, could I have a look at your driving-licence, please?' But when they laughed at him for being such a softy, he learnt to change his ways and stopped putting a 'please' on the end of his request, unless they were polite to him, of course. But he found it hard getting into the habit. Especially with the regulars – for some of the vehicles went backwards and forwards so often between the Republic and Northern Ireland that their drivers became well known to the soldiers on the check-points. At the first VCP he and Stirling were on, some of the locals had got so used to being stopped and questioned that they used to spell out their car registration numbers in the phonetic alphabet – saying Charlie India Lima and so on, the way the army did. But so far there hadn't been any real dramas, just the odd stroppy drunk or the occasional driver who wouldn't let you search his boot, and when that happened you just sent for the RUC and left it to them to deal with.

They got a lot of tourists through as well. A lot of English people on fishing trips. One day at the last place, he'd had a car that tried to drive through without stopping, and when he ran after it and opened the door and asked them what the game was they turned out to be French people on holiday who didn't speak a word of English and didn't think the road-blocks had anything to do with them. They were lucky he hadn't shouted out to the guy in the Sanger to pull the cord that worked the caltrops. The spikes on that would have punctured all their tyres and slowed them down a bit.

In spite of being stuck on VCPs all the time, Rod Stoner was generally happy with army life. His new bride had just moved into a flat in Aldershot; he was managing to save nearly all his pay – mainly because there was nothing to spend it on, but also because the army was kind enough not to charge them board and lodging for the pleasure of living in a VCP; and he was looking forward to getting the Northern Ireland medal. It would be nice to have, even though he didn't think they really deserved it. Not in view of the short time they'd been there, and the little he felt he'd done stuck in VCPs all the time. Others had fewer qualms on that score. Thirty days in Northern Ireland qualified you for the medal. They would be doing about sixty days. So they were perfectly entitled to get the medal. In any case they felt they could do with something to wear on their chests. It wouldn't be much fun going to 2 and 3 Para with a completely bare number two suit. After what that lot had done in the Falklands, they'd all be heroes and pretty big-headed about it. Pete O'Hare, for one, had a nasty feeling that he and the rest of 480 were going to get a hell of a lot of stick when they finally reported to their battalions.

One thing they all liked about Northern Ireland was being transported everywhere by helicopter. Army vehicles were vulnerable to bombs on the roads. Helicopters had so far proved harder to hit. So all movements of troops between VCPs and platoon and company headquarters tended to take place by chopper – either by Army Air Corps Lynx or RAF Wessex. The helicopters were also used for something called an Eagle Patrol, which – as Corporal Barry Gray of B Company explained – was basically a roving VCP designed to catch terrorists on the hop. Not all the roads leading into Northern Ireland were controlled by permanent VCPs. The chopper's job was to cover those that weren't, to fly around till they saw a car and then to zap down on it and land some way ahead, so the patrol could jump out, question the driver, ask him where he was going, what he'd got in the vehicle, all the usual sort of stuff. Basically they were looking for firearms, ammunition and explosives, said Cunningham, who thought flying around in helicopters was great fun.

Many of them also did ground patrols – some lasting forty-eight hours, others as long as four or five days at a time – and it was these operations that gave perhaps the truest flavour of what soldiering in Ireland was really like. What they had been training for in Wales had now become reality. Everything their corporals had taught them there had suddenly become relevant to the situation they now found themselves in. Even before they came to Ireland Tattum had sung Corporal Slater's praises for what he had done with their section at Brecon. Really switched them on, he had. Really pulled them all together and given them the confidence they needed when they went to their battalions. Corporal Slater, said Tattum, was the sort of guy you wanted to be with in Northern Ireland. And these were exactly the kind of sentiments the other two sections expressed about Corporals Baker and Priestley. They knew the score. They'd got the experience. They were switched on. If you were out on patrol with people like them, you knew you were in safe hands. The way you were with the corporals of 1 Para who had had the misfortune to get stuck with you for a couple of months because it didn't suit the powers-that-be to post 480 to 2 and 3 Para till October.

Basically, said Corporal Barry Gray, 1 Para didn't want 480. Certainly not half-way through an emergency tour. Because if there was an incident of some kind, the first thing they'd have to do was see if the new boys were all right. That was why they didn't really want them around, because they had a habit of flapping at first until they'd settled in and got into the swing of things. But since they were there, the best thing to do was get them on the ground as soon as possible, get them working with a brick, and brief them not to flap if they made a mistake or something.

480 were all a bit nervous about how they would be received when they first came over, but in fact they had no complaints about 1 Para. They'd treated them all right, knew they didn't know sweet FA, just showed them the tricks of the trade, and it wasn't long before they started to fit in. There wasn't half as much bullshit as there was at the Depot either, said Tattum. They were just told to do a job and left to get on with it. Some people gobbed off at them, called them Crows, but they were usually the ones who hadn't been with the Battalion long themselves. Mind you, nothing like the real thing for switching you on, said Pete O'Hare. In Wales, when you were doing patrols, you sometimes just bumbled along with a don't-care sort of attitude. But out here it was different, you paid attention to everything that went on, made sure you didn't get split up and always kept your eyes peeled.

O'Hare was involved in one of the few major incidents that occurred while 480 were with 1 Para. He was out on a 48-hour patrol, and they were just going to lie up for the night when word came over the radio that they had to go and set up a snap vehicle check-point on the road nearby. The Intelligence blokes had found a 600-lb bomb they'd been looking for. So the patrol O'Hare was on had to go and OP it – watch it to make sure nobody came and moved it. They were there for two days. Then the ammunition technical officers came and blew it up. It was a 600-lb bomb in six beer-kegs and they were blown up one by one. And that was it. All over and done with. A heavy day's work in a couple of minutes.

Not all such searches ended as harmlessly in Northern Ireland. The RCIED – Remote-Controlled Improvised Explosive Device – was the IRA's major weapon against the British Army in Northern Ireland, as Chris Hall, a Signaller in B Company, 1 Para, has good reason to remember. On 16 December 1981, he was one of twelve men on patrol near Bessbrook in South Armagh. They had been given two tasks. One was to clear a railway line that had been bombed several times. The other was to visit a post office in the area that had been robbed pretty often too. So the patrol was put in by Puma, deployed, and did the job on the railway line. Then they called at the post office and set up a snap VCP for about fifteen minutes. But everything was quiet, so just as the local school was turning out they set off down the road towards their pick-up point.

Chris Hall remembered noticing at the time that none of the kids were coming up the road in their direction for some reason but were all going away from them. The patrol was split into three four-man bricks. He was third man in the lead brick and walking down the right-hand side of the road. He had just decided to cross over, and had taken his first step in that direction, when he saw smoke and felt something sweeping him across the road where he ended up on his back in the hedge. It was only as he hit the ground that he realised it was a bomb. But in spite of the shock, the pain in his back, and his apprehension about what might happen next, he immediately sent off an initial contact report on his radio. Only after he had done that did he look across the road and see the two beer-kegs, now lying exposed to view in a hole in the road a few feet from where he had been walking. So he got up and ran down the road to join the rest of his brick. As he did so he heard them cocking their weapons, because at first they didn't believe it was Chris running towards them. They thought the lumps of frozen mud they had seen thrown up by the explosion were all that was left of him. And if it hadn't been for a rare piece of luck, that might very well have been the case. Afterwards the sappers reckoned the reason the bomb had not gone off was because that winter's exceptionally hard frost had rendered the explosive ineffective. Only the detonator and the 20-lb booster charge had fired. Enough to blow a hole in the road and blast Chris Hall into the hedge, but not enough to kill him or any of the others.

Meanwhile the rest of the patrol had gone to cover in the knowledge that the normal IRA procedure on these occasions was to follow one bomb with another – a secondary, as it was called – or with a shooting of some kind. So the patrol lay doggo and awaited developments. While doing so, they saw some people running and felt tempted to open fire. But they resisted the temptation. It had been deeply impressed on them they were not to shoot unless absolutely certain that their targets were enemy gunmen.

The bomb was fired at ten minutes to four on Wednesday 16 December 1981. The time and the date have stayed very firmly in Chris Hall's mind. But he did not tell his parents about the incident until he went home on leave to Nottingham in the New Year. And then, he said, he sort of dropped it casual-like, so as not to upset them. But it hadn't put him off the Paras. Although due out in 1986, he was planning to stay on.

There were those who believed the Parachute Regiment should not be used in Ireland. They argued that the Paras' training was not appropriate to the kind of patient, low-key security work they had to undertake out there. The Paras themselves did not agree with this. Although – like all the other units – they did not much care for the policing jobs on check-points and in the towns, what they were asked to do out in the country seemed perfectly proper soldiering in their eyes. Corporal Baker said he would be happy to spend the rest of his army career in Northern Ireland, out in the field, putting everything he'd learned into practice. Out there you were up against it just as you would be in battle. You weren't doing the routine stuff like they were in Aldershot. It was just you and your brick, or section, pitting your wits against everybody else, defending yourselves against the guys from over the border. You didn't even feel any particular animosity towards them, except temporarily perhaps, after something like Warrenpoint, because most of the time you were just concentrating on ensuring the security of the area.

In any case, soldiering wasn't just about acting aggressive, as some people seemed to think – and it certainly wasn't about behaving like a thug. The Paras had no time for thugs. If any strayed into their ranks they very rapidly got rid of them. What they wanted were men with enough self-discipline to keep their aggression for the battlefield. General Sir Anthony Farrar-Hockley, their Colonel Commandant, and Corporal Al Slater saw absolutely eye to eye on this point. They also agreed that self-discipline stemmed from total obedience to military discipline. As Corporal Slater said, if you wanted someone to move over to a tree and set up his gun, and he started telling you he could see a better place to put it, then things were going to start breaking down. So if you were told to go to Northern Ireland you didn't want people to start arguing the toss about that either.

In that respect the Parachute Regiment was no different from any other unit. So long as Northern Ireland remained one of the British Army's responsibilities, then the Paras would have to take their turn out there like everybody else. They must take on whatever task they were given and do their best, said the General – however much it tried the patience, however long and tiring the hours might be. The Parachute Regiment was a regiment for all seasons, or it was nothing.

Such thoughts, however, were not very much consolation to 1 Para as they slogged unglamorously towards the end of their second emergency tour in Northern Ireland in less than twelve months. It seemed to them that some seasons were a great deal more exciting than others, and that what 2 and 3 Para had done in 1982 would be remembered long after 1 Para's equally conscientious work that summer in Fermanagh had faded from the memory.

When the Falklands crisis first arose, of course, most people believed that Britain and Argentina would manage to resolve their difficulties before the Task Force reached the Islands. Karl Warden, a twenty-year-old machine-gunner from A Company, 2 Para, certainly did. But, like the rest of his battalion, by the time he was heading towards the beach in San Carlos Water in a landing-craft on 21 May he no longer had any confidence in that supposition. Worse still, he was expecting the landing to be opposed. So it came as a considerable relief when the ramps went down and nobody opened fire on them. Once ashore he dug in on Sussex Mountain with the rest of the battalion and watched the air attacks on the ships in the bay until it was time to set out for Darwin and Goose Green. They went a day and a night without sleep during the approach march, and on the morning of 28 May – while it was still dark – 2 Para began their attack.

Night assaults are difficult and confused operations at the best of times, and this one was no exception. At one time B Company were firing right across A Company's position. At another A Company didn't know whether they had reached their objective or not. As it got light, said Warden, they began to advance again, and when the Argies finally opened up on them they legged it forward looking for dead ground to take cover in amongst the gorse bushes. As the rounds started coming down, Warden began firing at a pillbox while the bloke next to him set fire to the gorse with a shot from a 66. Things got into a bit of a shambles from then on. All the drills went to cock and the sections split up, but everybody kept on doing their job. In Warden's case, this meant putting down controlled fire, together with other machine-gunners, onto a series of pillboxes and trenches up on the ridge facing them, and he did that on and off for the next five hours, though the time seemed to go by in a flash. It was during this period that 2 Para's CO, Lieutenant-Colonel 'H' Jones, arrived with Captain Dent and some others and asked to be given covering fire while they went up the hill to the Argentine positions. Later, when Warden and the other machine-gunners also moved up to the ridge, they heard that the CO had been hit, and soon afterwards the Argentinians started surrendering.

The blokes were great, he said. Fantastic. Did the job they had to do. Couldn't have done it without self-discipline. It was a hard thing to get up and go when you were under fire and you weren't being ordered to. You were lying there and you'd think, should you get up now or wait till it quietened down? So you'd leave it for a bit and then you'd get up, and

Top: *Men of Support Company, 2 Para, after landing from a Sea King helicopter on Mount Kent.*

Middle: *Men of 2 Para en route for Goose Green.*

Bottom: *During the battle at Goose Green.*

Men of 3 Para on Mount Longdon with their Argentinian prisoners.

they'd fire at you, and you could hear the muck whanging past, and you'd go down again and wait for another ten minutes or so, wondering what to do. It was a hard decision. Hardest decision you could ever have to make.

In some ways he found their last action, Wireless Ridge, worse than Goose Green. On Wireless Ridge, they were being bombarded, having to lie there and take it. Then, when the time came to attack, they all had to stand up and go towards the Argie trenches, knowing they were going to start shooting any minute. You knew it was going to happen, he said. You knew you could get killed. But you all got up and started advancing, even though to advance when people were going to fire at you was completely crazy. You just did it because you'd all done the same sort of training and that was the way it was. But if the Argies had defended better 2 Para could have had a lot more people killed. Still, even if they had been a bit lucky, he reckoned they'd proved themselves. And so had 3 Para. They'd done a good job. And they'd had to tab all the way across the mountains, too.

One of 3 Para who didn't make it all the way across was Julian Barrett. Also known as 'Bas' or 'Gargoyle' to his friends, he had started his military career at the age of sixteen in the Junior Parachute Company and was still well under eighteen when the time came for 3 Para to set sail for the Falklands. At Port San Carlos the ramp on his landing-craft jammed, so he and the others on board had to climb over the side to get ashore. Like 2 Para they were very glad their landing was not opposed.

The march across the island was hard and uncomfortable. At each stage they expected a fight, at each stage they found the Argentinians had withdrawn before their arrival, until finally they came to the foot of Mount Longdon where they found the enemy had decided to stand and fight. He was in 6 Platoon, B Company, and his platoon had to take the top of the mountain while 4 and 5 Platoons had other tasks. So after a briefing from their section commander, Corporal Trev Wilson, they set off up the slope. He wasn't so much frightened as nervous. Like everybody else, he felt nothing was going to happen to him, but the adrenalin was pumping all right as they came up towards the crest. It was rocky and they were all climbing with their rifles in one hand and grabbing hold of the rocks with the other to pull themselves up. But they reached the top all right and were just beginning to spread out in their platoon formation when the rounds started to come. Barrett could see loads of lights through a gap in the rocks, which looked like a massive city but was really Port Stanley, and further down the slope in front of him he could make out land features like big rocks, but no way could he see if there were any bodies amongst them, it was just too dark for that.

Then they got under cover and Trev Wilson gave them another very quick brief. 'Remember what I told you,' he said. 'Whatever happens, keep going, don't stop moving, and if your mate gets hit and he's screaming, leave him alone, don't go near him, or you might get knocked off yourself.'

After that they started moving forward again and Barrett saw an Argentinian position in front of him which he fired into, and he thought he probably hit the blokes in it because he didn't get any fire down on him from there. At that time there was a lot of tracer whizzing past their heads, just missing them, and Nick Rose, one of his section, shouted out, 'You're doing all right, keep going,' and got into a crack in a rock and opened up from there, and that was when Julian got hit, shot from the flank where blokes had been waiting in ambush for them.

Like being plugged into the mains, it was. A sudden bang and he started screaming, funny really, because he'd always seen these films where people get hit and get up and run on, but no way, not him, it completely blew him out, he couldn't move at all. A couple of minutes later his platoon sergeant came up to give him some treatment, and he got hit in the arm, and next thing they knew everybody was getting popped off all round them. His mates Stewart Gray and Den Dunn got hit, and then a bloke who came up to treat him and the sergeant got shot in the head and fell about five yards away. By then half the section had been hit, sniped by Argentinians with night sights, and it was two and a half hours before even the walking wounded could be got back. In Barrett's case, it was ten hours before Trev Wilson managed to get four blokes up there to fetch him out on a stretcher. And when he got down to the Regimental Aid Post there was an even worse shock waiting for him. Three of his mates he'd come from Junior Para with had been killed in the fighting on top of Mount Longdon, all of them like him from B Company.

Fortunately his wound proved less serious than it might have been. A bullet which had struck him near the base of his spine emerged from his thigh without hitting bone or any vital organ on its way through. But it had badly bruised his sciatic nerve, and it was this which had caused him such intense pain. After treatment at the RAP, he was flown out in a Wessex helicopter with three Argentinian wounded to Teal Inlet. Later he sailed on the *Uganda* and the *Hydra* to Montevideo from where he was flown back to England via Ascension Island.

Battle casualties for 3 Para were twenty-two killed and fifty-four wounded. 2 Para lost eighteen killed and thirty-nine wounded. Although by some standards these casualties were relatively light, the toll was still heavy enough to ensure that it would be some time before either battalion got back to full strength. In some compensation for the fact that 3 Para had suffered the heavier casualties, only six of 480 Platoon had been posted to 2 Para. The remainder – including those who passed out subsequently with 482 and 483 Platoons – were allocated to 3 Para.

On 1 October 1982 a memorial service was held in Aldershot for those members of the Parachute Regiment and Airborne Forces who had died in the Falklands. That same weekend 1 Para's emergency tour in Northern

Ireland came to an end, and the battalion moved back to its base in Edinburgh to complete its two-year tour there. The Scotsmen from 480 Platoon went with them, flying by VC10 from Aldergrove and dispersing on arrival to their homes for the six days' leave everyone was getting.

The rest flew south by Hercules to Lyneham – except for Hunt who had opted to stay with 1 Para and been granted a change of posting. Soon after arriving in Northern Ireland he had answered a request for volunteers to join the battalion boxing team. Its organisers – unaware that his posting was temporary and his boxing experience more or less limited to his bout of milling with Ward during Pre-Parachute Selection – accepted him. By the time higher authority discovered what was happening, Hunt had got so involved with the battalion that he was reluctant to leave it, and what had begun as an accidental transfer ended by being officially confirmed.

On arrival in Lyneham, the English contingent – together with Tattum, the last of the Welshmen – also dispersed to their homes. Like their Scottish comrades they were disgruntled with the amount of money issued them. Several reckoned they had about £600 in credit, most of it accumulated while they were in Northern Ireland, but due to some bureaucratic hitch it could not be made available and they had to be satisfied with a mere £75 advance to take on leave.

Stoner set off for Aldershot and a welcome reunion with his wife in their new flat. Unfortunately, there was confusion about his estimated time of arrival and she was away for a few days staying at her Mum and Dad's. And as Stoner didn't have a key to his flat, he had to kip under the stairs in the block – which, after two months in VCPs, didn't bother him terribly much. Next day though, the pain in his stomach he had thought was wind got worse, and when he went to the military hospital about it at eleven o'clock that night, he was immediately admitted and operated on for appendicitis – so joining 3 Para a little later than the others.

All of them found that, when the time came to return from leave and report to their battalions, the experience was less daunting than they had imagined. Although no one – apart from Hunt – had applied to stay with 1 Para, several had left with mixed feelings. Stirling said he wished in some ways they'd never been sent there in the first place. He'd got to like the people he'd met in C Company so much that it was a great shame having to leave them. And there were others who echoed his sentiments. They'd met a lot of nice guys in 1 Para. They'd been well treated.

But very soon they were saying the same things about 2 and 3 Para. Their fear of having to take stick because they were raw squaddies and hadn't been to the Falklands turned out to be unfounded. They discovered 2 and 3 Para didn't talk about the Falklands much. They were still busy settling back into the routine of regimental life that had been so unexpectedly shattered for a few short months in the spring and early summer of 1982. Barring acts of God, temporary absence on courses and occasional trips abroad on company exercises and foreign attachments, Bruneval and Normandy Barracks at Aldershot would be the two battalions' homes for the next four years or so. From now on it would be mainly nine to five soldiering. In anticipation of this they had all put their names down for the rare privilege of being accepted on a free-fall parachuting course and had begun to plan what areas of military skills they ought to specialise in. Meanwhile Butler and Birrell, for instance, could look forward to a trip to Cyprus in February 1983 with A Company of 3 Para. Others would be going the following October with B Company. Another group would be going to the USA with C Company in March.

These were the high points of the following year and helped to sustain them through that period of anti-climax they experienced after their first few weeks with their battalions. Day in day out for nearly six months they had worked with one aim in mind – to pass out as trained soldiers, fit to serve in what they not unnaturally considered was the best regiment in the British Army. When they had joined in January they all thought it was the best regiment, and to their minds what had happened since in the Falklands had proved them right. Now it was up to them to make sure that everything they did while they themselves were Paras would help it to stay that way.

480 Platoon

In this nominal roll of 480 Platoon the two recruits from Dublin – one AWOL and the other a DAOR (£75) – are not included. Each name is followed by date of birth and home town, civilian job, and final posting or discharge details. Those who passed out later with another platoon have its number in brackets after their posting.

The following abbreviations are used:

AWOL   Absent Without Leave

DAOR Discharge as of Right (cost £75)
IE   Illegal Enlistment (non-declaration of some medical condition that makes them unsuitable as soldiers)
NFA Not Finally Approved (during selection week)
SNLR Services no longer required (after attempts to reallocate have failed)
TU Training unsuitable

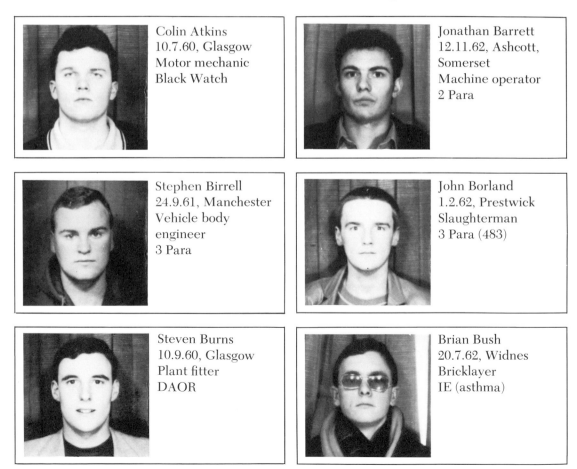

Colin Atkins
10.7.60, Glasgow
Motor mechanic
Black Watch

Jonathan Barrett
12.11.62, Ashcott, Somerset
Machine operator
2 Para

Stephen Birrell
24.9.61, Manchester
Vehicle body engineer
3 Para

John Borland
1.2.62, Prestwick
Slaughterman
3 Para (483)

Steven Burns
10.9.60, Glasgow
Plant fitter
DAOR

Brian Bush
20.7.62, Widnes
Bricklayer
IE (asthma)

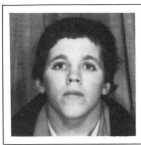

Anthony Butler
8.1.61, Wilmslow,
Cheshire
Carpet fitter
3 Para

Kevin Byrne
28.10.59, Liverpool
Lubrication bay
operator
IE (blood pressure)

Alistair Campbell
20.11.60, Fort
William
Electrician
IE (knees)

Paul Chant
20.8.62, Northampton
Motor mechanic
SNLR

Mark Chard
1.11.63, Dulwich
Factory worker
In military hospital

Lee Clark
21.12.63, Bexley
Heath, Kent
Police cadet /
Unemployed
1 Para Band

James Craddock
29.12.63, Astley,
Lancs
Plasterer
2 Para

Andrew Cunningham
18.10.62, Dalry,
Ayrshire
Police cadet
3 Para

Ewan Fleming
17.12.59, Dundee
Storeman
3 Para

Graham Harrison
29.10.63, Blackburn
Joiner
Royal Corps of
Transport

Michael Healey
10.1.61, Anglesey
Fitter
NFA

Austin Hindmarsh
2.6.59,
Middlesbrough
Heating insulator
SNLR

Frazer Hooper
25.10.57,
Pumpherston,
Midlothian
Tinsmith/Welder
3 Para

John Hughes
23.2.62, Liverpool
Photographer's
assistant
IE (asthma)

Mark Hunt
13.6.63, Pontypridd
Toolmaker
1 Para

Paul Kentish
9.6.62, London SE17
Trainee office
manager
DAOR

Joseph Killey
9.4.61, Catterick,
Yorks
Storeman
3 Para (483)

Alistair Melvin
1.6.62, Dundee
Wood machinist
2 Para

Nicholas Moy
3.3.64, Tadcaster,
N. Yorks
Farm labourer
3 Para

Peter O'Hare
13.9.60, Whitehaven,
Cumbria
Machine operator
2 Para

Alex Preston
21.6.59, Cropston,
Leics
Labourer/Driver
DAOR

Gary Price
30.7.63, Hereford
Labourer/Unemployed
AWOL

Peter Richards
4.2.62, Exmouth
Labourer
TU

Graham Robertson
19.3.64, Perth
Shop assistant
3 Para

John Stirling
30.11.60, Cumnock,
Ayrshire
Factory worker/
Unemployed
3 Para

Rod Stoner
21.11.63, Basingstoke,
Hants
Labourer
3 Para

Philip Tattum
21.5.60, Llanrwst,
Gwynedd
Lumberjack
3 Para

Stephen Thomas
20.9.61, Glyn Ceiriog,
Clwyd
Trainee hotel
manager
Queens Division

Dean Ward
30.6.63,
Loughborough
Labourer/Laminater
2 Para

Andrew Way
10.3.63, Liphook,
Hants
Police cadet
3 Para (483)

Stephen Wood
25.5.62, Sedgeford,
Norfolk
Glass cutter
IE (knees)

Ian Woodcock
5.3.61, London N20
Labourer/Train guard
3 Para (482)

Nigel Woof
21.8.62, Shipley,
W. Yorks
Electrician
Royal Pioneer Corps

Further Reading List

Airborne Operations (Salamander Books, London, 1978).

Bragg, R.J. and Turner, Roy, *Parachute Badges and Insignia of the World* (Blandford Press, Poole, 1979).

Buckley, Christopher, *Greece and Crete, 1941* (HMSO, London, 1977).

Comeau, M.G., *Operation Mercury* (William Kimber, London, 1961).

Dover, Major Victor, *The Sky Generals* (Cassell, London, 1981).

Frost, Maj.-Gen. John, *A Drop Too Many* (Cassell, London, 1980).

Gale, Lt.-Gen. R.N., *With the 6th Airborne Division in Normandy* (Sampson Low, London, 1948).

Gregory, Barry, *British Airborne Troops* (Macdonald & Jane's, London, 1974).

Kuhn, Volkmar, *German Paratroops in World War II* (Ian Allan, London, 1978).

Liddell Hart, B.H., *The Other Side of the Hill* (Cassell, London, 1948).

Low, Professor A.M., *Parachutes in Peace and War* (John Gifford, London, 1942).

Miksche, F.O., *Paratroops* (Faber & Faber, London, 1943).

Millar, George, *The Bruneval Raid* (Bodley Head, London, 1974).

Mrazek, James E., *The Glider War* (Robert Hale, London, 1975).

Newnham, Maurice, *Prelude to Glory* (Sampson Low, London, 1947).

Norton, G.G., *The Red Devils* (Leo Cooper, London, 1971).

Popham, P.E., *The German Parachute Corps* (Hutchinson, London, 1941).

Ryan, Cornelius, *A Bridge Too Far* (Hamish Hamilton, London, 1974).

Saunders, Hilary St George, *The Red Beret* (Michael Joseph, London, 1950).

Sims, James, *Arnhem Spearhead* (Imperial War Museum, London, 1978).

Spencer, John Hall, *Battle for Crete* (Heinemann, London, 1962).

Weeks, John, *Airborne Equipment* (David & Charles, Newton Abbot, 1976).

Weigley, Russell F., *Eisenhower's Lieutenants* (Sidgwick & Jackson, London, 1981).